A CASEBOOK

OF CHILD

PSYCHOTHERAPY

Strategies and Technique

by

Shirley Cooper, M.S.

and

Leon Wanerman, M.D.

Brunner/Mazel, *Publishers* • New York

Library of Congress Cataloging in Publication Data

Cooper, Shirley, 1923-
  A casebook of child psychotherapy.

  Includes bibliographies and index.
  1. Child psychotherapy—Case studies. 2. Child
psychotherapy. I. Wanerman, Leon R., 1935-
II. Title. III. Title: Case book of child psychotherapy.
RJ504.C617   1984   618.92′8909   84-12678
ISBN 0-87630-369-6

Copyright © 1984 by Shirley Cooper and Leon Wanerman

Published by

BRUNNER/MAZEL, INC.
19 Union Square
New York, New York 10003

MANUFACTURED IN THE UNITED STATES OF AMERICA

For Robin, Phillip, Brian, Todd, Laura
and all the other children.

Contents

Foreword by Calvin Settlage, M.D.   ix
Introduction   xiii

PART I. OVERVIEW

1. The Relationship Between Theory and Practice   5
2. The Aims and Goals of Child Treatment   13
3. The Conditions Necessary for Treatment   32

PART II. CASEBOOK

4. Stalled Cases and Other Vexing Problems   51
   Carmen Taylor   52
   Douglas Watson   67

5. Seriously Disturbed Children   86
   Sherry Turner   88
   Peter Martin   99
   Terry Frank   117

6. Selectively Disturbed Children   129
   Cornell Wilson   131

Ellen Hodges   139
Jennifer Parsons   149

7. Crisis Intervention   164
The Lindquist Family   167
Anthony Wilkins   185
Alicia Compton   191
Monica Reifer   196
Tommy Smith   201
Julie O'Connor   203

8. Adolescence   212
Mary Morishita   217
Jeffrey Murphy   228
Larry Scott   233

Index   253

Foreword

This book presents a valuable and unique approach to the practice of psychotherapy with troubled children and their families. Drawing upon and correlating an extensive knowledge of theory and a wealth of clinical experience, the approach translates concepts about human development and behavior into practical principles governing the therapeutic situation.

In their earlier volume, *Children in Treatment: A Primer for Beginning Psychotherapists,* the authors addressed concepts and principles bearing on the initial phases of treatment. In this new volume, they address concepts, principles, and issues of psychotherapeutic technique throughout the ongoing process of therapy. The content of this volume spans early childhood through adolescence, covers the range of psychopathologies, and addresses specific clinical problems as well. It includes a wide variety of clinical illustrations presented for broad understanding or close examination in the form of detailed therapeutic process. Both volumes honor and attest to the value and irreplaceability of the psychotherapeutic interchange between patient and therapist.

In its objectives, the authors' psychotherapy model blends a view of the ideal and the optimal with a respect for what is realistically feasible. The model's theoretical base embraces psychodynamic theory and the theory of psychoanalytic psychotherapy as it includes the con-

ix

cepts of conscious and unconscious mental functioning, transference and its interpretation, and working with and through the ego and its defenses in the process of undoing pathology and furthering development. The authors' psychotherapy model serves the function of selectively and meaningfully reducing, organizing, and focusing their knowledge and experience and relating it to the otherwise incoherent and eclectic array of human psychologies and treatment modalities.

Distinctive to the authors' translation of theoretical concepts into practical principles are the bridging ideas which they term *middle-level conceptualizations*. These conceptualizations are derived in part from elements of abstract theory and in part from day-to-day and moment-to-moment clinical assessments and interventions. Citing the capacity of an intercurrent event to organize an individual's subjective reality and behavior, they show, for example, how the death of a 5-year-old boy's father and its sequelae shaped the boy's fear and eventual mastery of intimacies and commitments. The authors convincingly propose that middle-level conceptualizations, when fully developed, will provide a coherent body of ideas having the virtues of making it possible to draw upon diverse theories and of bringing an immediacy and vitality to clinical work.

The authors' overarching goal for the child psychotherapist is the promotion of optimal development. Pursuit of this goal rests on a comprehensive developmental perspective. This concept is defined, amplified by a series of related specific goals and principles, and clinically applied to the case material. The presentation holds firmly to the time-tested concepts and principles of psychodynamic psychotherapy but also is up-to-date. It introduces and applies newer concepts, among them: separation-individuation theory; the development of the sense of self; object constancy and self-constancy; self-regulation including the regulation of self-esteem; and the relatively greater importance of mutuality and relatedness in female development and of autonomy and individuation in male development.

As noted, the authors' therapeutic objectives are tempered by considerations of reality. To this end, factors that can enhance or limit therapeutic potential are identified and taken into account, and are regularly reassessed. The aim is to create the best possible conditions for therapeutic work on a specifically individual basis. Similarly, technique is flexibly and appropriately employed. A less-than-desired but "good enough" therapeutic result will be accepted, but with a view to the future and the possibility of further treatment on the basis of further development and better conditions.

This realistically framed treatment approach recognizes that psychotherapy is a mutual, cooperative endeavor involving not only the child patient and the therapist but the parents and significant others within and outside of the immediate and extended family. This recognition leads to a therapeutic stance that respects each participant's need for autonomy of function in relation to inner urges and external demands and for defenses aimed at maintaining mental and emotional equilibrium and important relationships. The authors' appraisal of the conditions for therapy employs a thorough assessment of all of the relevant environmental, interpersonal, and intra-individual factors. A workable therapeutic situation is something to be thoughtfully, sensitively, and mutually structured as both the vehicle for and an important element of therapeutic process.

In their introduction to this volume, the authors state that this book is addressed to all therapists who are still in the process of evolving and modifying ways of treating children and their families. Although the volume is focused on childhood and adolescence, the employed developmental perspective conceives development to be a life-long process. The combination of the potential for adult development and the continuing emergence of new knowledge about human development and behavior means that the process of evolving and modifying one's therapeutic method and capability is also life-long. In this important regard, all therapists can learn much from this volume and can seek to emulate its authors in their demonstrated openness to new ideas, their integrative grasp of concepts with therapeutic utility, and their steadfast pursuit of the best ways and conditions for imparting psychotherapeutic help.

Calvin F. Settlage, M.D.
Clinical Professor of Psychiatry
University of California
San Francisco

Introduction

Mrs. Harris phoned her local Community Mental Health Center concerned about her four-and-a-half-year-old son's nightmares which started very soon after many homes in their town were destroyed or damaged by floods and landslides. An appointment was arranged in which Mrs. Harris reported that their home was not severely damaged, that her son had had no previous difficulties with nightmares, that family relationships were good, and that her son was generally a cheerful and competent child. He played well with other children and his nursery school teacher had often remarked on his fine abilities. Mrs. Harris noted that the mothers of other children in the nursery school were also aware of some changed behavior in their children since the flood. The therapist was impressed with Mrs. Harris' detailed and perceptive observations.

Any therapist would now be confronted with an important question: How to intervene? A reflective therapist might pursue the following line of reasoning: "(Is) . . . working at the individual case level . . . necessarily the most effective way to assist a family? . . . Beyond the case level is this a class of problems of which this is only one example? . . . Are there common situations which provide difficulties for people and to which this child's reaction is predictable and expectable, given his or her temperament and familial environment? . . .

At what point does this child really need individual therapy, family therapy, group therapy, etc., or how far can some of these situations be dealt with by discussion groups of parents and children in common situations? . . . Perhaps the most parsimonious way of dealing with some of these situations would be to offer people going through . . . life crises opportunities for discussion . . . that could aid them in working through the sorts of problems that are common to families in such situations. From . . . these groups is likely to be sieved one or more families who require more intensive therapeutic work" (6, pp. 222-223). Such a line of reasoning acknowledges the following realities:

1) Psychotherapy is not the only way of helping people.
2) People helped one another long before there were psychotherapists.
3) Despite increasing knowledge about events which stress children, evidence mounts that not all children facing stress succumb to emotional problems. One person's trauma may be another person's triumph—and the why is simply not yet understood.

    It is also not yet understood why some individuals' efforts to cope with stress or trauma lead to solutions where others' efforts lead to additional difficulties. The best current view is that coping styles derive from an admixture of constitutional and temperamental factors, existing strengths and vulnerabilities, and a large dose of chance events which includes the behaviors and attributes of important others. Some efforts to cope/defend result in denial and constriction with a resulting impoverishment of the inner world and/or a distortion of reality. Still other coping patterns and defensive styles may endanger the child's relationship to others.
4) In a better-organized society many forms of help, particularly of a preventive nature, would be a common and natural part of the landscape.
5) Even those children who, in theory, need psychotherapy will not necessarily get it. Some families will be unable to afford it. Some will be unable to find it. Some will be unable to use it. Some will not be motivated to seek it out or will be deterred by the mystery and stigma which still surround it.

Nonetheless, psychotherapy—under the right conditions—remains an effective way of helping. This book is about the practice of psychotherapy with troubled children and their families. To suppose that this or any other book could teach the knowledge, skill and art of therapy would be as much an illusion as the supposition that the violin could be mastered from the reading of a printed page. Both require extensive practice under careful tutelage with an ever widening grasp of the principles, the techniques and of the possibilities and limitations of the instrument.

However, we believe that this book provides an array of portraits of numerous children and numerous approaches and interventions which their therapists have made in the process of psychotherapeutic work. Some of these portraits are detailed and fairly complete; others are partial or fragmentary. Some are successes, while others fail. Some examine the therapeutic work microscopically, other portraits are presented with much broader brush-strokes. In all of the cases we have attempted to delineate the thinking and the principles which guide the technical interventions. Such exposure to a wide range of children, pathologies, principles, therapeutic strategies and tactics, and common problems encountered by therapists is essential in the evolution and modification of any therapist's unique style of working.

The book is, therefore, addressed to all therapists who are still in this process of evolving and modifying ways of treating children and their families. It is also addressed to the teachers and supervisors of such therapists.

The book is intended to be a companion and extension of our earlier work, *Children in Treatment: A Primer for Beginning Psychotherapists* (7). That volume focused on the first set of conceptual and practice principles in the initial phases of child treatment. By contrast, the focus of this book is on issues of psychotherapeutic technique throughout the ongoing process of therapy and on the principles which support them. Given this focus, we assume that the reader has some existing knowledge about child development, theories of personality formation, psychological structures and processes and the important interrelationship between the environment and the individual. We also assume that the reader has had some experience with the practice of child psychotherapy.

The book is organized in two sections. Section I (Chapters 1-3) is a broad overview of general principles which govern psychotherapeutic practice. Chapter 1 is a discussion of the relationship between theory and practice and includes some conceptual efforts to bridge this relationship. Chapter 2 takes up the question of establishing the aims and goals of treatment, the importance of doing so and some specific, common goals which can be established. These are illustrated with a number of case vignettes. The conditions necessary for treatment, as distinct from the aims and goals of treatment, are the subject of Chapter

3. Illustrative examples of how these conditions affect child therapy and treatment planning are included.

Section II (Chapters 4-8) is a casebook. It begins in Chapter 4 with a discussion of common problems and pitfalls encountered by therapists with special attention to cases which get stalled. Chapter 5 addresses technical issues in the treatment of seriously disturbed children in contrast to Chapter 6, which takes up the techniques of working with children whose problems are more selective and circumscribed. Chapter 7 considers various types of crisis situations and interventions, including cases involving suicide attempts, child abuse, serious illness and surgery, divorce and child placement.

The treatment of adolescents deserves and receives fuller consideration in Chapter 8. The special issues related to this shifting developmental stage and the technical problems of working with teenagers are explored and discussed. We have taken the broadening world of the adolescent as an opportunity to discuss, in this chapter, the importance of culture and its significant impact on personality and on psychotherapy.

There are many important issues in the treatment of children and their families which are not included. The significant advances in the understanding of biological and biochemical factors and the therapeutic developments which arise from these are not addressed. The importance of this knowledge and these therapies is not to be underestimated, and all therapists must have at least some acquaintance with this area. Our emphasis, however, remains on the psychotherapeutic interchange between patients and therapists. Although some of the cases include group and family therapy, our emphasis is on the model of individual work with children and adolescents combined with collateral work with their parents and other important caretakers. This emphasis is not intended to devalue such alternative modes of treatment. Our experience as practitioners and as teachers, and consequently our bias, is heavily weighted toward the model presented here. There is an extensive and excellent literature from others more expert in these alternative modalities. For similar reasons our focus is on work whose understanding and interventions are based on a psychodynamic orientation as opposed to a purely behavioral perspective. However, the careful reader will note that many of the interventions described are aimed at modifying behavior, and not merely at interpreting conflict or promoting insight.

The cases draw upon the work of very experienced therapists, as well as relative beginners. It would be incorrect for the reader to assume that all of the elegant work comes from the more experienced clinicians or that the examples of awkward or inept technique come only from the novices.

We would like to express our gratitude and our thanks to the many students and colleagues who have generously provided us with many of the case illustrations which appear throughout this volume.

To Sol Cooper and Paddy Wanerman, who suffered with us and without us as we brought this work into being, very special thanks are due. Sol's many by-the-way suggestions and criticisms have been incorporated here.

Special thanks are also due to those who typed our often indecipherable notes and pages—Roxie Berlin, Yvonne Kanis, and Janice Chinen Walt.

Finally, a general acknowledgment and commemoration are due to the trainees and the teaching staff of the Department of Psychiatry at Mount Zion Hospital and Medical Center, San Francisco. Since 1939 the training programs of the Department have been a model of excellence and a unique environment in which professionals from all major mental health disciplines have worked closely and collegially, and learned together in an atmosphere of intellectual stimulation, rigor and mutual respect. It has also been an atmosphere of warmth and often, of joy. Its graduates are numerous and, by now, far-flung, with many occupying important leadership positions in our field.

As of 1984, the training programs, which have been the center of the Department's life, will come to a close. Among the programs are the training programs in child psychotherapy. Unfortunate events, largely beyond the control of the Department, account for this unhappy circumstance.

The ending of an enterprise of such significance should not go unnoted, unhonored or unmourned.

REFERENCES

1. McDermott, J. F., Jr., Indications for family therapy: Questions or non-question. *J. American Academy of Child Psychiatry*, 1981, Vol. 20(2): 409-419.
2. Eisenberg, L., Social context of child development. *Pediatrics*, 1981, Vol. G8(5): 705-712.
3. Murphy, L. B., and Moriarity, A. E., *Vulnerability coping and growth from infancy to adolescence*. New Haven: Yale University Press, 1976.
4. Fraiberg, S., Pathological defenses in infancy. *Psychoanalytic Quarterly*, 1982, Vol. 51: 612-635.
5. Cowen, E. L., The wooing of primary prevention. *American J. of Community Psychology*, 1980, Vol. 8(3): 258-284.

6. Rae-Grant, N., The implications of primary prevention for the training of the child psychiatrist. *J. American Academy of Child Psychiatry*, 1982, Vol. 2(13): 219-224.
7. Cooper, S., and Wanerman, L., *Children in treatment: A primer for beginning psychotherapists*. New York: Brunner/Mazel, 1977.
8. Rappoport, J. L., and Ismond, D. R., Biological research in child psychiatry. *J. American Academy of Child Psychiatry*, 1982, Vol. 21(6): 543-548.

A CASEBOOK
OF CHILD
PSYCHOTHERAPY
Strategies and Technique

PART I

Overview

CHAPTER 1

The Relationship Between Theory and Practice

A natural starting point for any discussion of psychotherapy is a consideration of the relationship between theory and practice. The "pure" theoretician, placed in a room with a patient, will simply not know what to do. The "cookbook" practitioner may have some recipes for what to do but may have no understanding of why it is done. The most vexing aspect of the relationship between theory and practice is how to get from one to the other.

Margaret Frank described this vexing problem in the form of useful metaphor. "We could say that theory builders are the map makers while practitioners are the travelers along the roads. It is obvious that maps cannot tell us the precise conditions of the roads, the nearest potholes and frost heaves, where a bridge is out or the sharpness of a turn. They can only give an overall view of our direction" (6, p. 394).

To complicate the problem further, there are dozens of theories, some which are complementary, some that only partially overlap, and some which are completely contradictory. The practitioner must choose among these in the theory market. This marketplace, although highly competitive, is a small "Mom and Pop enterprise" when compared to the supermarket of endlessly proliferating how-to-do-it practice ideologies. Wittingly or unwittingly, therapists do make choices among the theories and practice styles which suit each of them best.

No matter what choices are selected, no clear and complete set of guidelines exists as yet for the direct translation of theory into practice. Each therapist working in each clinical situation must tailor-make and improvise the translation. There are, however, some important, albeit fragmentary, ideas which help to bridge the gap and promote the integration of theory and practice. These ideas can be thought of as "middle-level" conceptualizations which are derived both from parts of more abstract theories and from day-to-day and moment-to-moment assessments and interventions. The following are a few examples of such "middle-level concepts."

I. Concepts About the Clinical Interchange From the Point of View of the Therapist

1) The making of observations as differentiated from inferences about observations: observations are simply a catalog, in descriptive, phenomenologic terms, of one's sensory impressions. What is seen, heard, smelled and sometimes tactilely experienced (such as a hand-shake) about the patient is the raw material of this catalog. One's own reactions—I'm uneasy; I'm bored; I'm intrigued—form another part of the observational field. The breadth and quality of life experiences and the relative freedom to observe will be major determinants of what enters the observational field.* To say to oneself, "I smell something sweet," is an observation. To say, "This person is wearing perfume," is already an inference which may exclude other possibilities.

2) The making of inferences is the process which orders and makes sense of observations. Inferences are those tentative ideas and conclusions which are derived from the intersection of the raw observations with one's beliefs, values, experiences, temperament and personality. Multiple inferences can be drawn from the same observation and multiple observations can lead to the same inference. There is a hierarchical order to inferences; some are simple and have a higher probability of accuracy, while others are more complex and abstract requiring more caution and more evidence about their validity. "This person is wearing perfume" is a very different order of inference from "The sweet smell of perfume means that this person is exhibitionistic

---

*This idea is related to the ideas of suspended but focused attention, and the act of active listening which have been written about by many authors.

or narcissistic." Simpler inferences are also more easily tested, whereas more complex conclusions typically require more time and effort to substantiate.

3) Inferences and sets of inferences serve as signals to the therapist to begin the process of forming and testing hypotheses. An hypothesis illuminates and guides exploration and intervention: the patient confirms, modifies or refutes. This mutual process selects certain material, excludes others and points the way to the most significant material of the moment. It is in this sense that every interchange has both a diagnostic and a therapeutic function. This process of observation, inference and hypothesis testing has, of course, its counterpart in everyday life. The following excerpt is a charming example.

Once, among a group of colleagues engaged in specialties different from my own, we were discussing the learning of foreign languages. One of the group, a most accomplished and unusually gifted doctor, told us that he had acquired his rather fluent knowledge of German from a German chef when, as a high-school boy, he was employed as a dishwasher in a Boston restaurant. He then added with an amused, almost mischievous smile (at least this is how it impressed me), that in spite of this sound preparation he very nearly flunked his German exam in college. Continuing with this account, he related the special circumstances which had unsettled him on this occasion. The examiner had asked him not to translate the German text word by word, but to read the whole page carefully first, and then translate it. The student found himself incapable of doing so, and when the professor offered him another chance with a second page of the book, he again failed almost completely. At this point I asked curiously and quite spontaneously: "Was it Thomas Mann?" "How did you guess this?" my friend asked. "I did not guess," was my reply, "I inferred it." This somewhat superior statement provoked the appropriate reaction, the request that I should demonstrate the process of inference drawing. Not to be found deficient, I did my very best to meet this challenge and what I could retrieve of my thoughts runs as follows: "This is a highly intelligent and gifted man. In all probability he was a very promising youngster, from Boston, earning his living as a dishwasher—a classical combination for a scholarship at Harvard."* Then there was the question of the German text: A Harvard language exam would not use a mediocre writer

---

*"I hope it will be understood that our innermost thoughts frequently have this unequivocal directness which when said aloud or seen in print acquires a quality of irreverent or jocular unconcern" (2, pp. 8-9).

but an important one. Was this responsible for the doctor's special, amused smile, instead of a wistful expression at the recollection of his failure? Perhaps there was something amusing and intriguing about the assignment? Moreover, why was he asked to read the whole page? Not to translate word by word seems an appropriate request in a first-rate institution of higher learning, but why a whole page, why not just sentence by sentence? And at this moment, an idea, a recollection, an image emerged in my mind: what writer of first-rate standing, comparable to that of a first-rate college, would write sentences that are a page long? Then my question took shape: "Was it Thomas Mann?" (2, pp. 8-9).

4) Psychotherapy adds another dimension to the process—intentional helpfulness. From the small, moment-to-moment interactions a therapeutic plan and direction ultimately evolves. Central to the overall plan and direction of a therapy are the methodologic strategies which are constructed from observations, inferences and hypothesis testing and which shape the overall plan and direction of the therapy. These strategies take the form of the specific helpful interventions which earn the therapist's keep.

II. Concepts About the Clinical Interchange From the Point of View of the Patient

All patients enter a therapist's office with a combination of hope and fear. This is true in the first meeting and in all subsequent meetings, although the balance and nature of the hopes and fears change with time.

Most of the time the patient's hopes lie within the realm of psychotherapeutic possibilities—even though the degree of expectation may need to be modified in the course of therapy. On occasion, however, patients bring to therapy only hopes which are unrealistic, inappropriate and beyond the scope of therapeutic achievability. Hopefulness is an attribute which is essential for psychotherapeutic work. It is a personality attribute which is a part of every person's perception of self and world.* Regardless of how a request for help is phrased, patients' hopes are an inevitable mixture of desires for relief of pain and anxiety (including the anxiety of telling their story), for greater comfort in their daily lives, and for the development of new adaptations and

---

*In Erikson's developmental scheme, hope is the positive outcome of the earliest developmental phase (Basic Trust vs. Mistrust) and affects all subsequent phases.

greater mastery. These hopes are a central part of the more complex concept usually called motivation.

The other face of hope is fear. Therapists usually view patients' fears about therapy as exaggerated and unwarranted. However, from the patient's perspective the fears are just as real as the hopes. Typically a patient fears exposure, the unknown, and the vicissitudes of change. The fears are another element of the patient's motivation. The manifestation of the patient's fear is typically called resistance, which is constructed from the patient's characteristic defenses. The relationship between resistance and defense is a good example of the distinction between a "middle-level" concept (resistance) and the more abstract, theoretical concept of defenses which includes defensive structures, defense mechanisms, and defensive operations.

III. *Concepts About the Relationship Between Content and Form*

Every communication contains two elements: the *content* of the communication which conveys information about the what, the why, the where and the when of ideas and experiences, and the *form* of the communication which conveys different but no less important information. How a patient tells something can add to the meaning of the content, change the meaning of the content, as well as provide more general and vital information about the person. Issues of form can be outlined in the following way:

> *Appearance*
>> Physical factors
>> Stylishness, care of person
>> Dress as clue to person's self-perception
> *Motoric Styles*
>> Posture, walk, activity level
> *Eye Contact*
> *Mood*
>> Affects (labile, stable, appropriate, inappropriate)
>> Anxiety manifestations
>> Depressive manifestations
> *Gestures and Mannerisms*
> *Modes of Speech*
>> Loud, soft, monotonous, shrill tones, etc.
>> Modes of speech as an index to thought processes, such as concrete vs. abstract, discursive, tangential, constipated, halting, open, direct, related, incisive, and dramatic

Modes of speech as indicators of intelligence and judgment, such as reflective, insightful, reasoned, and constricted

Since the form of communication is often related to character organization, it changes less readily and less frequently than the content.

IV. Concepts About the Contents

The content of any communication will encompass some element or elements in the following diagram.

FIGURE 1. Content of Observational Data*

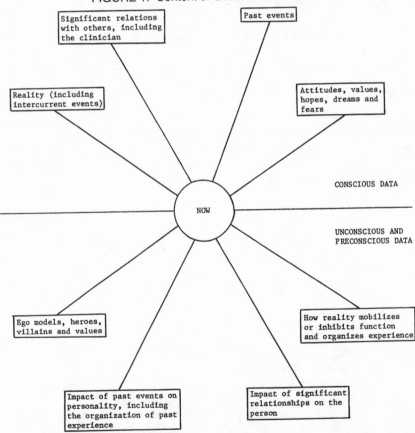

*Copyright 1977, National Association of Social Workers, Inc. Reprinted with permission, from Cooper, S., Social work: A dissenting profession, *Social Work*, Vol. 22, No. 5 (September, 1977), p. 365, Fig. 1.

The manifest content always lies above the line dividing conscious from unconscious data, but is always connected to some element of below-the-line latent content. Frequently the connection is direct as shown in the diagram. At other moments, not infrequent, the connection is less direct and even obscure. The schema is useful in helping the therapist think about why one is being told what one is being told, as well as what is left out of the telling. Obviously the diagram has roots in an array of higher level abstractions, including developmental theory, object-relations theory, identity formation, psychodynamic theory, ego psychology, communication theory and learning theory.

Each of the elements of the diagram contains other middle-level conceptualizations. For example, the current reality of a person's life includes not only ordinary day-to-day events but also those experiences which are referred to in the diagram as *intercurrent* events. This term refers to those highly colored events which punctuate a lifetime, such as losses, moves, graduations, etc. The events have the capacity to organize a person's subjective reality and behavior. Through their connections to important earlier related experiences, intercurrent events have a filtering and magnetizing quality. For some people such events will touch on existing vulnerabilities; for others they will create opportunities for new or re-worked mastery.

Russell Baker, in his book, *Growing Up* (1), provides an artist's illustration of this concept in relation to the death of his father when he was five. He describes sitting in the kitchen of his neighbor, Bessie Scott.

> Bessie said I would understand someday, but she was only partly right. That afternoon, though I couldn't have phrased it this way then, I decided that God was a lot less interested in people than anybody in Morrisville was willing to admit. That day I decided that God was not entirely to be trusted.
>
> After that I never cried again with any real conviction, nor expected much of anyone's God except indifference, nor loved deeply without fear that it would cost me dearly in pain. At the age of five I had become a skeptic and began to sense that any happiness that came my way might be the prelude to some grim, cosmic joke . . . (p. 61).
>
> . . . The three of us—Doris, my mother and I—were people bred to repress the emotional expressions of love . . . (p. 163).

This portrayal of how the death of a five-year-old boy's father and its sequelae shaped the future fear of and eventual mastery of intimacies and commitments is an excellent example of this "middle-level concept"; the organizing effects of intercurrent events. The concept has its obvious roots in more abstract, theoretical ideas drawn from stress theory, crisis theory, developmental theory, defense work and adaptation, and object theory. As a middle-level concept it has greater utility in guiding the practitioner's consideration of such issues as how a request for help may be initiated by a precipitating event, areas of vulnerability, coping mechanisms, focused historical inquiry, and the development of the patient's unique manner of relating to the therapist.

Obviously, these few illustrations of "middle-level conceptualizations" need elaboration and expansion. Such conceptual development would lead, ideally, to a coherent body of ideas which would bring theory and practice closer together. These concepts have the additional virtues of making it possible to draw from diverse theories, thereby bringing an immediacy and vitality to clinical work.

The focus of this book addresses day-to-day practice principles derived from cases and the experiences of a number of therapists who work with children and families. The emphasis is on method and the format is the case study. However, two additional and major considerations must precede the cases: the aims and goals of child treatment and the conditions necessary for treatment.

REFERENCES

1. Baker, R., *Growing up.* New York: Congdon and Weed, Inc., 1982.
2. Bibring, G., *The teaching of dynamic psychiatry.* New York: International Press, 1968.
3. Cooper, S., Social work: A dissenting profession. *Social Work,* 1977, Vol. 22: 360-367.
4. Erikson, E., *Identity and the life cycle.* Psychological Issues, Monograph Series No. 1. New York: International University Press, 1959.
5. Frank, J. D., Mental health in a fragmented society: The shattered crystal ball. *American J. of Orthopsychiatry,* 1979, Vol. 49(3): 397-408.
6. Frank, M., Boundaries of theory and practice: Problems in integration. *American J. of Orthopsychiatry,* 1979, Vol. 49(3): 392-396.
7. Gould, S. V., *The mismeasure of man.* New York: W. W. Norton & Co., 1981.
8. Greenacre, P., Reevaluation of the process of working through. *International J. of Psychoanalysis,* 1956, Vol. 37: 439-444.
9. Korner, A., Individual differences at birth: Implications for early experience and later development. *American J. of Orthopsychiatry,* 1971, Vol. 41(4): 608-619.
10. Scheflen, A. E., *How behavior means.* Garden City, NY: Anchor Press, 1974.

CHAPTER 2

The Aims and Goals of Child Treatment

Those who treat children must have a "knowledge of children's basic . . . needs, a clear way of defining normalcy without losing normal variability and an ability to differentiate between momentary discomfiture and abiding unhappiness. [Therapists] must be able to distinguish stressful events that will lead to growth and greater ability to cope from those stresses that are excessive for that particular child at a given time" (4, p. 5).

These "requirements" for child therapists immediately suggest the importance of a developmental perspective for the assessment of a child's difficulties, the development of a treatment strategy, and the delineation of specific aims and goals of a particular child's treatment. The overriding goal is always the promotion of optimal development. The realization of the goal is, of course, an ideal and as such not always possible. The goal dictates that every therapist must aim to understand where and how development became delayed, arrested, or distorted. This developmental perspective obliges the therapist to focus attention simultaneously upon the innate, forward moving processes which, as far as can be understood, seem to be built into the human organism, as well as those external, ongoing events and experiences which influence, and are influenced by, the inexorable ticking of the developmental clock. This is the essence of diagnostic thinking and treatment planning.

Given this view of the primary goal, child treatment bears certain obvious similarities to parenting. Therapists and parents alike strive to promote growth, to create the best possible circumstances in which growth can occur, and offer themselves as models to the child for identification and internalization. In this sense, therapy serves development and is also a developmental situation. There are, of course, important distinctions between therapy and parenting. Parents are typically continuous figures in the child's life, while therapists are invariably temporary figures. Ideally therapists relate to the child in a planned, conscious, deliberate fashion, whereas parents usually simply live with their children without thinking out every interaction. Parents are real objects to the child while therapists serve both as real people and as transference representatives.

With the aim of promoting optimal development established as both the general and ideal goal of all child therapy, it is possible and necessary to specify further aims and goals. Some of these specific objectives will be part of all therapeutic work with children and families and markedly resemble parenting objectives. Others will be more unique to the treatment of a particular child at a certain time and under certain circumstances. Some of the particular goals discussed below will not be objectives of all therapies, or will assume much less importance than other therapeutic goals.

The importance of making an effort to formulate tentative, specific aims and goals at the outset of treatment cannot be overemphasized. It is even important to discover that it is not yet possible to do so in the early phase of some treatments because this discovery provides a frame of reference for what further information must be obtained to allow the development of more precise goals to occur. Furthermore, the presence of goal-hypotheses at the outset enables the therapist to reassess and modify objectives and to develop alternative technical interventions as the therapeutic data unfold. The continuous presence of particular goals also provides the best possible barometer for evaluating the course of treatment including what has been accomplished, what is possible to accomplish, what remains to be accomplished, and when to stop.

The following attempt to delineate specific aims and goals is, like all other categorical frameworks, artificial, somewhat arbitrary, partial and only a pale approximation of reality. Such a listing promotes the idea that these goals are discrete and separable when, in fact, they are rarely so. More often they combine and overlap, altering as the work proceeds. With this caveat in mind, the following list may help therapists to articulate and define the aims of their work with a given patient.

CREATING SAFETY AND A SENSE OF SAFETY

Being safe and knowing one is safe derive from appropriate amounts of protection which, in turn, permits the freedom to be curious and experiment. Safety is closely related to trust; it both leads to and depends upon trust. Safety is threatened by an absence or insufficient supply of nurturers and caretakers; by the unreliability of one's own body; by frightening and poorly regulated fantasies and impulses; by unrealistic demands and expectations; and by lack of consistency, reliability and predictability in one's life and environment. Generally, therapy cannot proceed without adequately insuring real safety in the child's outer world, in the therapy sessions, as well as the safety which allows the child to know and want to find out. When a child feels unsafe, excessive energy must be devoted to building systems of defense. These systems sometimes appear as hypervigilance to imminent dangers, as excessive risk taking and impulsivity which deny the differentiation between safe and unsafe, as an inhibition of curiosity and achievement, as a pervasive need to know everything, or as a failure to distinguish between reality and fantasy.

Alan

Alan is a seriously disturbed 11-year-old, whose strange and troublesome behavior has exacted an enormous toll on his parents who are tiring of the need for constant vigilance and the disproportionate amount of energy, funds and effort which they are expending upon him.

In his own efforts to make sense of the world and more order for himself, Alan has recently become preoccupied with learning all the public transportation routes in his city. He spends endless time travelling on the buses and streetcars. Out of exasperation, his parents have decided to allow him free-rein in this new activity. His therapist learned of several incidents which occurred during his travels, which were potentially dangerous and quite frightening for Alan. These events led to Alan's devising increasingly bizarre and grandiose schemes which he inappropriately believes will protect him. In fact, his effort to make greater order and sense of spatial relationships is leading to even greater disorganization.

The therapist recognized the necessity to intervene with Alan's parents and to assist them in limiting this activity and replacing it with a safe and structured after-school environment in order to ensure true safety and real stability for Alan. Parenthetically, but not unimportantly, this reality intervention is necessary for the safety and stability of the psychotherapy as well.

Lilly

Nine-year-old Lilly is brought to the doctor for severe abdominal pains, and hospitalized for a workup which reveals that Lilly is suffering from a kidney infection. In addition, the doctors learn that Lilly has been nocturnally enuretic for some time. She has also been recently sent to live with her father.

Lilly's parents have been divorced since Lilly was one. For some time thereafter both parents lived in the same city, so that Lilly has known and been attached to both. When Lilly was six, she and her mother moved to another city where a half sister was born a year later. Lilly's mother worked the graveyard shift, leaving Lilly alone to care for her sister. When Lilly's father learned of this, he arranged to have Lilly come and live with him. Lilly's illness occurred a few months after her return to her father.

The nurses were tremendously impressed with Lilly's intelligence, precocity and cheerfulness. They described Lilly to the pediatric social worker who became interested in the fact that Lilly had become an expert on the I.V. treatments she was receiving. Observing the child on her rounds, she noted Lilly's hypervigilance and made time to talk with her.

The social worker remarked on Lilly's knowing so much about the I.V. treatments—were there other things she knew about her illness? Lilly's story poured out. She didn't know what was wrong with her, or why she was in the hospital. When the social worker noted that Lilly hadn't asked before, Lilly replied that she had not wanted to bother the busy doctors and nurses. The worker assured Lilly that *she* was not too busy to listen to Lilly's questions or her worries. Lilly talked of missing her mother, and her concerns about who was now taking care of her little sister. Her mother was often so busy. At night, when

Lilly was alone, she was often frightened—too frightened even to get out of bed to go to the bathroom.

The social worker said that she understood that Lilly's worries about her mother and her sister, about her illness, and about the hospital must make her feel frightened and unsafe. She also guessed that Lilly liked to know and said that maybe she learned so much about the I.V. so she could feel a bit safer. When so many things are hard to understand, knowing can help. Lilly nodded vigorously and the social worker explained more about her kidney infection. She began to prepare Lilly for a urethral catheterization scheduled for the next day. Lilly wanted to know exactly what would happen. She agreed vigorously with the social worker's comment that being prepared helps a little girl know, and knowing is some help in feeling safer—less scared.

Regrettably, the catheterization was moved up to that same afternoon. Lilly became enormously upset, for the first time crying bitterly as she insisted that she was not ready—"it was tomorrow—not today!" The pediatrician heeded the child's plea and rescheduled the procedure. The second time, although Lilly cried about the pain, she accepted it, announcing that "now is the better time."

When the social worker and Lilly met again, the social worker told Lilly that she had been right to protest, and reinforced that being prepared, knowing and feeling safe are very important.

Lilly's experience illustrates the importance of creating for the child the maximum amount of safety possible in such a trying circumstance. Lilly is struggling with the effort to cope with a series of recent traumatic events: the loss of her mother and sister, other familiar landmarks, her illness and her medical treatment. To counteract her fear, she seeks to master these difficulties by a selective hypervigilance and need to know—while remaining unclear and bewildered about other important events. Given the fact that Lilly is hospitalized, that no one is asking for an extensive psychotherapy and that Lilly's panic resides centrally in a profound sense of unsafety, the pediatric social worker was well advised to set the expansion of Lilly's sense of protection as her primary goal.

PROMOTING OR RESTORING STABILITY AND CONSTANCY

There are, in fact, two components to this therapeutic goal. One of these is the insurance of an adequate level of stability, constancy and orderliness in the child's external world. Since there are insufficient societal resources to assist families in helping to organize stable care-taking arrangements for their children, more and more, therapists are confronted with families which have been disrupted, moved or otherwise altered. In other instances, the psychological realities within the family may create chaotic and unregulated environments. These psychological realities may reside within any member of the family, including one of the other children, and not always within the parents. The therapeutic task in these instances must be directed first at efforts to improve the environment to "good-enough" levels. This objective is, obviously, closely related to the goal of creating safety for the child.

A second component of this therapeutic aim is the promotion or restoration of internal stability and constancy. These two processes are inextricably linked, although the importance of either component will vary with the child's developmental phase, the degree of actual disorder in the environment, the innate endowment and resiliency of the child, and the availability of important potential substitute parental figures.

The importance of the development of internal object constancy as the successful outcome of the separation-individuation process has been a major emphasis of and contribution to the theory of child development and the child psychiatric literature in recent decades. The process has been described with major emphasis on the first three years of life. Important as these years are, it is clear that the separation-individuation process and the development of object constancy are lifelong affairs. When the promotion of internal stability and constancy is a central therapeutic goal, therapists are aided by the very nature of the treatment structure with its built-in regularity of time, place, person and materials and the establishment of regular ways of working together with common and explicit ground rules. For example, games which have rules and procedures assist children in understanding that stability is essential and valuable in true game-playing and other comparable goal-oriented activities.

In addition to the general structure of therapy, therapeutic interventions also promote internal stability. Furthermore, numerous specific opportunities arise in the course of therapy which permit a more focused effort in the service of this goal. These opportunities often come up in relation to real and recapitulated separations from important people.

Carlos

Carlos, age four, is seen for extreme willfulness and defiance. An only child, Carlos has begun to tyrannize his parents, who are recent immigrants to this country. While in their homeland, much of Carlos' care was given over to servants. Carlos lost much in the immigration—the regularity of his life, important people, a beloved dog, and the protection of adults who were competent in caring for small children. His parents were forced by political conditions to leave their country, and found resettlement extremely difficult. They lost economic status and comforts, important people, their home and their homeland. In addition, they were attended by servants in their own country and were ill-prepared to deal with the many practical matters they now faced. Carlos' father did find work in this country—work, however, which involved a lot of travelling.

During the first year of Carlos' treatment, he and the therapist became good friends. She helped him to replace some of the orderliness of his previous experiences and to understand his grief about so many losses. In the process, Carlos was able to manage impulses with greater control.

Helping the bewildered parents, on the other hand, was demanding work and not always successful. The therapist found it very difficult to help Carlos' parents to make order for him, to set appropriate limits and to acknowledge his grief. Thinking that Carlos' parents would be better served by a therapist of their own, she suggested a referral. The father was particularly offended by this suggestion, with its implication that he needed help himself, and its overtones replicating his exile. He terminated Carlos' treatment precipitously.

The reappearance of Carlos' disruptive behavior at home, and now also at school, led to a resumption of the treatment. The renewed sessions were drastically different from the earlier work. Carlos destroyed toys, seemed unable to play in a sustained way, and was often sadistic and provocative. A physically precocious child, Carlos seemed bent on hurting himself and his therapist.

It took some time for the therapist to link and explain to Carlos that his angry behavior was a response to her inability to protect his treatment. She had been unable to make his parents continue to bring him to see her regularly—and so Carlos was very angry with her. His whirlwind behavior stopped when she finally made this interpretation. With great sadness he put his question: "Why couldn't you? I thought you were my friend?"

The case of Carlos illustrates the need to focus on different therapeutic goals at different stages of treatment. In the first phase of this treatment, the therapist's aim focused on the restoration of order and constancy, which had been disrupted by the family's enforced move with the many attendant losses. Considerable progress toward this objective was realized in the work with Carlos, but less so with the parents. In fact, the attempt to help the parents work toward greater stability through a referral for their own therapy precipitated another disruption, recapitulating for Carlos the prior losses of important people.

When treatment resumed, Carlos' behavior required a re-casting of the priorities of the therapeutic goals. Clearly, Carlos was now out of control and unable to regulate or contain his destructive impulses. These ongoing difficulties seemed exacerbated as he resumed treatment and helping him to control himself became a primary focus. This goal was linked, as well, to the therapist's recognition that the treatment disruption paralleled Carlos' earlier traumatic experiences. Carlos was helped to gain greater control by the therapist's interpretation of his anger toward her for failing to maintain their relationship.* This intervention succeeded in promoting the goal of greater impulse control and served the simultaneous aims of working through previous traumatic loss, its recapitulation in the treatment disruption, and the aim of repairing a relationship. Although there are additional goals to this second phase of treatment, the restoration and promotion of stability and constancy remained central throughout.

PERMISSION TO HAVE APPROPRIATE WISHES AND "GIMMES"

This goal, like promoting and restoring stability and constancy, also has two potential facets. In those children whose experiences of disappointment and deprivation have led to their developing excessive expectations of their "entitled rights," the therapeutic objective becomes the translation of greed into realistic needs. This carries with it the recognition that, while some wishes can be granted, others will remain unfulfilled. By contrast, other children who have repeatedly experienced disappointment and deprivation often find themselves unable to wish, want or hope: They experience themselves as undeserving. The therapeutic aim in such instances becomes lifting the repression, constrictions and inhibitions which prevent appropriate understanding

---

*Carlos' behavior was modified by the therapist's verbal interpretations alone. Other children so lack the capacity to control impulsivity that verbal requests or insistence that they stop their behavior are required. In more extreme instances physical restraint or ending the hour may even be necessary.

and behaviors about what one may want, what one may have, and what one may keep. It remains something of a mystery why such similar experiences can lead to opposite outcomes.

A frequent and important aspect of this therapeutic goal is the assistance which the therapist provides the child's parents in balancing gratifications and frustrations.

The recent theoretical contributions to the understanding of appropriate and pathologic narcissism and the psychology of the self are useful in delineating this therapeutic goal.

Trudy

Trudy, age nine, is the middle child of three with two brothers whom she has mothered and looked after since her mother was placed in a state mental hospital when Trudy was almost five. The children presently live with their father who finds their care overwhelming. He is the sole custodial parent. The mother, who now lives in another part of the state, visits the children infrequently.

Trudy was referred for treatment by her teacher who noticed how sad and inhibited this child was. She often asked the teacher whether she might help with school chores when other children were out on the playground.

Trudy came to each of her therapy hours either early or on time. She worked diligently in the waiting room on school assignments. However, she remained hyperalert, watching for her therapist's arrival, and always appeared shyly pleased to see her. In the office, she rarely made a choice or initiated any spontaneous play. Often she elected to continue her homework. It was clear that Trudy's history of deprivation and her sense of undeservingness prevented her from wishing, hoping or asking. The early goal in this treatment aimed toward helping Trudy loosen some of her prohibitions against having appropriate needs and wishes and asking that these be met. These efforts went very slowly. A vivid illustration of Trudy's resistance occurred five months into the treatment as Trudy was approaching her ninth birthday. The therapist inquired how Trudy was planning to celebrate. Trudy insisted that she neither wanted nor expected to have a party, declaring that it would be too hard for her father to arrange one and that she really didn't care anyway. It had not even occurred to Trudy that she and the therapist might celebrate her birthday. Even when this was clarified, Trudy had great difficulty suggesting what she might like for this special event.

THE DEVELOPMENT OF A SENSE OF SELF AND OF SELF-ESTEEM

All children are in the process of developing the sense of who they are and their value as human beings. For younger children, body function and integrity are the most important organizing framework for this process. As children grow older, intellectual and social ability and special talents take greater precedence. When this process goes awry, its restoration becomes an *essential* therapeutic objective. This goal encompasses the child's recognition of his or her own worth, talents, skills, capacities, and limitations. Included are such issues as what one's body can and cannot do and what one's intellect can and cannot accomplish, as well as the recognition of what is possible now and what may be possible in the future. As with all other important life processes, the sense of identity is worked and re-worked throughout the life cycle and the therapeutic process.

Mark

Eight-year-old Mark began treatment because of enuresis and occasional encopresis. Although he lives with his father, and his six-year-old brother lives with his mother, the boys continue to have close connections with both parents. In spite of Mark's symptoms, there are many precocious areas of his functioning which served to compensate for his parents' chaotic style of living and their difficulties in offering consistent and effective guidelines for their sons.

The early therapy hours were characterized by Mark's swift and erratic movements leading to many spills, falls, and broken objects. This was particularly evident when he became excited by a competitive game or his need to recount an event with great rapidity and intensity. Initially, Mark reported to his therapist without any apparent distress that he understood himself to be a "klutz." His therapist adopted a questioning attitude about Mark's self-assessment and his seeming lack of concern about the way he managed himself and his body. Using the unevenness of Mark's behavior in the sessions, the therapist was able to demonstrate that Mark was capable of more coordinated and effective action. In addition, she began to interpret Mark's clumsiness as a response to excitement and anxiety, a view of him which began slowly to interest Mark as an alternative to simply viewing himself as inept. Following these interventions Mark began to ask if he could sit in the therapist's chair during a game, noting that he wasn't as likely to knock things over or drop things when he sat in her spot.

The boy's inability to manage and control his body in a variety of ways was clearly leading to the development of an impaired sense of self and an identity as a damaged, incompetent, and ineffective person. The therapist identified as the central goal of this treatment the acquisition of better impulse control, the development of body integrity and the connection of these to Mark's sense of self and self-esteem. She began to work systematically on helping him see his clumsiness as reactive and comprehensible, rather than as a fixed and inherent part of his being. His growing identification with her was a major process through which these goals were achieved.

THE DEVELOPMENT OF INCREASED CAPACITY FOR TOLERATING CONFLICT, ANXIETY, AMBIVALENCE AND FRUSTRATION

The appropriate management of impulses is central to this goal and is closely related to the acquisition of self-regulatory mechanisms and the ability to convert overwhelming, free-floating affect into signals for this regulating process. This objective is furthered by the therapist's efforts to promote delay and clarification of time, sequence, and structure. It is further enhanced by the provision of appropriate gratifications and frustrations, by naming and explaining affects and ideas and their relationship to events in and out of the treatment, and by the explication of multiple and sometimes opposing wishes. An obvious part of this treatment aim is the reduction of excessively harsh self-condemning and punitive ideas and behavior and their replacement with appropriate degrees of guilt and remorse.

Chris

Chris is an intelligent, sensitive and talented 17-year-old, whose difficulties with his family bring him into treatment. He is the middle of five children, whose two older siblings are considerably older than he. When he was about six, his mother's deteriorating behavior led to the first of several hospitalizations, and the father's decision to divorce Chris' mother. Following the divorce, Chris' father married again, and Chris' stepmother joined her husband in the care of the five children.

For Chris, these events were critical. The older siblings were sufficiently far along in their development to have a more balanced view of their mother's illness; the younger children retained few memories of her. Chris' memories of his mother were all good and protective; he thought that she might have been wrongly considered ill and hospitalized. These memories and ideas were never tested by subsequent contact with his mother. To protect his strong feelings of loyalty to his mother, Chris found it difficult to make a positive attachment to his stepmother, and repressed warm and loving feelings toward his father as well. Thus, Chris continued to perceive himself as "different" from his siblings who had formed attachments to both their father and stepmother. This sense of his own difference from other members of his family was further reinforced by his father's and stepmother's inability, at times, to understand Chris' need to hold himself apart from them. They did not sense his intense need to remain loyal to his idealized mother and often their puzzlement led them to interpret Chris' behavior too literally, adding to their own hurt and bewilderment about Chris' struggles.

Treatment focused on the goal of helping this appealing boy tolerate ambivalence and conflict in order for him to develop an appreciation of his own dimly-perceived positive and negative thoughts and feelings about various members of his family. An expanded capacity to tolerate mixed and complex ideas and feelings helped him to more realistically understand the world and those in it, and to begin the process of reducing harsh and punitive judgments about himself and others.

Additionally, the growing tolerance for ambivalence and ambiguity led to a detachment of psychic energy from his loyalty struggle, freeing this for use in the more age-appropriate tasks of learning and experimenting, and the testing of ideas against experience. Chris' fine mind, his sensitivity, along with his growing cognitive maturation were important aids in this process. So, too, were his parents' real interest and concern for Chris.

THE DEVELOPMENT OF REAL RELATIONSHIPS

This goal includes the development of appropriate assertiveness, mutuality, sensitivity to the needs and feelings of others, and pleasure derived from satisfactory affiliations. This objective implies the permission to seek out others, to identify with an expanding cast of characters, and to invest in each relationship a differentiated and realistic degree of intensity. It subsumes the capacity to tolerate and accept authority, dependence, autonomy, and leadership, as well as privacy and sociability.

Recent contributions to developmental thinking have suggested that the interplay between culture and personality leads to a greater importance of mutuality and relatedness in female development, by contrast to the greater importance of autonomy and individuation in male development (9)

Work with children is heavily dependent upon the therapist's self-presentation as a real object, along with the careful management of the transference relationship in which the therapist represents various figures from the child's past and present life.

Steven

Seven-and-one-half-year-old Steven plagued his therapist with his quiet but never-ending and ever-perplexing questions about why he was seeing the therapist. He was also hyperalert to things in the office, searching an overstuffed chair during every hour for pencils, paper clips and other debris, which, to his therapist's surprise, he occasionally found. The office was shared by several therapists, an arrangement that Steven was aware of. Other than his persistent questions Steven had little to say to his therapist. He asked repeatedly, "Why are these things in the chair? Who puts them there? Who uses this office? Are these pictures and toys yours or do they belong to the other guy? Why aren't things in their proper place?"

Steven used none of the toys in the office. Instead, he brought books or puzzles with him that were often beyond his ability to put together, although he would try again and again. In connection with these puzzles, he announced that he had learned to spell "puzzlement" and that it means, "not knowing what is going on." The therapist acknowledged that it was hard not knowing what is going on, but failed to recognize that Steven was completely bewildered about who the therapist was, about what therapy and its purpose were and about what he, Steven, was doing there.

In a later hour, Steven reported that his baby brother had spilled ink on his bedspread and had also dumped something in the goldfish bowl which had killed the fish. Leaving no time for the therapist to respond, Steven launched again into his questioning: Did the therapist have a brother? Which things in the office belonged to the therapist? etc.

He then told a story about Snoopy and Charlie Brown. In the story, Charlie Brown lectured Snoopy, telling him what to do, and warning Snoopy about the many places where dogs are not welcome. Although Snoopy's feelings were hurt, Snoopy persisted in defying Charlie Brown's bossy warnings. As he told this story, it was clear that Steven was identified with Snoopy's wish to feel welcome.

Steven is the second of three sons and his mother's favorite child. His father is devalued by his wife and also by Steven who shares his mother's view of his father. All transactions with Steven's father are negotiated by his mother. She is an energetic, competent woman who "overprotects" Steven by overlooking minor delinquencies and frequently intervening for him with school personnel when Steven complains about teachers or assignments. In spite of the school's dissent, Steven's mother has managed to change his classroom several times, although Steven is never satisfied about these alterations. These interventions have in fact permitted Steven to make important life decisions which he is far too young to be able to assess properly.

Steven's youngest brother was an unplanned pregnancy, and Steven did not "know" about his mother's pregnancy and his brother's birth until the baby was brought home from the hospital. Steven's maternal grandmother was persistent in trying to get her daughter to seek help for Steven's stealing, which his mother could no longer deny. The decision to bring him for treatment was one of the few times in Steven's life when his mother made an important life decision for her son which was not based on his avowed wishes or complaints.

Steven's history and the early hours of the therapy suggested that a primary goal of his treatment must be an effort to help Steven develop an effective, safe and age-appropriate relationship to his therapist. If successful, this would provide Steven with a model for other relationships and an opportunity to detach himself from the intense symbiosis with his mother. The promotion of cognitive progress is a closely linked goal but one which cannot be realized until Steven has the freedom to establish new and differentiated relationships.

In this early stage of therapy, these goals are becoming more and more obvious as is the great difficulty which the therapist is experiencing in his efforts to help Steven. Steven cannot understand why he is there or how he can permit himself to let the therapist help him know what therapy is about. Instead, he persists in asking one question after another without the capacity to either tolerate or assimilate a response. To permit an attachment to the therapist or even to trust a response might interfere with his intense primary attachment to his mother. Unprotected by her "overprotection" and her failure to set clear guidelines for age-appropriate behaviors, Steven steals things and knowledge which remain unintegrated and unclarified by true exploration. Clearly some things are too dangerous to know about and must remain hidden and secret under the facade of wanting to know and know and know.

It is probable that Steven cannot make progress without the assistance of his mother. Unless the therapist can find some way of forging an alliance with her to help her to relinquish her part in the symbiotic dyad, Steven will be unable to establish a true relationship with the therapist, a sense of autonomy, relationships with others and true learning.

THE PROMOTION OF COGNITIVE PROGRESS

To some extent this goal is present in all therapies. However, it becomes a more focused goal for those children whose cognitive development has been impaired by emotional difficulties. Problems with learning are one of the most universal manifestations of a troubled child, although the sources may differ markedly. It becomes particularly important to distinguish innate cognitive limitations from the more emotionally bound cognitive impairments such as an inhibition of curiosity, an inability to assimilate or integrate knowledge, or a withholding or fear of expressing that which is known. Depending upon this assessment, the therapist may aim to help the child enjoy and master new tasks and skills, to value his/her own knowledge and efforts, or to have greater freedom to risk trial and error.

Closely related to this goal—as well as to several previously described—is the firmer establishment of a sense of reality.

Stacey

Thirteen-year-old Stacey is brought to therapy by her distraught mother after a four-month period of lethargy and depression. Mrs. White is utterly perplexed by this new behavior which has not been relieved by the mother's massive efforts to distract Stacey by providing a continual round of presumably pleasurable and engaging activities. In desperation, Mrs. White sought the advice of Stacey's pediatrician who referred her to a therapist.

Stacey's "funk" seems to have been precipitated by being ostracized by her friends and classmates at her exclusive private school. This exclusion followed a dance at the school during which Stacey accepted an invitation to dance from a boy who was considered the "property" of one of the other girls. Although Stacey "knew" of the relationship, she cannot now understand why she didn't realize the consequences of accepting the invitation, nor can she understand why her friends reacted so violently and persistently. She is depressed and bewildered by this turn of events.

Stacey's family is wealthy and socially prominent. From her earliest years, Stacey's life had been organized to the minute by her mother. No wish has been denied and no activity unavailable. An endless frenetic round of parties, lessons, shopping tours, trips and sports has been provided. Any quiet, reflective activity prompts her mother to ask why Stacey isn't keeping busy, keeping herself entertained and taking the fullest advantage of her opportunities. The demand to keep active is a continual external stress. By now, it is an equally internal stress since Stacey is so identified with her ambitious and socially successful parents.

In addition to the presenting problem, the therapist also learned that Stacey's schoolwork has always been considered mediocre in light of everyone's assessment that she is an exceptionally bright and gifted child.

Early on in her contact with Stacey, the therapist understood that this child's cognitive abilities were significantly impaired by her inability to pause, reflect, consider alternatives and allow her own feelings to be part of the useful information that could inform her thinking and behavior. Stacey has always leapt before she looked. The goal of treatment will be to try to reverse this process by helping Stacey value pausing, thinking, reflecting and feeling. At the same time, the therapist knows that this goal will be more easily achieved if the parents can be helped to allow Stacey this new approach.

THE DEVELOPMENT AND IMPROVEMENT OF EGO-FUNCTIONS

Once again, this is a general and ubiquitous goal. It takes on more precise importance with those children whose ego-functions are obviously deficient and inadequately developed. In these instances, the therapeutic aim resembles "ego-muscle-building" in which the therapist demonstrates his or her "good" ego capacities and gradually assists the child through the sequence of incorporation, imitation, assimilation, identification, and autonomous ego functioning. This goal requires some precision in identifying the deficient ego functions and, once identified, some ingenuity in designing specific "exercises" to strengthen them.

Ricky

Ricky is nine, the older of two children whose mother has supported both her children since her divorce some years ago. Ricky's mother is a woman with exacting standards who finds Ricky's problems exasperating. His school work is sloppy and erratic, he whines about being teased, is friendless and wets his bed frequently.

In the very first hours, Ricky quickly demonstrates a serious inability to take in information and use it effectively. Rather he offers whatever comes to mind impulsively; as if guessing is as good as knowing. This becomes evident in a game of Ricky's invention. He asks the therapist to clasp his fingers together and to hide some fingers from view. Ricky will tell how many fingers are hidden and which these are. As the game unfolds, Ricky blurts his answers instantly and without examining the therapist's hands.

The therapist becomes very curious. How does Ricky know how many fingers are out of sight and which are not visible? Each time Ricky gives the following typical response: "I don't know but it's just two and it's the two pinkies." Once again, the therapist puzzles about how Ricky knows and how Ricky might truly figure this out. Ricky is bewildered but intrigued. The therapist can now offer a suggestion, if Ricky is interested, in how the therapist would figure out the answer. The therapist would need to really look, examine the clasped hands, count the fingers, subtract from ten and identify which of the fingers he sees and doesn't see.

This process seems to be a revelation to Ricky. Together therapist and Ricky play this game repeatedly, devising new forms and adding variations to this simple presentation.

The finger game becomes a paradigm for the many new functions Ricky must learn. Early on the therapist has identified Ricky's serious deficits, and recognizes that the aim of this treatment will be to help Ricky build new ego-functions. He is aided at the outset by the boy's hunger for attention and interest, and by Ricky's readiness to use the relationship with the therapist as the basic mode for developing new capacities. Lending Ricky a more effective ego, over time, helps this impaired boy incorporate, imitate, identify with and, subsequently, own new-found competencies. In turn, these new skills will reduce Ricky's strangeness, loneliness and those exasperating qualities which have estranged him even from his mother.

THE RELIEF OF SPECIFIC SYMPTOMS

The common recognition that symptoms are a compromising effort to adapt to and cope with conflict must not obscure the view that the symptoms create additional suffering and may, in fact, further impair or slow development. In some cases direct attention to the specific symptom becomes a central therapeutic issue. This is particularly true when children have been exposed to recent traumatic events. Even when more general goals are taken as central to the therapy, the specific symptoms and their course should not be ignored.

Freddie

Freddie, age five, began having nightmares after learning that his parents had decided to separate. In the third therapy session he told his therapist his worst fear: that when his Daddy left the house he would never be able to find him again. The content of his nightmares clearly reflected this terrible fear. Both parents were advised to let Freddie know very clearly that his father would not disappear and that they would make sure that Freddie and his father would continue to see one another and that his Daddy would never stop being his Daddy. Neither parent had realized what Freddie feared and were able to utilize the therapist's suggestion ably and directly. The therapist and Freddie worked together on his fear for a very brief time and the nightmares ended. Some six months later, on an agreed upon follow-up visit, Freddie seemed to be doing well and there had been no recurrence of the nightmares.

The work with these children illustrates some of the areas and goals which evolve from the therapist's understanding of each child's unique needs and problems. Although the development of appropriate aims and goals is a necessary step for treatment to proceed, it does not guarantee that treatment can proceed. Certain necessary conditions must be fulfilled before psychotherapy is truly underway.

REFERENCES

1. Bernstein, A., *The flight of the stork*. New York: Dell Publishing Co., 1978.
2. Brody, S., Aims and methods of child psychotherapy. *J. of American Academy of Child Psychiatry*, 3: 395-412.
3. Chess, S., Selectivity of treatment modalities. *Canadian Journal of Psychiatry*, 1981, Vol. 26(5): 309-315.
4. Chess, S., and Hassibi, M., *Principles and practices of child psychiatry*. New York: Plenum Press, 1978.
5. Coopersmith, S., *The antecedents of self-esteem*. San Francisco: W. H. Freeman & Co., 1967.
6. Erickson, E., *Identity and the life cycle*. Psychological Issues Monograph Series No. 1, New York: International Universities Press, 1959.
7. Fraiberg, S., The origins of identity. *Smith College Studies in Social Work*, 1968, Vol. 38(2), 79-101.
8. Freud, A., The concept of developmental lines. *Psychoanalytic Study of the Child*, 1963, Vol. 18: 245-265.
9. Gilligan, C., New maps of development: New visions of maturity. *American J. of Orthopsychiatry*, 1982, Vol. 52(2): 199-212.
10. Greenspan, S., and Lourie, R., Developmental structuralist approach to the classification of adaptive and pathologic personality of organizations—Infancy and early childhood. *American J. of Psychiatry*, 1981, Vol. 138(6): 725-735.
11. Inhelden, B., and Piaget, J., *The growth of logical thinking from childhood to adolescence*. New York: Basic Books, 1958.
12. Kernberg, O., *Borderline conditions and pathologic narcissism*. New York: Jason Aronson, 1975.
13. Mahler, M., Pine, F., and Bergman, A., *The psychological birth of the human infant—Symbiosis and individuation*. New York: Basic Books, 1975.
14. McCall, R. B., Challenges to a science of developmental psychology. *Child Development*, 1977, Vol. 48: 333-344.
15. Mishne, J., *Clinical work with children*. New York: Free Press, 1983.
16. Ornstein, P. (Ed.), *The search for the self: Selected writings of Heinz Kohut, 1950-1978. Vols. 1 & 2*. New York: International Universities Press, 1978.
17. Palumbo, J., Theories of narcissism as related to social work practice. *Clinical Social Work*, 1976, Vol. 4: 147-161.
18. Perlman, H. H., *Relationship: The heart of helping people*. Chicago, IL: University of Chicago Press, 1979.
19. Redl, F., *When we deal with children: Selected writings*. New York: Free Press, 1966.
20. Settlage, C. F., The psychoanalytic understanding of narcissism and borderline personality disorders: Advances in developmental theory. *J. of the American Psychoanalytic Assn.*, 1977, Vol. 25: 805-833.
21. Thomas, A., Current trends in developmental theory. *American J. of Orthopsychiatry*, 1981, Vol. 57(4): 580-609.

CHAPTER 3

The Conditions Necessary for Treatment

BETSY JAMES

Betsy is eight, the eldest of three children, having two sisters, ages six and one. She lives with her parents, Mr. James, 35, a computer programmer, and Mrs. James, 33, a homemaker. Betsy is referred because of speech and behavioral problems.

Up to the age of five, Betsy did not speak any conventional language, but, instead, designed a private one which only the family could understand. During the past few years, she has been in speech therapy and is gradually learning to speak English. She's also described as always getting into things, difficult to discipline, and impervious to punishment. The school she attends is insisting that she be in psychotherapy. While the parents are concerned about Betsy, they are bringing her largely under pressure from the school, although they've known something was wrong for many years. When she was three-and-a-half, they asked a pediatrician about her not speaking and were told not to worry, that she would certainly begin talking when she started school. They found this a comfortable position to take. At the school's urging, however, they sought out a speech therapist and finally a psychotherapist.

Mrs. James is the youngest of three children whose mother abandoned the family when Mrs. James was four. Her childhood was marked by numerous moves. She sometimes lived with her father or her grandmother or several aunts and finally back with her mother when she was ten. By then, she had learned to be "self-sufficient and not need mothering." She left high school to marry for the first time at age 17. Four years later, she met Mr. James, divorced her first husband and married him.

Mr. James grew up in a strict family from the rural South. He was rarely allowed to have friends over since his friends were always ridiculed by his mother. When his grades fell in ninth grade, he was sent away to an uncle for disciplining. After high school, he joined the Army, where he received his beginning training in computer programming. Upon his discharge, he came to California where, shortly afterward, he met his wife-to-be.

The marriage has been extremely stormy, with numerous fights and separations. When Mrs. James became pregnant, Mr. James felt tricked. He wasn't ready. Betsy's birth did not bring them closer together, and the fights, which often included physical violence, continued. Periodically, Mrs. James would leave, sometimes to return to her parents, sometimes with other men. Her absences would last from a few days to months. From the time Betsy was six months old until she was almost six years old, these separations occurred on the average of twice a year. Usually Betsy, and later, Betsy and her younger sister, were left with Mr. James. Occasionally, Mrs. James would take the two girls with her. Finally, when Betsy was five-and-a-half, Mr. James sought a divorce and received custody of the girls. However, shortly after the divorce was final, the parents reconciled and have lived together, though not married, for the past two years. During this time, Betsy's sister was born. Although no further separations have occurred, the relationship continues to be strained and confusing. During a conjoint interview held as part of the psychiatric evaluation, their interaction was described as exceedingly tense and their communication as confusing and bizarre. The father was described as a rigid, insecure, highly guarded man, who struggles to minimize and deny the seriousness of Betsy's problems. Mrs. James seemed more realistic about Betsy's difficulties but was herself quite nervous and depressed, with limited capacity to deal with frustration.

As might be anticipated from the marital history, Betsy's development was quite uneven. Her birth was reported as very difficult. Apparently, there was so much molding of the head that Mr. James was sure her head was "all bashed in," and to this day wonders about brain damage. She had a milk allergy with much diarrhea for the first two years. Her motor development was not unusual, and she walked by 12 months. Toilet training was reported as easy and fully achieved by three years. However, she did not learn to speak but rather developed her own language which, by the time Betsy was three, Mrs. James says she and later the younger sister could understand. As might be expected, Betsy had great difficulty when she began school and was placed part of the time in a regular class and part of the time in a class for "aphasic" children.

Betsy is a small, very thin and appealing child with huge eyes and huge eyeglasses. During the evaluation, she was immaculately groomed and appeared "dressed up" for the occasion. She made an immediate—perhaps too quick and intense—attachment to the therapist. Her speech is blurred and mushy, with poor sentence structure, making her very hard to understand. By contrast, her motor behavior, both in play and in drawing, is much more communicative and considerably less retarded than her speech. In the initial two hours, her play had little sustained focus as she moved from toy to toy and game to game, with few discernible rules. The third hour was marked by a distinctive departure from the first two, as follows:

Betsy arrives carrying a teddy bear which she is glad to introduce to the therapist, making sure that the therapist knows the bear's name. The therapist is interested in Betsy's bringing a friend from home to the hour. Betsy asks if the folder on the therapist's desk is hers and examines the two drawings which she remembers having made.

She moves to the toy cabinet and more slowly examines the toys, coming upon two small magnets. She is interested in what will stick to them and experiments with these. The therapist comments that Betsy seems curious about what things stick together, which Betsy acknowledges with an "Uh-uh."

The major part of the hour is then devoted to sustained play with the dolls and the dollhouse. She puts the father in his bed and the boy and girl in their beds in the other rooms. A dog is put in a hiding place under the stairs, and the mother is placed outside of the house some distance away. The therapist says, "Mom is not home!" Betsy says: "Yes, Mommie not home." Betsy rings the doorbell and the therapist wonders aloud what she should do. Betsy answers: "Have girl answer door." As she says this, she moves the mother toward the front door. The therapist has the girl answer the door, but as it is opened, Betsy hides the mother doll so no one is there. The therapist comments that no one is there. Betsy laughs nervously and tells the therapist to put the girl back in bed. This game is repeated in the same way several times.

The therapist says that it looks like the family is waiting for Mommie to come home, but that Mommie doesn't come but hides instead. Betsy laughs nervously as she says, "Uh-uh."

The same sequence is repeated another three or four times. Then Betsy asks the therapist to seat everyone at the kitchen table, including the dog. Then she has the mother appear, placing her at work in the kitchen. The therapist notes that it must be very confusing: "Sometimes Mom is home and sometimes she's not." Betsy says yes and once again giggles nervously. The therapist reflects that even though Betsy is laughing, she thinks that Betsy may be worried. This time, Betsy acknowledges the therapist's comment, but without the nervous laughter.

The hour comes to a close with Betsy's request for a balloon for her teddy bear. She wants it blown up and tied with string so her teddy bear "won't lose it."

Altogether Betsy's is a complicated and sad story; it is one about which a plan of intervention must be evolved from a wide range of choices. Which intervention should be chosen? Further speech therapy? Special education? Play therapy for Betsy? Therapy for Mr. and Mrs. James? Family therapy? An activity program for Betsy? Any combination of these? Which is preferable and which is possible? How shall the decision be made?

In this instance, the therapist evaluating Betsy and her family developed an initial treatment plan which included the following:

1) Individual play therapy sessions with Betsy. This seemed indicated in the sessions with Betsy, most notably the third session, which suggested that she was struggling with internal conflicts and confusions, as well as serious lags in development. The therapist felt this would be a useful intervention because of Betsy's evident ability to make use of the therapist and to convey important problems in her play.
2) Conjoint meetings with Mr. and Mrs. James aimed at stabilizing their relationship and helping them establish greater consistency for Betsy, and, indirectly, for the two younger children as well.
3) A careful review of Betsy's school placement along with a review of the speech therapy. Betsy's therapist anticipated being actively

involved in planning for Betsy's special educational needs in the future.

This initial plan will be subject to constant review and modification. For example, the early assessment leads, in Betsy's case, to the reasonable hypothesis that she can make use of individual play therapy. This hypothesis rests on two pieces of evidence: Betsy's ability to relate to the therapist, and her progressive ability to communicate important content over the first three hours. However, what remains to be confirmed over a lengthier period of time is whether she can continue to reveal her inner world and whether she can make use of the therapist's help to modify her perceptions and her behavior. Frequently, these changes cannot come about without a supporting set of conditions in the outer world.

For Betsy, the need for a supportive external environment led to the recommendation for conjoint sessions with the parents—a plan that was soon modified. As the conjoint work with the parents proceeded, it became clear that each wanted and could make use of separate time with the child's therapist. The therapist agreed to this alteration from the experience of working with the two together. While both parents attended most of their early appointments, as therapy progressed they began, on occasion, to come separately, announcing that child care or work requirements made joint attendance difficult. Different, but equally important, work was accomplished in the individual and the conjoint sessions. Each parent, however, was conveying a clear message to the therapist that each needed some private time with her, although they continued to productively work on their conflicts in parenting, together. Individual sessions were then added to the conjoint sessions—all of which focused largely on the James' relationship and their parenting. Sometime later, Mr. James requested a therapist of his own; a request made possible only after Mr. James experienced significant trust in and help from Betsy's therapist.

The beginning plan for Betsy's treatment illustrates the general principle that a "case plan" must recognize the existence of two overlapping universes—the *ideal* and the *real*.

The *ideal* universe consists of all the interventions available in the field of child treatment. As knowledge and the "state of the art" expand, the ideal universe of interventions grows larger and larger. Already, more is known than can be effectively implemented. For example, more is known than ever before about how affiliations are developed, disrupted and restored. Similarly, knowledge is expanding about individual temperamental differences, about the proximal conditions in the physical and emotional environments which promote development, about vulnerabilities and resiliencies, about those conditions which put people at risk and even about how one might prevent some disorders.

The ideal range of choices is immediately circumscribed by the limitations of the therapist's own knowledge, as well as by the ideological persuasions which he or she may hold. These limitations will inevitably dictate certain therapeutic choices. Some hypothetical options will simply not occur to the therapist, while others may be thought of but quickly discarded—since even though they can be entertained intellectually, they will not match one's theoretical biases.

Above and beyond the limitations imposed by the particular therapist's fund of knowledge and theoretical biases, the ideal range of choices is further constrained by the limitations imposed by the real world. These include:

1) The Realities of the Particular Family

At the simplest level, these realities include who is involved in the problems being presented, how amenable these people are to change, what kinds of changes may need to occur, what strengths each of the principal players has, what time and funds the family has available, and what ability they have to bring themselves to the therapist or the therapeutic center. For example: No matter how much one is certain that weekly family therapy sessions might be the best intervention plan, if one of the parents cannot find time to attend these, such a plan simply will not work.

Mr. and Mrs. Spencer are intensely involved in the lives of their son and daughter, ages 12 and 15. Mrs. Spencer had problems in school during her own education which left her with a pervasive sense of inadequacy. The residue of this unhappy past is now being projected into her present intense investment in the academic achievement of her children. Mr. Spencer is deeply committed to his wife, which leads him to support her "program" for the children and prevents him from a full appreciation of the impact this has upon them.

The household is in constant uproar as the children ally together to resist the overwhelming pressures Mrs. Spencer imposes on them for school performance. They are battling for their own autonomy, without being fully conscious of the dimensions of this struggle.

They consult a therapist who recommends that the family meet as a unit, based on the assessment that the family is split into two warring camps which permits none of its members to develop independently. Unfortunately, this plan is rendered untenable by Mr. Spencer's work schedule, which regularly takes him away from home on business trips all over the country.

Some other interventions will need to be found though they may be less ideal.

2) The Motivations and Interests of the Family Members

In fact, the realities families face and their psychological states combine to create their motivations. Often, motivational factors are complex and only partially understood by the members of a family, and function as another limiting factor. Frequently, different family members will have differing and even discordant motives. For example: Jane, 12, is the younger daughter of a hardworking widowed mother. Since the death of her husband, Mrs. Howard has been entirely occupied with finding and keeping a job and providing the necessities for her family. This has included great effort in maintaining the care of her children while she is at work. With so much of her energy caught up in realistic problems, she has had little time or opportunity to attend to her growing awareness that Jane is indeed quite different from other youngsters. This awareness was further screened by Mrs. Howard's insistence that Jane's clumsiness, lying, and poor schoolwork were intentional. Gradually and painfully, she acknowledged that Jane is different and troubled. At first, she attempted to help Jane by placing her in a different school. When she finally sought a psychiatric evaluation for her daughter, her motivation was strong and her relief that help might be available was quite evident. As the evaluation proceeded, Mrs. Howard revealed still other factors in her earlier motivational hesitancy. She grew up in a family where culprits were sought out and accused regularly. Such a background prepared her to assign intentionality and blame to all behavior—including her own. This made it virtually impossible for others who might have offered assistance earlier to "read" her very weak signals for help.

The state of Jane's motivation was quite another matter. She had no wish to see a "shrink." She came late or on the wrong day, "mistakes" which seemed confusional as well as oppositional. Early hours were spent in superficial, very concrete interchanges. With the therapist's help, Mrs. Howard persisted in her insistence that Jane continue.

It became increasingly clear over the first two months that Jane was struggling with a profound conflict between her wish to make an alliance with the therapist in order to get some help and her intense need to ward off her awareness that there was something very wrong. This conflict was graphically portrayed in the twelfth week. Jane's chattering was interspersed with many long periods of silence. She spent a good deal of time rummaging through her book bag and later in the hour, silently spun in the therapist's swivel chair, which permitted no eye contact. The therapist commented that Jane seemed different today, and that she had the idea that Jane was feeling very sad. Mutely, Jane nodded her agreement. The therapist added that she had another idea. Perhaps Jane was finding it hard and sad to think about the things that were worrying her. Jane experienced the therapist's remarks as an invitation to engage in an alliance for which she clearly hungered and simultaneously as a confrontation with her intense denial. Jane's motivation had now shifted. She was ready to engage, but the price of this was her great sadness, a prelude to the work that was to follow.

This situation is not uncommon. The treatment of children, in contrast to psychotherapeutic work with adults, is marked by the varying motivations of various family members, which emerge as differing defenses and resistances. How these hidden or overt agendas and motivational factors are understood and negotiated is a critical determinant in the case planning and therapeutic work to come.

Closely related to differing motivations among the various family members are differing perceptions of the nature of the problems. Naturally, people see things differently and some discrepancies are to be expected. However, occasionally, the differences are so great that one must consider how they came about and the meaning of such extensive distortion. In these extreme situations, the initial case planning for the various family members may well need to be very flexible and experimental until further clarity about the extent and nature of these distorted perceptions is achieved.

An early clue to such difficulties can often be found in the therapist's inability to identify the child who walks into the playroom as the child described by the parents. Michael is such a child. Recommended for treatment by the school psychologist because of his inability to read, Michael is entering the third grade, having already repeated the first grade.

Michael's parents seem attractive and bright. They are both employed. In addition to Michael, there is a brother who is two years younger. The mother is evidently the more concerned of the two about Michael. The father is a jovial man who talks of Michael as outgoing, athletic, skillful at making friends easily and "with everyone." He is, however, troubled by Michael's school difficulties, which his own tutoring has not remedied.

The mother's view is quite different. At times, she is vague, complaining that Michael is "hyperactive," unable to play by himself, easily distracted and tempestuous. The father smilingly suggests that each parent has a favorite child; Michael is his, while Dennis is his wife's.

Both parents are concerned about introducing Michael to the first therapy session. He has already been tested many times and the mother complains that they have learned little from these experiences. The father wonders whether the therapist can be introduced as a family friend, noting again that Michael "can make friends with the devil." The mother, on the other hand, thinks Michael may not be so readily engaged, and predicts that there will be difficulties.

In a separate session with each parent, the therapist learns of Michael's birth history. The mother was sure that something was wrong during her pregnancy and that he would be born prematurely and damaged. Unfortunately, Michael was born with a tracheo-esophageal fistula, which required immediate surgery and which kept him hospitalized for a week. Each parent reports these facts similarly. However, the mother is more reticent about her reactions but associates to a memory when Michael was four. She saw a TV film about the damaging effects which may occur when parents don't hold their babies enough. The father reported that his wife was extremely fearful of holding Michael during the hospitalization and the first weeks at home and that he had assumed the major responsibilities for feeding and caring for the baby.

Three months after Michael's birth, his mother returned to work, leaving Michael with baby-sitters.

After these meetings with the parents, the therapist is unsure who to expect. Will he meet a hyperactive, tempestuous, difficult, damaged child as portrayed by his mother or the affable, outgoing, and easily engaged youngster seen through his father's eyes?

In fact, he meets a totally different boy. In the waiting room, Michael is weeping quietly behind his mother's shoulder. He is only willing to come in the playroom if accompanied by his mother. In this session, the mother persistently talks to her son, verbally encouraging him to talk or play with the therapist, while making it virtually impossible for this to take place by her constant interference, distractions and introductions of new topics from their "private" conversations. In an "aside," she reminds the therapist that Michael did not like talking to the school psychologist. At the conclusion of the hour, the mother says to Michael: "See, it wasn't that bad."

In the second session, Michael does come into the playroom alone and without difficulty.

He begins by making a colorful and beautifully executed drawing, followed by a series of play-dough models. The play is interspersed with conversations with the therapist about some things Michael does at home and at school.

Clearly, there are four different Michaels, so far. Neither Michael of the two therapy sessions matches either parent's version of him. The therapist is left struggling to find a coherent view of Michael's internal structure, to fit this with his parents' obvious misperceptions and to understand the origins, nature and extent of these distorted views of their son.

The father's distortions seem to be more immediately comprehensible. They appear to be in the service of protecting Michael from his wife's pervasive message to Michael that he is a severely damaged and troubled child. At the same time, the father's denials seem aimed at reassuring his wife by attempting to ameliorate her guilt and worry. It is probable that these denials also serve other, unknown needs of his own.

The distorted view which Michael's mother holds seems far less understandable. The nature of this incorrect view, the history of its very early appearance, and the manner in which she behaved in the joint session with Michael suggest that her view of him probably has its roots in her early experiences, and that Michael represents to her some figure from her past about whom there is much unresolved conflict. As a consequence, Michael is in danger of becoming mother's self-fulfilling prophecy rather than his own person.

The initial therapeutic plan will need to address the task of assisting both parents to yield their different fantasies of who Michael is and find a more realistic appraisal of their son. Failing this, it is highly unlikely that Michael can be helped psychotherapeutically.

3) Attention to the Separate Value Systems of the Family Members

Attention to the family members' separate value systems, particularly those of the parents, as these interact with the value systems of the therapist, is inherent in arriving at a feasible case plan.

Every family and every therapist brings these value systems to the encounter. At the very least, these will include values about appropriate parenting and child rearing, values about the efficacy of treatment in general, and about certain modalities in particular—to say nothing of basic mores and ethics. Some therapists cannot work with a family which fundamentally believes that regular physical punishment is important for a child's moral development. Who can work with whom is a question with finite borders. These borders cannot always be stretched beyond certain limits of discordance. Unfortunately, these questions are often ignored or quickly buried under the value system of many therapies which hold that one should be saintly and skillful enough to be able to provide help to anyone, at any time, in any place.

More recently, there has been a trend to narrow such therapeutic zeal by another value system which holds, in the extreme, that those with particular life experiences and attributes are exclusively suited to treat given groups of people. Carried to its most logical extension, this belief would assert that only children should treat children.*

To illustrate: An immigrant family came to this country when their eldest son—one of four children—was about four years old. Through the entire extended family's strenuous involvement in a small business, they acquired considerable economic advantages, though they remain anxious that these may not endure.

The core of the father's self-esteem rests on his capacity to earn in spite of being totally illiterate in both his native and adopted languages. Acquisition is central to his life and, defensively, he insists that learning and school achievement are superfluous and vastly overvalued in this country. Naturally, he and the school have been at odds about his son's many school absences and school failures. Finally expelled, the boy was placed in a day treatment program. Neither the mother—for her own reasons—nor the father can understand the Center's insistence that they take time from work to participate in the boy's treatment.

In addition to participating in the prevailing family value which places acquisition above all else, this 14-year-old boy has faced many other experiences which leave him feeling utterly unprotected, damaged and unable to find a place with peers or family. The boy's thinking is fragmented and chaotic, subject to intense disorganization, while his level of anxiety is pervasive and intense. He cannot understand what

---

*We do know of one case in which a parent withdrew her child from treatment on the grounds that if he were going to play, he should play with someone his own age. While amusing, this anecdote must not obscure the serious and important element which values play in determining treatment planning.

is wanted of him by the various helpers who have entered his life and left defeated. His relationship with his new therapist is tenuous and easily disrupted. Attempts to label his anxious feelings are denied and vigorously warded off by a pseudo-macho stance which leaves the therapist puzzled and helpless. To help the boy remain longer in the treatment room, they finally hit on Monopoly, a game which the boy seems to enjoy. However, the therapist is puzzled as the child does not play by standard rules. And though this boy can count, he seems uninterested in the actual scores. Instead, he stacks his winnings, preferring small denominations to the larger bills, and is pleased as his pile mounts and exceeds the therapist's—regardless of its value. He is puzzled when the therapist offers to make a record of where they have gotten to in the game, so they may continue in their next meeting.

Aside from the value discrepancies between the family and the various settings concerned with this boy's care, it becomes clear that this boy is intent on acquisition alone. He is unable to hold representations of people or things in his mind from one moment to the next. He has and owns the things of the moment, concretely estimating their worth *and* his own by what he can see, touch, and measure competitively against the other's winnings. In this instance, the therapist is playing Monopoly; the boy is playing quite another game. Unless she can penetrate to the level of this boy's concreteness and the basic value system he derived from his family's view as well as the many deprivations he has experienced, this treatment will fail, even if the therapist is, by dictum, successfully able to insist upon the family's participation.

No one is overly hopeful in this instance; however, case planning and prognosis aside for the moment, the case illustrates that value discordances do influence the understanding and interventions one makes on a microscopic as well as a macroscopic level.

4) The Skill and Style of the Therapist and Their Effect on Choices Offered Patients and the Way in Which the Work Is Conducted

In our wish to be scientific and objective, it is tempting to view the diagnostic sessions as a data gathering process, in which the facts will ultimately be ordered towards a set of reasonable recommendations. However, while this computerlike process is underway and needs to take place, other equally or perhaps more important events are occurring. For the child, the parent and the therapist, the initial diagnostic sessions are a sample of the actual experience of treatment. It is in this unfolding experience that patients determine *if* they will contract, *how* they will contract and *what* the terms of the therapeutic contract will be. Viewed from this perspective, these initial diagnostic sessions pose particularly difficult and complex tasks for the therapist. Among these tasks are the gathering and processing of data, the establishment of a relationship that includes some degree of safety, trust, mutual understanding and respect, and a view that the plan which is "finally" portrayed is, at best, tentative and always subject to review and modification.

For example: Marshall is five-and-a-half. His parents separated when Marshall was 18 months old. Each has since remarried, the mother when Marshall was almost three. Marshall now has a two-month-old stepsister. Although his father visits him, Marshall has always lived with his mother.

Recently, Marshall's father asked the court to alter the custody award to joint custody to permit him to have his son for longer periods of time. This has once again activated the alternatingly strident and dormant struggle between the parents.

Marshall's mother believes that Marshall becomes more anxious before and after visits with his father. His father believes that, if this is so, it is because the mother criticizes him, and because Marshall visits too infrequently. Whatever the cause, Marshall is indeed a tense child whose anxiety is displayed in stomachaches and some sleep disturbance. It is these symptoms and the impending court action which prompt the parents to agree to a psychiatric evaluation.

In the first session, Marshall behaves with considerable caution. He seems precocious, engages warily, and looks at the toys, remarking that he need not play with the office toys, since he has so many similar ones at home. After some time, he becomes interested in the stacking barrels, carefully lining up the barrels in two lines against the wall so they are symmetrically organized, each side duplicating the other. He remarks that they now look like "a road without an end"—and seems somewhat bothered when he discovers a tiny animal on one side in the smallest barrel.

He leaves the play quickly.

In the second hour, Marshall draws a picture of a simple human figure with arms extended. When asked if the picture has a story, Marshall remarks, "The boy is being pulled." The therapist asks, "How come the boy is pulled?" Marshall does not reply and returns to the barrels, again lining them up neatly on both sides of the room. Later, he returns to his drawing and, as though scribbling, draws a line down the center of his figure. The therapist asks about the line and Marshall wonders which side of the boy the therapist likes best. He replies, "I'm on *your* side."

While this therapist is empathically alert to Marshall's struggle and clearly wishes to portray himself as Marshall's ally, his comment may not be the most helpful. In asserting that he is on Marshall's side, he may have unwittingly reinforced Marshall's sense that one must take sides in this embattled child's life. This intervention, as a sample of the therapy to come, has the potential of defining the treatment plan as one which will seek to define the correct choice of sides. Perhaps a more effective portrayal of the therapy would be an acknowledgement of how difficult it is to be faced with hard choices as a preliminary to an inquiry about how this must feel to Marshall. While this is a subtle differentiation, it seems important in determining how the therapist's skill and style of intervention may influence the treatment.

5) Attention to the Interplay Between the Child's Inner World and the Environment in Which He Lives

The degree to which the real and psychological environments support or undermine the specific therapeutic efforts to resolve conflict, alter behaviors, or assist in promoting development must be viewed as equally important as understanding the child's intrapsychic difficulties.

For example, to focus on a child's constriction and phobic defenses naturally suggests an intensive, uncovering treatment whose objective is to help the child resolve those distortions which promote his view of the world as unrealistically dangerous. However, if the child continues to be confronted with an environment which promotes a lack of safety and stability, such uncovering would not only fail to resolve neurotic conflict but would also promote confusion and further disintegration.

Therapists are not infrequently confronted with a surprising end to a treatment which they believe to be going well. As a disturbing symptom may mute or disappear, a parent may feel that all is well again and terminate the treatment. Or the new behaviors made possible by the symptom abating may be in conflict with the parents' expectations and wishes leading to termination.

Josie, once an excellent student, entered high school at a time when her divorced parents again escalated their ongoing struggle about visits, child support and child-rearing practices. Josie became listless and apathetic, and her grades began to drop sharply. Josie's mother, whose academic standards were exceedingly high, sought help from the school counselor, who recommended psychotherapy for Josie. While Josie's mother approached treatment with some conflict, she readily gave Josie and the therapist her support as Josie's academic performance steadily improved. The therapist correctly understood that Josie's learning difficulties were a symptomatic expression of her conflicts about extricating herself from her family and the imperative each parent placed upon her for primary loyalty. As a consequence of this correct view, the therapist and Josie worked toward developing a more autonomous posture separate from both parents. This afforded Josie considerable relief and allowed her to make strides academically and socially. Less compliant now, Josie's developmentally appropriate social interests brought her into sharp conflict with her mother, who insisted on complete obedience, and who held a much more limited view about appropriate and acceptable social activities. Josie's mother moved forcefully to end the treatment, informing Josie's therapist: "I don't care what progress you think Josie is making; in my family children obey their parents!"

Despite the abrupt termination, Josie's treatment can be considered successful. For the moment, the treatment cannot go further since it will founder on her real dependence upon her mother, in whose home she must remain for some time. Josie was able to acknowledge that she must abide by her mother's wishes, though she can still retain her own point of view. "I may not altogether like it and there may be some fights, but I know that when I'm old enough I'll decide myself how children should be raised!" said Josie on leaving.

Here, an adolescent meets a psychological reality in her immediate world which conflicts with her inner needs and the therapeutic objectives.

A related, larger-scale dilemma which often presents itself in the assessing of the probability of undertaking a successful psychotherapy is socioeconomic pressures that permit little time and energy for reflection. It may be self-evident, but it is worth underlining that people faced with hunger, inadequate housing, poor medical care or unemployment will be afforded little relief from psychotherapy unless this goes hand in hand with concrete services to ameliorate their crushing environmental realities.

6) Realities of the Available Treatment Resources

An individual therapist or agency may not have at their disposal all the ingredients needed to arrive at a realistic and reasonable treatment plan for a particular child. A child who has failed to learn because of emotional conflicts will need assistance to catch up, in addition to assistance in resolving those conflicts which make the child less receptive to learning. An isolated child may need help in making friends or finding opportunities for social contacts when he or she is psychologically ready to do so. If the therapy is to have optimal benefits, therapists must frequently look at the larger community or evolve programs to enrich the child's life and provide essential experiences for the child. Services such as activity programs, group experiences, learning assistance, respite care medication or special treatment settings may be required as part of a complete treatment plan.

It will not suffice, however, for the therapist simply to think of the various elements in a comprehensive plan, and send the family off to find them. Therapists should have a working knowledge of these resources, take an active part in helping parents locate them and hold themselves accountable for ongoing coordination and collaborative work with other professionals.*

7) Administrative and Bureaucratic Realities Which Increasingly Limit the Capacity to Help

Like it or not, more and more parties, outside of the therapist and the family, dictate how long patients may be seen, how frequently treatment can occur, and in some instances, whom and in what modes to treat. While the growing role of bureaucracy cannot be denied, administrative rules and regulations should, ideally, be the least influential of the conditions determining the best possible treatment plan. Resistance to intrusive bureaucracy must be maintained in the face of the pressure to compromise and collude with such bureaucratic goals as cost effectiveness, utilization review, accountability, and management-by-objectives.

REFERENCES

1. Ainsworth, M., Bell, S. M. V., and Stayton, D. J., Individual differences in the development of some attachment behaviors. *Merrill-Palmer Quarterly*, 1971, Vol. 18(2): 123-143.

---

*A particular pet peeve of the authors in the current "mental health treatment system" is the emphasis on case management. This is a useful idea intended to correct the fragmentation of services particularly needed by "multiproblem families." "Linkages" and "networking" are the current vogue. However, their implementation too often leads to a situation in which everyone is coordinating and being coordinated while no one provides essential services.

2. Ainsworth, M., and Bell, S. M., Mother-infant interaction and the development of competence. In K. J. Connelly and J. S. Bruner (Eds.), *The growth of competence.* New York: Academic Press, 1974.
3. Bowlby, J., *Attachment and loss I: Attachment.* New York: Basic Books, 1969.
4. Bowlby, J., *Attachment and loss II: Separation, anxiety and anger.* New York: Basic Books, 1973.
5. Bowlby, J., Attachment and loss: Retrospect and prospect. *American J. of Orthopsychiatry*, 1982, Vol. 52(4): 664-678.
6. Bronfenbrenner, U., Is early intervention effective? Facts and principles of early intervention: A summary. In A. M. Clark and A. D. Clark (Eds.), *Early Experience: Myth and Evidence.* New York: The Free Press, 1976.
7. Chess, S., and Thomas, A., Temperamental individuality from childhood to adolescence. In S. Chess and A. Thomas (Eds.), *Annual Progress in Child Psychiatry and Child Development.* New York: Brunner/Mazel, 1978: 223-244.
8. Cooper, S., Social work: A dissenting profession. *Social Work*, 1977, Vol. 22: 360-367.
9. Fanshel, D., and Shinn, E., *Children in foster care: A longitudinal investigation.* New York: Columbia University Press, 1978.
10. Fraiberg, S., and Fraiberg, L. (Eds.), *Clinical studies in infant mental health.* New York: Basic Books, 1980.
11. Fraiberg, S., Adelson, E., and Shapiro, V., Ghosts in the nursery. *J. Amer. Acad. of Child Psychiatry*, 1975, Vol. 14(3): 387-421.
12. Galt, J., *Systemantics: How systems work and especially how they fail.* New York: Pocket Books, 1975.
13. Garmezy, N., Children under stress: Perspectives on antecedents and correlates of vulnerability and resistance to psychopathology. In R. A. Zucker and A. I. Rabin (Eds.), *Further Explorations in Personality.* New York: John Wiley and Sons, 1980.
14. Germain, C., and Gutterman, A., *The life model of social work practice.* New York: Columbia University Press, 1980.
15. Horowitz, F. D. (Ed.), *Review of child development research, Vol. 4.* Chicago, IL: University of Chicago Press, 1975.
16. Kagan, J., Emergent themes in human development. *American Scientist*, 1976, Vol. 64(2): 186-196.
17. Klaus, M., and Kennell, J. H. (Eds.), *Maternal infant bonding.* St. Louis, MO: C. V. Mosby Co., 1976.
18. Maccoby, E., *Social development: Psychological growth and the parent-infant relationship.* New York: Harcourt, Brace, Jovanovitch, 1980.
19. Murphy, L. B., and Moriarity, A. E., *Vulnerability, coping and growth from infancy to adolescence.* New Haven: Yale University Press, 1976.
20. Noshpitz, J., Toward a national policy for children. *J. of Amer. Acad. of Child Psychiatry*, 1974, Vol. 13: 385-401.
21. Perlman, H. H., In quest of coping. *Social Casework*, 1975, Vol. 56(4): 213-225.
22. Pilisuk, M., The future of human services without funding. *American J. of Orthopsychiatry*, 1980, Vol. 50(2): 200-204.
23. Rutter, M., Maternal deprivation, 1972-1978: New findings, new concepts, new approaches. *Child Development*, 1979, Vol. 50: 283-305.
24. Rutter, M., Social-emotional consequences of day care for preschool children. *American J. of Orthopsychiatry*, 1981, Vol. 50(1): 4-28.
25. Settlage, C. F., Psychoanalytic developmental thinking in current historical perspective. *Psychoanalysis and Contemporary Thought*, Vol. 3(2). New York: International Universities Press, 1980: 139-170.
26. Stone, J., Smith, A., and Murphy, L. (Eds.), *The competent infant.* New York: Basic Books, 1973.
27. Wachs, T. D., Proximal experience and early cognitive-intellectual development: The physical environment. *The Merrill-Palmer Quarterly*, 1979, Vol. 25(1): 3-41.

PART II

Casebook

CHAPTER 4

Stalled Cases and Other Vexing Problems

All child therapists meet common vexing problems in the course of treating children and their parents. The case histories of Carmen and Douglas presented in this chapter involve the treatment of children, in which the case bogs down and, ultimately, seems to come to a halt. These "stalled" cases often have a resistant, repetitive and ritualistic quality about them: The child comes to his hours engaging in the same play and behavior over and over again. Some become increasingly disengaged from the therapist, revealing little new material while demonstrating no progress in important life spheres. Such cases require the most rigorous review, including:

1) a thorough examination of the entire course of treatment;
2) the goals;
3) an effort to discern when the case became mired;
4) an effort to link the stagnation with events and experiences in the life of the child;
5) a review of the disposition including a rethinking of whether all the appropriate people who influence the child are being properly included in the work;
6) the frequency with which the treatment occurs;

7) the need to appraise whether the child is acting for himself or is acting out for important members of the family;
8) the method chosen for the treatment of the family; and
9) the all-important question: whether the therapist's countertransference is in some way interfering with therapy.

At times, the most skillful child therapists find themselves unable to fathom why they cannot help the child. There is still much that remains unknown in this field. In some instances, the essential "chemistry," so central to the highly personal interactions in treatment, seems to be missing. Too often our understanding of why it is missing remains elusive. At other times, an essential ingredient in the conditions for treatment is lacking (see Chapter 3) and only becomes apparent as the case unfolds.

The following cases are instances in which the therapy got "stalled" until two therapists found ways to initiate progress in the therapy once again.

CARMEN TAYLOR

Carmen was referred by her school because of her poor academic performance and disruptive behavior in the classroom. She would not pay attention to her teacher's directions, fought with the other children and was described by her teacher as aggressive, domineering, hostile, and extremely manipulative. She was also fearful of trying any new activity. She avoided her classmates and was not invited by them to participate in group activities.

At the time of the referral Carmen was nine-and-a-half, and lived with her widowed mother and five-year-old brother. Her father died in an accident when Carmen was five. A year after the father's death, Mrs. Taylor took a secretarial job which she has held ever since. Both children have been in day care since that time, and they continue to go to day care after school. The day care center staff have noted similar problems as the school.

In the initial meetings Mrs. Taylor confirmed the problems at school and at the day care center and was concerned that Carmen might be expelled. She added her own complaints about Carmen: "She won't listen to me. Can't keep her mind on things. Can't follow directions or does it half-assed. She talks adult-like but acts like a baby, whining all the time." When asked for further details, Mrs. Taylor conveyed her expectation that Carmen take responsibility for various household tasks. The therapist thought that many of these expectations were beyond the capacity of most nine-and-a-half year olds.

Mrs. Taylor's complaints about Carmen's failure to live up to these expectations were at odds with her account of Carmen's early precocity. She described Carmen as a superbaby who did everything very early. She had four teeth by age five months, which brought breast feeding to an end. Carmen reportedly had an extensive vocabulary and was completely toilet trained without difficulty by the time she was one. All developmental achievements were accomplished simply by the mother's request that Carmen behave "like a big girl." Nursery school and the start of kindergarten seemed to go well. Both parents were actively involved in the nursery school. Similarly, Mrs. Taylor reported no notable problems connected with the birth of Carmen's baby brother.

Within a year of the new baby's birth, the family's situation altered dramatically. Mr. Taylor was killed in an automobile accident. Mrs. Taylor was so absorbed in her own grief that she could recall very little about the year following her husband's death, including how her children had responded to it. She was able to recall her surprise when, one year later, Carmen asked when her father would be coming back. Mrs. Taylor had presumed that Carmen understood that her father was dead and noted that after explaining that "he had gone to heaven" and would not return, Carmen never asked further about her father.

Mrs. Taylor has had several boyfriends since her husband's death. Carmen was described as not liking any of them, except the current one. Mrs. Taylor described this relationship as the most stable and serious one in which she'd been involved, and that she was expecting to marry soon.

Carmen had done reasonably well at school until the year prior to the referral. There had been occasional minor disciplinary problems which seemed to disappear when Mrs. Taylor advised the teacher to provide Carmen with additional attention and to treat her "like a star." Mrs. Taylor was unable to explain the great difficulty during the past school year except to speculate that it might be related to Carmen's first experience of having a male teacher. She did acknowledge that Carmen was also causing her more and more trouble at home. Although somewhat baffled, Mrs. Taylor was inclined to view these problems in terms of willfulness, stubbornness and laziness. On the other hand, Mrs. Taylor did suggest to the therapist who first saw Carmen and her mother that "something mental might be going on."

Mrs. Taylor's own history provided some important clues toward understanding her relationship to Carmen. Mrs. Taylor was born in Texas to a Mexican-American family. Her mother was 18 and had a one-year-old daughter at the time of Mrs. Taylor's birth. Her father was in the army and visited only occasionally during Mrs. Taylor's early years. When she was six months old, her mother left the care of the two children to her husband's grandmother and disappeared. When her great grandmother's health began to decline, the two children were sent to California to live with their father's mother. Mrs. Taylor was five. Shortly thereafter, the great grandmother joined them in California where she lived with the children and her daughter until her death eight years later.

When Mrs. Taylor was eight, her mother re-appeared and began visiting the family several times a year. Mrs. Taylor remembers her as a woman who brought candy and presents but toward whom she felt little connection. A few years later Mrs. Taylor's mother sought the custody of her two children which was resisted by the grandmother. Ultimately the court decided in favor of the grandmother, largely because the children expressed their preference for remaining with her. Mrs. Taylor remembered being very frightened that her mother, who felt like a stranger, might be able to take her away from her real home. When the legal battle was over, her mother disappeared again and Mrs. Taylor has not seen her since.

Mrs. Taylor recalled feeling very safe and well cared for by her grandmother and great grandmother. In retrospect she described being sheltered and protected with few demands made upon her to learn skills or self-sufficiency. This became particularly evident to her at age 21 when she married Mr. Taylor and discovered that she knew little about cooking, shopping or housekeeping even though she had always imagined a future for herself as wife and mother. She had worked briefly before her marriage in several clerical jobs. She described her marriage as extremely happy and fulfilling. Carmen was born a year later and everything went "wonderfully" until her husband's death.

Despite Mrs. Taylor's apparent motivation and seemingly open manner, there was considerable difficulty in scheduling during the evaluation. Several appointments were cancelled at the last moment, and Mrs. Taylor and Carmen were late for almost every meeting. In the three sessions with Carmen, the most notable feature was her rather constricted, superficial and infantile play. Her play, drawings and her interactions with the therapist were either minimal or oppositional. At the end of each hour she passively resisted leaving saying that she was having fun, although this was not evident from her demeanor. Her speech was soft, timid and sparse. In the third hour she was sullen and obviously angry about her brother's having received candy when she had not. She remained unresponsive to the therapist's efforts to engage her, choosing instead to play by herself with Tinker Toys. She left the room, ostensibly to get a drink of water but returned instead with some candy which she greedily and victoriously ate.

Psychological testing was requested in view of questions about possible intellectual impairment and the need for clarification of underlying conflicts and dynamics. The testing confirmed the clinical impressions of a child with average intellectual potential stunted by depression and an array of constricting and oppositional defenses. Further clarified was the issue of how thought about things lost and missing roused anxiety and how this was defended against by denial and inhibition of curiosity and activity. Carmen did, however, persist at tasks despite frustration, which was viewed as a hopeful prognostic indication for therapy.

Mrs. Taylor was accepting of the recommendation for therapy and Carmen was transferred to a therapist who had time available. The following is the account, by her therapist, of a year of work with Carmen and her mother.

When I first saw Mrs. Taylor her primary concern was about Carmen's behavior at home. She said that Carmen frequently refused to do her chores (cleaning own room, washing dinner dishes four times a week), saying that she could not, or was not able to do the work. Mrs. Taylor stressed the importance of Carmen needing to learn responsibility, knowing how to do things when she grows up, and being prepared for the real world. Mrs. Taylor said that, instead, Carmen acted like a baby much of the time, complaining that her brother was better treated and less was expected of him, and crying, whining, or throwing temper tantrums when Mrs. Taylor pushed her to finish her undone chores. In part, Mrs. Taylor thought that Carmen was "just lazy." Yet Mrs. Taylor also wondered if "there was something in Carmen's mind" that caused her to behave the way she did.

Description of Work with Mrs. Taylor

Mrs. Taylor is an attractive 33-year-old woman who is slim, well groomed, and always stylishly dressed. She is appealing and personable. She has a frank, outspoken manner which belies what is in fact both a lack of sophistication and a certain naivete, as well as an emotional closedness and significant discomfort in expressing feelings of vulnerability. Mrs. Taylor is somewhat concrete in her thinking and she seems unpsychologically minded, as though unwilling to consider Carmen's behavior in terms of emotional variables because she would then have to acknowledge the painful reality of her own emotional world. My first impression of Mrs. Taylor concurred with those of the intake worker. Some of her expectations of Carmen's behavior seemed unrealistic, rigid, and age-inappropriate, with a corresponding intolerance for Carmen's more dependent, "babyish" behavior. Initially I decided to see Mrs. Taylor on a weekly basis in order to further assess whether her difficulties with Carmen stemmed largely from her own psychodynamics and/or a lack of information about appropriate expectations of a nine-and-a-half-year-old.

During the first four months of weekly appointments, there were three cancellations and one failed appointment. I found this first series of encounters frustrating and essentially non-productive, so that I acquiesced with some relief when Mrs. Taylor asked to discontinue our meetings because of time difficulties and "really not needing it anymore." She seemed to fill each hour with talk, and quickly moved from one topic to another, often unrelated to her daughter. Talk about Carmen was mainly in the nature of repetitive complaints. Mrs. Taylor often invited my advice or opinion and stressed my professional expertise. Yet each time I made even the mildest attempt to look at the emotional basis of Carmen's behavior, Mrs. Taylor would respond with vehement disclaimers which emphasized Carmen's willfulness, laziness, etc. As a result of these contacts, it seemed clear that Mrs. Taylor's unrealistic expectations of Carmen were not simply due to lack of information, but rather reflected a psychological need to view Carmen as an irresponsible, recalcitrant adult rather than as a dependent and emotionally needy child.

Shortly after the start of the new school year, and around the time that Mrs. Taylor discontinued our appointments, Carmen was suspended from school for deliberately hitting another girl with a stick. Carmen refused to discuss any of this in therapy. Mrs. Taylor maintained that Carmen had been picked on, bullied, and threatened by this girl on previous occasions, that Carmen had never complained about the girl because she was afraid to, and that Carmen had then armed herself and acted only in self-defense. Mrs. Taylor stated that the school had taken the other girl's side in the episode, and because Carmen was so unfairly treated, Mrs. Taylor immediately transferred

Carmen to another school. From her mother's description Carmen has no real friendships with girls her own age, but plays with several younger girls in the neighborhood. Mrs. Taylor denies that this is something to be concerned about. However, she is planning to start Carmen in Girl Scouts—a move which I strongly supported.

I began seeing Mrs. Taylor again on an ongoing basis after a four month interval. Our resuming contact was prompted by my wanting to touch base. Relatively quickly, perhaps within the space of a month, Mrs. Taylor began presenting herself quite differently. In fits and starts she disclosed much more about her concerns and wondered whether she was handling the problems correctly. Such concerns were given sporadically and, once voiced, Mrs. Taylor would quickly turn, in anxiety, to another topic. But briefly she touched on such things as: 1) Carmen fighting with her brother; 2) Carmen having once stolen from a candy store and Mrs. Taylor's feeling that this was somehow her own fault, that she must have done something wrong in raising Carmen; 3) Carmen telling Mrs. Taylor that she was being threatened with physical violence by girls at the new school and Mrs. Taylor's anger with Carmen for "being a baby about it and not handling it herself." Mrs. Taylor wondered if Carmen was fabricating the whole thing and then worried that maybe Carmen was telling the truth after all and that she was being too harsh; and 4) Mrs. Taylor having "caught Carmen playing with herself" several times and being careful not to make Carmen feel guilty, but rather telling her that "she shouldn't mess around down there because she might hurt herself."

In the last few months of our work together Mrs. Taylor became increasingly more focused on Carmen and specific reality concerns. She genuinely seemed to want, and did use, my thoughts and advice about such questions as: Should Carmen go to a better, but out of district, junior high school, or to a nearby school which has a bad reputation? Could Carmen manage the buses or would she get lost? How could she best prepare and teach Carmen to make the bus ride? Mrs. Taylor was able to acknowledge pangs of conflict about seeing Carmen take this more adult step and her own impulse to "protect" Carmen from this move toward growing up. Mrs. Taylor also asked my opinion on questions regarding whether she needed to have a sex talk with Carmen and what to say and how to say it.

Mrs. Taylor also became less guarded regarding her own personal concerns. She expressed some anger and dissatisfaction with her boyfriend who, though he lives with the family, still maintains his own apartment and insists on Saturdays to himself. Although Mrs. Taylor continued to deny any feelings of vulnerability and neediness, a clearer sense emerged of her defending, through denial, in these areas. When I informed Mrs. Taylor that I would soon be leaving for another job, she seemed shocked. However, she composed herself rapidly. She denied any reactions except to note that she was pleased that Carmen was doing better in school and that they were getting along better at home. I offered the possibility of transferring Carmen to another therapist, but Mrs. Taylor decided that Carmen had made significant enough progress to get along on her own. Mrs. Taylor did understand that she could resume contact with the clinic at any time.

Description of Carmen

Carmen is an attractive, somewhat chubby child with brown eyes and hair. Although she is always well groomed and nicely dressed, her outfits are often purposefully big enough "for room to grow into," and she holds herself and moves in an awkward, clumsy manner that gives her a sloppy look. Although Carmen is probably within the range of average height for her almost 11 years, she seems, rather, like a younger child who is big for her age. Carmen's behavior conveys the impression of an almost deliberately created and held-onto infantilism; her speech is often indistinct with near-lisps and pouts; simpering, drooling, and temper tantrums are a regular part of her behavioral repertoire.

Course of Treatment

Certain characteristics and patterns were consistent in Carmen's behavior throughout most of the course of therapy.

Beginning the hour

Carmen immediately instituted a way of beginning the hour which continued during the entire year. Upon entering the office she would proceed to my swivel chair where she would sit down and eat her pre-dinner snack (almost always provided by her mother because of the late dinner time on therapy days). Occasionally Carmen would briefly comment on some event of the past week, but frequently she would say nothing, sometimes spinning herself around in the chair as she ate her food. Usually this was a golden moment: oneness with the therapist and the fullness of the whole, unused hour spread out ahead of her. It seemed to me that she enjoyed the, as yet, unspoiled illusion that all of her needs would be met without obstacles and frustrations.

Play

Frequently Carmen would go through four or five activities in one session, rarely remaining with any one thing for more than ten minutes, often tiring of and discarding an unfinished activity embarked upon only moments before. Play involved painting and coloring, block building, jacks, cards, and checkers. Usually the quality of Carmen's play was constricted and unrelated. Her involvement often seemed superficial and uninvested and she would hurry through what she was doing with clumsy, rushed movements that produced a sloppy, inferior product. In response, Carmen would frequently disdain her creation or label it as ugly or no good. At times Carmen would be bored. Her boredom seemed appropriate in the sense that she was engaged in a non-challenging activity or doing something that involved monotonous repetition.

Carmen's selection of play material rarely involved doll or puppet play—and her play, in general, was conspicuously devoid of imaginative content. With rare exceptions, the pictures she produced were of two kinds. She let herself take more time with her coloring and these were balanced, symmetrical abstract designs in which she would systematically divide up the page into even spaces which she would carefully color. In contrast, her paintings fell into what I called the "surprise" category. Carmen would hastily slop puddles of color onto the page, then fold the paper in half, and press it. She would then open up her creation and see whether it turned out "pretty" or not. Other "surprise" activities included hastily cutting out a folded paper design, and writing or drawing with eyes shut and then seeing how she'd done.

Leaving the office

Until the last few months of therapy Carmen rarely went through a session without several abrupt, unannounced departures from the office during the hour. "To get more water," "to go to the bathroom," "to ask mother something," etc., would be her response when asked. Neither questions, requests to stay, nor interpretations worked to keep Carmen in the office once she'd made a move for the door. She acted first and might talk about it later. At first these excursions seemed to reflect Carmen's concerns about being separated from her mother and her mother's availability. However, this activity continued, though less frequently, even after Mrs. Taylor began taking her son to the library during Carmen's hour. It was my impression that Carmen would suddenly become anxious during the hour, perhaps about mother's whereabouts, but possibly also about whether she, Carmen, was free to come and go. It seemed that Carmen's departures often coincided with moments of intensity or involvement for her and that the experience of involvement, itself, was anxiety-provoking.

Brother

Initially, Carmen seemed unable to leave her brother out of the sessions. For approximately the first three months of therapy he would frequently knock at and/or open the door and ask to come in. Or Carmen would dart out of the office and reappear with him at her side, having either explicitly invited him or implicitly enticed him with teasing talk of all the great toys inside the office. Carmen would then ignore his knocks and presence or she would plead with me to let him in or give him toys. After sending him away, saying that the toys stayed in the office and that this was Carmen's time, she would usually say nothing about the incident. When asked how she felt about his appearance she would deny any feeling, saying she didn't care, or that it would be fun to have him to play with. In one session, soon before the issue died down, Carmen demanded that I ask her mother to let him come too, that it was boring and no fun without him. Yet, in the next session Carmen giggled with great enjoyment when I sent him away. After this there were no further incidents or mention of him in the hours.

Questions about the time

Carmen's questions about the time ("How much time left?") were posed with varying frequency in every session from the first through the last. Usually the question was first asked a few minutes into the hour, Carmen's response being "oh, good—I have plenty of time." Sometimes the question would be noticeably absent until the end of the hour, and at other times Carmen would ask every other minute. Her preoccupation with the time itself seemed to reflect the wish for having all she wanted, as opposed to her sense of impending loss and uncontrollable and unanticipated endings. However, as I discovered when it finally occurred to me to ask about it, Carmen also did not know how to tell time. Different pieces of the necessary conceptual framework were partially understood, but not fully mastered, or the parts not fully put together.

Ending the hour

Carmen usually had difficulty ending every hour. She'd ask for more time or, more frequently, ignore my statements about the time being up. Frequently Carmen teased me about taking something home with her from the office—my chair, a toy—or she would ask me if she could take something home—paper, a pen, etc.

Transference, countertransference, therapeutic tactics and therapeutic gains

For much of the year Carmen persisted in calling me "Miss Lee" despite my protests and my observations and explorations about this. Carmen, who had had a Ms. Lee as a day-care worker and, coincidently, a Ms. Leeds, who did the psychiatric evaluation, offered no explanations, except at one point to comment that she "just like to" call me "that." Whatever else went into this behavior, it seemed to speak to her need to deny object loss by maintaining an interchangeability of people and pretending that everybody was one and the same. Thus, in March, when I told Carmen of my impending vacation, her first response was to ask if she could have a substitute in my absence! Perhaps out of such a dynamic, Carmen treated me, for much of the year, with a certain kind of impersonality and lack of involvement, which was certainly reflected in the countertransference I often felt; bland, boring, bored, uninterested, unengaging, and unengaged.

Two of Carmen's characteristic replies to my questions or explorations were that she "didn't know" or "didn't care." If I persisted with further questions or observations on the issue at hand, Carmen would often completely ignore me, acting as though nothing had been said. Carmen's need to experience and present herself as without thoughts or feelings was usually quite conspicuous and seemed to be a defensive function, involving denial and repression, in an effort to keep out thoughts or feelings which would evoke anxiety or depression. When I persisted in my observations or explorations beyond a minimal point Carmen would shout, "Too many questions! You ask too many questions!" and/or "No! No! No more questions!" Sometimes Carmen would put her hands over her ears in an effort to not hear me, or she would yell or raise her voice in an attempt to drown me out.

Carmen's ability to tolerate frustration in certain areas was initially, and indeed for a prolonged time, almost nil. She quickly became anxious and angry when I did not directly answer a question, and attempted to elicit more material. She would become more vehement in her questioning, sometimes becoming whiney and pleading, and would often say "Come on! Tell me! You know!" Frequently it was my impression that Carmen, in fact, did believe that I *did* know and was holding out on her—even when the subject in question was something nebulous, such as what Carmen herself meant by the use of the word "good."

Carmen also could not tolerate the experience of finding out about something that interested her if the key to the answer lay in any sort of problem-solving procedure that didn't yield immediate results. Instead she'd cut off her curiosity or interest in mid-air, become bored and then abandon the activity altogether.

The main countertransference snag of the early months of therapy centered around my own difficulty in tolerating Carmen's marked sense of frustration and the pull I experienced to give Carmen what she wanted, however unexamined and anti-therapeutic. These early months were exceedingly difficult for me. It took me some time to figure out that I needed to demonstrate to Carmen my capacity to tolerate her frustration and demandingness. Instead of giving in to her demands, I began repeatedly to puzzle out loud about what these demands could mean, despite her efforts to shut me out or shout me down.

The first area in which this work took place was the game of "school" which Carmen initiated in the fourth month. It involved Carmen, as the teacher, giving me lengthy spelling and arithmetic tests. Carmen was content to play this game for hours on end but became angry and would try to shout me down when I asked too many questions about the personality, etc., of the student I was playing. I also interpreted the activity as a resistance—an attempt on Carmen's part to keep away anxiety-provoking thoughts and to put me in the desired role of one who would do her bidding and cooperate unquestioningly. When I began insisting on more information about my role, Carmen dropped the game. A month later, however, she reinstituted it. I refused again to play without Carmen explaining what kind of student I was to be. Carmen would say only that the student, Mary, was "good." As I tried to understand what "good" meant Carmen became increasingly furious, and I finally noted that we seemed to be stuck. I wasn't willing to play without more information and she was not willing to give any information to me. Carmen cried, screamed, yelled, threatened never to come back and, after that session, did not try to play school again.

However, after that session our mutual play reflected an increased ability to make compromises and to engage me in a less dictatorial manner. For example, we played jacks, taking turns, with Carmen gracefully accepting a compromise—she wanted to play jacks all hour, I offered ten minutes, we agreed on 15 minutes. In following hours Carmen remembered this initial contract and stuck to it. In a cutting and pasting project she asked me to choose pictures from the magazine for her to cut out and when I insisted that in such games she would have to make her own choices, she immediately revised her request—I'd turn the pages, she'd choose the material, I'd cut it out and she'd paste it. When I said that in this game we were not stuck, she smiled coyly.

A similar effort focused on Carmen's questions about the time. Once it was established that she didn't know how to tell time I would offer to help her figure it out. Although Carmen would then refuse this offer and repeat the question with more urgency, I'd "answer" her by figuring out what time it was out loud. After a month or so Carmen began interrupting with "no—let me!" and she gradually made increasingly prolonged and successful attempts at figuring out the time. Soon Carmen had it mastered, although she would often still first ask me for the time and then giggle when I'd playfully wonder why she was asking me when she knew herself and also knew I wouldn't answer for her.

Termination

Six weeks before I left, I began to prepare Carmen for termination. Her first response to the news of my leaving was to ask if we could visit together sometime. She then looked sad and rapidly drew two pictures of black skies and rain coming from clouds. In the next hour, she agreed with my comment that she wished she didn't have to say goodbye, and could have the power to make people appear whenever she wanted. Carmen made no further direct verbal reference to my leaving until the final hour, but she listened quietly, and often with apparent interest, to comments about how I thought she might be feeling. In our next-to-last hour we exchanged presents—Carmen having apparently been prepared by Mrs. Taylor, who knew I was giving Carmen a present. She gave me stationery on which, I told Carmen, I'd write her a thank-you note. Carmen seemed delighted with her windup alarm clock, and she took what was for her a leisurely amount of time figuring out how it worked and reading the instructions. She proudly showed me her improved report card, and the rest of the hour was spent in cooperative cutting and pasting of female faces onto paper.

In our last hour Carmen questioned why I had to leave and suggested and semi-pleaded that maybe I could stay. She then discovered an old desk calendar in my drawer, looked up the days of the week on which her birthday was going to fall for the next five years, looked up my birthdays, and then asked a very interesting question about how the calendar worked. The concepts involved were quite complicated and I explained them poorly, yet Carmen made a number of attempts at understanding with only a minimal amount of impatience surfacing on the fourth try.

Closing Impressions

Ideally, Carmen should have continued in treatment even though it would have meant transferring to another therapist. Paradoxically, this was made impossible by Carmen's impressive school improvement, verified by her teachers and her report card. Her teacher no longer complained of much disruptive behavior, described some beginning friendships and reported that, for the most part, Carmen was working at grade level. Mrs. Taylor's pleasure in these achievements reduced her motivation to continue Carmen's therapy. Her excessive expectations of Carmen at home were also reduced by her pleasure at Carmen's progress. Concerning Carmen's continuing reluctance to do chores, Mrs. Taylor said, "I guess I cannot expect that *and* her being good at school, too, can I? I mean nobody is perfect after all."

While some changes in Carmen's behavior in the therapy sessions were apparent, these were not as dramatic as the notable improvement at school. Although there was obviously much therapeutic work still to be done, I did not press for her transfer to another therapist in view of the losses this youngster had already sustained and her mother's obvious sentiment that enough had been accomplished.

Discussion

Clearly this is a case which was stalled for many months and incomplete at its ending. Cases like this one are not often reported even though they are not all that unusual. What is unusual is the candor with which this therapist describes the countertransference bind in which she found herself and which she identified as central to the therapeutic "stall." The therapist puts this most eloquently: ". . . I often felt bland, boring, bored, uninterested, unengaged and unengaging."

That Carmen would pull such helpless, stuck feelings from her therapist is not surprising since Carmen herself is "stuck" in many ways. The case report makes clear that the therapist had a good intellectual grasp of how Carmen's difficulties may have come about. Carmen's mother reported that she was not well prepared for the tasks of parenting. However, her marriage and Carmen's early development are described in idyllic terms, too wonderful to be fully credible. Although it is not possible to be certain about the quality of the distortions, their direction is itself instructive. In her memories of the first few "wonderful" years, Mrs. Taylor remembers Carmen as being capable of far more than a young child would normally be expected to achieve. Following her husband's tragic death and the year which is blind to her, Mrs. Taylor's view of Carmen continued to have unrealistic expectations, now unfulfilled and burdensome. Although the quality of Carmen's early experiences with her parents remains obscure, her fourth to sixth years were highly traumatic. A brother was born, she lost her father and her mother was psychologically unavailable for almost a year. These losses coincided with her entry into school. Over the next few years she is perceived as more and more inadequate and troublesome at school and at home. She cannot please or be pleased. Whether some areas of difficulty existed prior to these traumatic years cannot be known with certainty. By the time she is seen in therapy it is evident that Carmen is locked into provocative, demanding, infantile behavior and into poor relationships with peers and adults.

Mrs. Taylor's own history of loss and abandonment combined with overprotection and lack of opportunity for autonomous development contributes to an understanding of her great difficulties in helping Carmen out of this bind. Indeed, she is unwittingly disposed to participate in it and reinforce it.

This background makes Carmen's behavior with her therapist comprehensible. She treats the therapist in a stubborn, impersonal, uninvolved, domineering and demanding way, conveying the feeling that the therapist is easily replaceable and can never gratify Carmen's endless and impossible expectations. In response to this treatment, the therapist feels compelled to give and give without effect, and to experience her efforts to give as submission. This leads to further frustration, irritation and a covert power struggle that is played out repeatedly in the therapy sessions, replicating Carmen's experiences elsewhere.

All therapists are subject to these pulls. This therapist candidly reports how her own vulnerability to Carmen's manipulative behavior caught her in a severe "countertransference snag" until she became aware of it and found a way out.

The snag with Carmen was compounded by the difficulty in working with Mrs. Taylor, whom the therapist found equally unrewarding and difficult. To help Carmen and her mother simultaneously was simply too burdensome. It was only after the therapist's "acquiescence" to Mrs. Taylor's request to discontinue their meetings that the therapist began to find her way out of the "box" that she was in with Carmen.

Her way out began with the recognition that the key was to tolerate Carmen's frustration, as well as her own, and to stop giving and giving in. She began this work with the simple acknowledgement that she and Carmen were stuck and that they both needed to find a way to get unstuck. An explicit solution to the problem of getting unstuck is never articulated. Rather it is experienced and demonstrated in a series of sessions in which mutual participation begins to be established around a variety of compromises and accomodations. This starts the building of a true connection between Carmen and her therapist. A major intervention is the therapist's demonstration of problem-solving approaches (figuring out loud how to know what time it is) instead of just giving answers. This appears to unlock some curiosity as is shown in Carmen's gradual efforts to take over the figuring-out process.

The good effect of these strategies is noted most impressively in Carmen's improved school performance and, less dramatically, in the changed tone of the therapy hours. The struggles between client and therapist diminish and the genuine connection which is established is most evident in the final hours concerned with the termination.

It is possible that the emergence of a solution to the bind with Carmen permits the therapist to resume contact with Mrs. Taylor and to find a more effective way of working with her. Carmen's improvement has, very likely, also altered her mother's perceptions of the therapist and the manner in which the mother and therapist relate. This certainly contributes to Mrs. Taylor being more available to the therapist's efforts to help with her real worries, confusions and guilt about her daughter.

The therapist is undoubtedly correct in her view that further therapy, ideally, would be indicated. Equally correct is her assessment that it would not be feasible at this time and that the year's therapy stands on its own with some significant accomplishments.

DOUGLAS WATSON

At the suggestion of Douglas's school, Mrs. Watson sought help for her 11½-year-old son who was falling further and further behind in his schoolwork. In addition to his academic difficulties, she was also concerned about his timidity, his fearfulness, his reluctance to play with children his own age and her mounting frustration at her not being able to get her son to tell her what was troubling him or why he was having these difficulties. Although she valued his cooperation in helping with the care of her two younger children and his efforts to earn money by taking small jobs, she worried that Douglas lacked sufficient assertiveness or skill "to make his way in the world." She, herself, was a scrappy and energetic woman who had raised the three children largely by herself and had worked at various jobs to support her family. Neither Douglas's father, who left soon after his birth, nor the father of the two younger children had contributed much to the family's support, nor did they have much contact with the family. Douglas' father would appear, unexpectedly, for a brief visit every few years and then drop completely out of sight again.

The psychiatric evaluation revealed that Douglas's intelligence was in the average range with some potential for superior functioning. His learning difficulties seemed to be a result of significant inhibition and restriction of curiosity, a fear of taking risks and a defensive confusion which appeared to serve the function of protecting Douglas from finding out about some presumably terrible secrets. Some significant depression was also evident.

Mrs. Watson accepted the recommendation that Douglas begin psychotherapy and a tutoring program which was also available at the psychiatric clinic. She indicated that her own very busy schedule made it difficult for her to see Douglas's therapist on a frequent or regular basis and that it would be necessary to schedule his therapy sessions and his tutoring sessions on the same day. The therapist and the tutor accepted these arrangements and Douglas began coming weekly, spending an hour with the tutor followed by his therapy hour.

From the outset, Douglas made a much more solid connection with his female tutor than with his male therapist. The therapy sessions were marked by minimal conversation in which Douglas revealed little about himself or his concerns. On occasion, he would talk briefly about his jobs and his interest in saving money and what he would like to buy. These desultory exchanges occurred as Douglas and the therapist played a variety of structured games. Douglas's play was cautious and without much apparent interest in the outcome. The therapist was able to piece together a few bits about Douglas's relationship with his younger siblings, some worry about his mother's hard life and his discouragement at school. Any effort to encourage Douglas to elaborate upon or explore these issues was met with apparent confusion and a series of "I don't know" responses.

After four months of this slowly moving therapy, the therapist reconsidered the initial treatment plan, particularly with respect to his very limited contact with Douglas's mother. He concluded that it was necessary to have more ongoing access to the day-to-day realities of Douglas's life, which he was not likely to get from Douglas, and that he needed to establish a connection and an alliance with Mrs. Watson in the hope of enlisting her as a more active participant in helping Douglas. To the therapist's surprise, Mrs. Watson was receptive to these efforts and was willing to find time to see him on some regular basis.

After these contacts were established, Mrs. Watson revealed that Douglas periodically wet his bed and that all her efforts to help him with his enuresis were to no avail. She had not reported this problem before because Douglas had insisted that she keep it secret and because she was also ashamed about it and puzzled as to why this persisted in the face of his competence at his jobs and other responsibilities. With some help and continued apprehension she agreed to inform Douglas that his therapist needed to know about this problem and that she could not keep her vow of secrecy.

At about the same time, Mrs. Watson reported that Douglas's father had made one of his unexpected and unannounced visits and that she believed that Douglas had again been very disappointed in his father's failure to keep his promises to visit often and do things with and for Douglas.

The therapist, after hearing from Mrs. Watson that she had told Douglas of her conversation with the therapist about Douglas's "secret," introduced the issue in the next therapy hour with Douglas. The therapist told Douglas that he and Douglas's mother both understood that a boy needed help with such a problem, even though he might want to keep it a secret. Douglas replied that he did not know how to talk about it. He sat stolidly in silence, appearing very ashamed. After a while a few tears trickled down his face. The therapist said that he certainly wouldn't want to force Douglas to talk about this, although he could understand that Douglas might feel forced since he hadn't chosen to mention this problem. He told Douglas that he also knew that his father had recently visited and that this must be an especially hard time for him.

The next hour was devoted to a discussion of Douglas's upcoming twelfth birthday and the plans he and the therapist made to celebrate it at their next meeting. The following three hours are reported directly by the therapist.

In the next hour Douglas declared that he wished to discontinue treatment. He had had a discussion with his mother in which he realized that he was feeling very lonely and that he needed to free some time. He could use the time spent coming to therapy to spend with friends. He was reluctant to give up his weekend job which allowed him to have some savings. He said again that he was lonely and needed more time. Tearfully he insisted that he knew that he could not just appear when he wanted to, but that he would come once more because he wanted to understand what I had to say. He acknowledged my previous comment that he felt forced to come.

In this hour he declined to eat or drink the refreshments that I had brought for his birthday, despite the fact that we had planned the party together.

The next hour began with my wondering whether he wanted to have the refreshments which we had agreed I would save. At the same time I commented that I knew that we had been talking about some very important things. He said that he would like to eat but hesitated when I offered to bring the refreshments to the small table between us. I asked him where he wanted to eat the refreshments, saying that it was up to him as it was his party. He said that he would like to eat at the larger play table where the refreshments were. We moved our chairs over there and I told him that I had gotten both root beer and Coca-Cola, not knowing which he would like. He said he wanted the root beer and the cupcakes.

Once we settled this, Douglas wondered whether we could eat and talk at the same time and I said that I thought that would be fine. He was quiet for a bit and I asked him if he had any ideas or new thoughts about what we had talked about last week. I knew that he was thinking about not coming anymore and that this was a very important feeling to him. He looked at me quizzically and asked me what I meant. I said I wondered if he thought anything new: "Were there any important things that stuck in your mind?" He sat blankly for a second and he said, "No, not really." I said that I had thought about it and I asked him if he wanted to know what I thought. He said that he did and I proceeded to note several issues. I knew he felt very discouraged about many things and I could tell that therapy was one of them. I said it must be hard for him to feel that if only he could get a helping hand things could get better and, at the same time, that coming to therapy was of no use. As he remained silent, I also said I thought it was a terrible thing to feel that the therapy that was supposed to be helpful to him was just something that was being forced upon him. This feeling could make a guy feel even worse. I added that in thinking about it I thought I could help him, but it would really depend on what he wanted to do. Therapy couldn't work if he felt forced to come and I wasn't going to force him. But, I told him, if we could find a way to talk about all those discouraged and painful feelings, maybe he would feel better and could do more of what he wanted. It wouldn't be easy, but it might be worth a try. We had to talk and think about it together. Just because I thought it was going to help wasn't reason enough to make him feel he should continue to come to therapy.

He said very little in response to these comments. I asked if he had any thoughts, to which he replied that he really didn't know what to say. After some silence I asked if there was something he was thinking that he was finding hard to say. He admitted to trying hard to find a way to put what he was thinking into words. I told Douglas I knew it was important for him to tell me what he thought and I would wait. After further silence, I inquired whether it would help him if he talked about why he was having trouble saying what he wanted to say. Douglas replied he was afraid to insult me. I agreed it must be very hard to feel that he had some ideas that would insult me and added that I knew he was a cautious guy and maybe in understanding why he hesitated now we would understand why he hesitated elsewhere. Douglas asked me to explain what I meant, and I tried to explain it in more detail, but it didn't seem very helpful or clarifying to him.

After some further silence Douglas asked me whether I wanted him to tell me what he was thinking. I said I thought it would be good if he could say what was on his mind because it would give us a chance to see what it was all about. But really I couldn't say it for him. I knew he was worried about being forced and that he had to decide whether or not to tell me what he felt. I could see that he felt very stuck and that's what we were really seeing together—the hard feeling of being stuck. In the continued silence I said I knew it was very important to him to be nice to people and that he worried about saying something to me that wasn't so nice. He nodded his head affirmatively and I asked him what it was like when he said things to other people that he felt might insult them. Had that ever happened? He said it didn't happen very often, but sometimes people would go away if they felt insulted. I said I could see that he might be worried that people would get mad and that they would leave him and not be there for him. Again there was a period of silence and he appeared to be struggling, unsure whether to say what he had to say. After a moment he said, "I guess I'll say it."

He asked me if I remembered when I told him that his mother had told me about his wetting the bed. I said yes, I did remember it and it had been a very hard time for him. He said "Yes." He told me that the next week he had seen a woman upon his arrival at the clinic who greeted him by saying, "Oh, so you're Douglas." He believed that I had told this woman his secret. He told me this painfully with tears running down his cheeks. He also said, "You told me you don't tell what I tell you to anybody."

I said that I could see that he would feel terrible about thinking that I told someone his painful secret, and that such a betrayal would hurt terribly. I could also see why he would think that it would be insulting to tell me this. I told Douglas I could understand his feeling very disappointed in me, and that nothing was more important than whether I would keep his secrets. I stated how terrible it must be to think that I would let someone know. He said "Yes" and nodded his head. I inquired further and it emerged that it was the receptionist who greeted him in that way. I told him, directly, that I hadn't told her or anyone else his secrets as I knew that his privacy was very important, especially when we talked about such painful and hard things.

He looked at me with a tear rolling down his face and I asked him what he thought. I said I knew that we had talked a long time ago about how hard it was for him to trust me, and that Douglas had important feelings inside that he was just starting to trust me with and now he thought I was going to take a painful secret and treat it with no respect. I asked him what he thought and he said, "Well, I'll just have to think about it. I'll have to think about what you said and I'll think about whether I can trust you." I said that it was clear that he needed to decide to trust me or not and that it seemed hard for him to trust people, especially people he thought he might get something from. I knew that he'd been disappointed in his life, trying to count on people and then being let down, and I knew that Douglas felt this about other people besides me. He might also feel that way about his dad. He interrupted me excitedly and said, "How did you know? Have you known that for a long time?" I said that I had known for a while, and asked what he was thinking. He said, "I was wondering how you knew." I said, "I knew because you told me and because I know it's hard for a guy when his dad shows up as yours did a few weeks ago and then disappears from the picture. That would be very disappointing again." He remained silent and the tears rolled down his cheek, and I asked, "Is this also something that's hard to talk about?" He said, "I don't want to talk about it. I'm just putting it out of my mind. I don't want to talk about it." I said, "It must be awfully hard to think whatever you are thinking, so that you want to put it out of your mind. Is it the kind of thing that would help to talk about?" He said, "I don't know what to talk about."

The hour was drawing to a close and I commented that we didn't have much time left, that we had been talking about important feelings about coming or not coming and that we were really in the middle of our talk. I didn't want to force him to come but that I thought that we ought to keep talking. When I said that I would like to see him next week he didn't respond for a moment and then he said he had a question to ask me. He asked me whether it was true that he would have to see me in order to see his tutor. I said that I could give him a short answer or we could have a talk where we could get some longer answers which would be better. But if he wanted a short answer I would give him a short answer. Then maybe we could talk more about it next time. I told Douglas that I believed he felt that he was forced to see me in order to see his tutor whom he felt helped him, while he wasn't sure at all that I helped him. I asked, "Can you tell me what was behind your question?" and he agreed that my interpretation was correct. As he wanted to know I said that I would give him a short answer, but I felt that there was a lot more to talk about. I told him that, as far as I was concerned, coming to therapy wasn't a condition of his seeing his tutor. I couldn't speak for her, but I could say that I wasn't going to make the requirement that he see me just to get to see her.

He was quiet for a minute and I asked what prompted the question. Douglas said he understood his emotional problems were keeping him from doing as well in school as he could and that I was supposed to help him with that. I said "emotional problems" was a big word which I supposed meant a lot to him, and it must be hard for Douglas to think that he had emotional problems without even knowing what it means. Douglas agreed. I asked him what he meant by emotional problems and he said something about keeping things inside that get in the way. I said that that was part of it, but I thought it was a big and complicated thing that we ought to take some time to think through. We really didn't have much more time today and maybe we could take some time next week. He said, "OK." I said it was about time to stop, and he said, "Oh, I just remembered, my mom asked me to find out if she was supposed to come to see you today." I said, "Yes" and went on to say that it might feel funny to him, after our discussion of my talking to other people, that I was going to talk to his mother. He said, "No," to talk to his mother was different, and he knew I didn't tell her things. I said, "Well, I'll let you know what we talk about, your mother and I, and we'll talk about it next time," and he said, "OK. Fine."

Unfortunately I had to change the time of Douglas's next hour. When we met he began by asking if I had gone away. When I said "No," he asked whether I'd had "an appointment," clearly asking if I had had something more important to do than see him. I verbalized this and Douglas affirmed this understanding. I told him that what I had done was not more important than seeing him, though a boy could feel that way when he was often disappointed.

It was evident that he was thinking hard. I asked if he was having a hard time finding words for the ideas he had in his mind. He nodded his agreement and continued to struggle to put his thoughts into words. Gradually he asked why he was continuing to see me. I rephrased Douglas's question by asking whether he wondered if he was coming because I thought it was a good idea and he was confused about what I could do for his "emotional problems." He spoke of having been told again that he had to see me "for emotional problems" but not knowing what that meant. I agreed that that was not a good state of affairs. He sat quietly a moment and then, rather forthrightly, said: "Can I give you some advice? You should tell kids why they come here." I said that his advice was very good indeed and that I would surely take it. He was right. Kids have a right to know as much as possible about why things happen.

As the hour neared its end he asked if I wanted him to come next week. I said I thought we were still in the middle of figuring out about his coming and his feeling forced by my ideas to do something he wasn't sure about. I waited while Douglas again took time to phrase another thought. Did I have the authority to permit him to discontinue meeting with him? I said I did, that I did not have a boss to tell me and him about his coming. I said this gave me a better idea of what Douglas might think: Either I was helpless to help him get what he wanted or

I was a forcer. That was a big problem. Gradually he was able to tell me that he didn't know how I could help him; he'd been coming here a long time and things were much the same. He came because he didn't do well in school. His tutor helped him with schoolwork but he was puzzled about whether I could help him. I said that I thought we ought to work that through to the end. He nodded and left.

Discussion

The case of Douglas illustrates the time-honored cliche that regular attendance at therapy sessions is no guarantee that much therapeutic work is taking place. Just as it is important to force oneself to make an initial formulation and plan, it is equally important to periodically re-evaluate what, if any, progress is being made and whether the initial plan needs to be re-fashioned.

After four months, it appears that Douglas's therapy is going at snail's pace with little obvious direction. Douglas's therapy parallels his life. He is in the dark about how and why things happen. His therapist appears to be equally in the dark about the events of Douglas's life and about Douglas's inner responses. The therapist is all too painfully aware that the hours reflect Douglas's constriction, repression, caution and depression, and that they are stuck. It is this realization that leads the therapist to re-evaluate the treatment to consider a different approach. This begins with a changed approach to Mrs. Watson and proceeds fairly quickly to the possibility of a different approach with Douglas.

The establishment of regular contact with Douglas's mother yields new and important information about secret symptoms and another disappointing visit by Douglas's father. Even more important than the content of these revelations is the fact that their secrecy must be understood as a central element in the lack of movement in therapy. The discovery of this withheld and missing information permits the therapist to identify the "ghosts" in the room, which he has sensed as impediments, and which are now possible to link more concretely with Douglas's general blocked view of the world as unknowable and too dangerous to reveal.

The hours which follow begin the difficult but essential effort to address these impediments with the aim and the hope of establishing a new treatment contract with Douglas, as well as with his mother. While these hours continue to demonstrate Douglas's fearful and blocked style, new behaviors appear which are uncharacteristic. Some assertiveness and risk-taking behavior are evident in relation to issues of secrets, trust and emotions.

These are tricky hours as the therapist knows a secret which Douglas has not, himself, chosen to divulge. In part, Douglas must experience his mother's disclosure as a betrayal and a violation of trust. This, however, is clearly not the only element in his experience of this event. His responses over the next several hours are indications that he has also experienced this as a relief—the adults are taking increased responsibility for his care—and as permission to explore why he is coming, how much this can be his choice and what he can know about the conditions of treatment. Perhaps most prominent, these are hours of talk and interchange in contrast to the uninvolved game playing of the earlier work—though the talk remains labored and fragmentary.

The first of the three hours which are reported in some detail begins with Douglas's announcement that he doesn't want to continue with therapy. His refusal to partake of the birthday refreshments is a behavioral version of this same refusal to accept the therapist's offerings, or to participate further. Nevertheless, he speaks about a feeling—loneliness—a highly atypical revelation for Douglas. Another difference is noted in Douglas's acknowledgment that he knew he could simply stop coming but that he wanted to hear what the therapist had to say. The issue of feeling forced to come is out on the table, to be explored more fully.

In the next session, Douglas begins by choosing to accept the therapist's "goodies." With considerable assistance from the therapist he is able to choose what he will take and where he will take it.

It is interesting to speculate about Douglas's choices: he selects some but not all of the refreshments; he chooses to eat these at the larger table, not the one he has used most frequently for games; the choice he makes does not put a table between the therapist and himself; and finally choosing to take something does not swerve Douglas from his resolve to discuss his reluctance about continuing treatment. Douglas's discouragement with the treatment, and his feeling that it has not helped, are considered, along with further discussion about feeling forced.

When Douglas's therapist straightforwardly answers that he does not want to force Douglas and that he believes still that he can help, Douglas begins an active struggle to convey some of his thoughts and feelings. His struggle is graphic and powerful. He wants to say something but he cannot; he wishes to phrase his thought but cannot find the words. That this struggle centrally involves coping with aggressive and insulting ideas is confirmation of the relationship between aggression and Douglas's learning problems. The therapist helps Douglas to clarify this by shifting from inquiry about the content to some brief exploration of the resistance to speaking his mind. This leads to discussion of very important material about being stuck and hesitant—not only in the office but elsewhere in Douglas's life as well.

Although Douglas appears to take in only part of this interchange, he makes clear that being "nice" is a necessary protection against abandonment. Only then can Douglas spit out his "insult." He suspects the therapist of having broadcast his secret, an obvious extension and displacement of his mother's "betrayal." This transference distortion plunges them into the issue of trust and secrets. In the face of the therapist's direct disclaimer, Douglas states only that he will have to think about whether he can trust his therapist.

The therapist uses this uncharacteristic response to broaden the issue of trust by linking it to Douglas's experiences with his father. Douglas's response is a complicated one. He is surprised and, one presumes, even a little pleased to be so well understood, and he is curious to learn more about how the therapist knows this about him. He appears not to recall that he previously conveyed his disappointment about his father to the therapist. It is as though the discussion of trust has shifted to a new context—who told what to whom. Douglas retreats from this discussion back into silence and the clearer assertion that he wants to put it out of his mind and not talk about it. This retreat may, in part, be dictated by Douglas's more urgent need to clarify the treatment contract. With initiative and directness he raises questions about the conditions of his treatment. The therapist's response is extremely skillful. By posing the distinction between long and short answers, the therapist conveys important, implicit statements about the ways in which one can know things and about the possibilities of their therapeutic relationship. In response, Douglas accepts the short answer with some willingness to hear the "longer answer" still to come.

In the closing interchange about his mother's appointment, Douglas reveals that he is less worried about the therapist's contact with Mrs. Watson than the therapist might have reasonably presumed.

The final hour of this sequence, which unavoidably had to be rearranged, begins with Douglas's presumption that other matters are always more important than he. This is very likely a reflection of his experience with his father, and possibly even with his mother. This session is marked by many questions from Douglas, who has obviously been thinking about the therapy and wants to know what it's all about.

These questions center on the meaning of the term "emotional problems" and culminate with Douglas's most vigorous assertion and risk:
"Can I give you some advice? You should tell kids why they come
here." Douglas has now turned the tables and advised his therapist not
to withhold information or to keep secrets.

It is by no means certain that the impasse addressed during these
hours will result in a guarantee that Douglas will continue treatment,
although the chances of continuation have been improved. Whatever
the outcome, these hours stand on their own and must be viewed in
juxtaposition to the prior months, during which little was taking place.
These hours have afforded Douglas the experience of making inquiries
and finding out, presenting his own concerns and points of view, and
taking risks—including disagreeing with and criticizing an adult. The
therapist has gained a more vivid picture of Douglas, confirming his
diagnostic impressions and promoting a greater sense of how to work
more effectively with Douglas and Mrs. Watson. This greater effectiveness becomes possible only when the therapist is able to free himself
from the concern about keeping the patient coming to the sessions, as
distinct from having the patient in treatment. This liberating realization that taking reasonable risks is not only the patient's task is one
from which most therapists profit, if and when they discover it out of
their own experience.

OTHER VEXING PROBLEMS

Even in cases which are progressing well, certain common problems
confront all child therapists. There is no one right way to manage these
problems that can be translated surely from case to case. In fact, different approaches to the same technical problem may be required at
different stages of the child's therapy. One way of responding may be
"right" for the time it is used; at another time in the case the same
intervention may prove to be far less useful.

A good number of these garden-variety problems are addressed in
the cases reported throughout this book. For example, how to answer
questions posed by children in flexible and varied ways is discussed in
the case of Peter (Chapter 5) and in the case of Steven (Chapter 2).
Cornell's questions require still another style of intervention (Chapter
6).

The issue of treats and gifts, and whether and how to use them, is
also reviewed in Peter's case, though it can be argued that he could
have been treated without any snacks at all. The impulse to give is a

strong one in treating children, particularly those who have experienced so much deprivation in their lives. Moreover, a child's thinking is far more concrete than the more cognitively developed thought processes of an adolescent or adult. A treat or gift is a concrete representation of the therapist's interest, care and value of the child. But these concrete representations are often a pale substitute for true nurturance or the ongoing recognition of a child's value which builds firm self-esteem.

For example: 12-year-old Amy was brought to treatment by her aunt, who was Amy's legal guardian. Her aunt was concerned about Amy's defiant behavior, precocious sexual interest, inability to take responsibility for appropriate chores and poor schoolwork which was far below Amy's obvious intellectual abilities.

Amy and her aunt had moved across the country six months earlier. This move was the culmination of a variety of efforts on the aunt's part to "rescue" Amy from her mother, whose life was in such disarray that she had been unable to properly care for Amy. After several years of squabbling about Amy's care—which included several previous periods in which Amy lived with her aunt—Amy's mother finally agreed to let her younger sister have custody of Amy.

Amy's aunt was particularly concerned and determined that Amy's life would not repeat the deprived childhood that she and her sister had experienced.

Once settled in the new city, Amy's aunt began to realize that, despite her determination, she might have bargained for more than she could deliver as a caretaker. This ambivalence was an implicit element of the request for help from the mental health clinic. Although this ambivalence was partially recognized by Amy's therapist, it was not confronted or explored with the aunt.

Amy's therapist was impressed with the child's brightness and seeming intactness, despite her chaotic background. Taken by Amy's appealing mixture of precocity and innocence, the therapist determined to overcome Amy's deprivation. The therapist set out to become a model of the kind of adult whom Amy had never known; loving, available, interested, predictable and reliable, nurturing and providing. In the service of constructing that model relationship, the therapist conceived two basic technical strategies. To avoid deprivation and frustration she would not pursue the discussion of any painful realities of Amy's past or present if Amy appeared to be distressed by or opposed to such explorations. Secondly, the therapist decided to provide numerous, tangible gifts and treats whenever the opportunity arose.

The therapy was marked by frequently missed appointments for which Amy always had a superficial explanation which the therapist would accept. Finally, the therapist decided that she would remind Amy of her upcoming appointment by phoning Amy on the evening before each session. After this decision, fewer sessions were missed. However, the sessions with Amy, which consisted almost exclusively of an ongoing Monopoly game, changed very little. Amy obviously enjoyed the Monopoly game and was clearly delighted at the frequent provision of snacks and gifts. Despite the obvious gratification, little changed in Amy's external world, nor did her difficulties with her aunt or her school alter.

This vignette is an excellent illustration of the therapeutic inadequacy of gratification—including concrete gift giving—as a substitute for 1) a careful effort to alter a child's environment in the direction of structure and safety. In this instance the work required a full exploration of the aunt's ambivalence and ability to provide proper care and 2) direct and sustained efforts to help the child change maladaptive behaviors, attitudes and defenses.

The case of Amy also serves as an example of the technical problems inherent in the treatment of a child whom the therapist likes too much. On balance, liking one's patient is generally an asset and an aid to therapeutic work. It becomes a problem when the therapist is so enchanted or so excessively compassionate that "therapeutic" interventions are dictated primarily by these feelings rather than directed by some objectivity, careful understanding of behavior, and efforts to bring about change.

The case of David is in sharp contrast to that of Amy. David, age seven and the youngest of three children, was deeply troubled when it became necessary to place him in a foster home after his mother's psychosis took on alarming proportions. An older sister had already been placed in a residential treatment center—a casualty of the poverty and mental illness which had shaped her life. The oldest child was sent to live with the maternal grandmother who, despite poor health, had tried valiantly to assist her daughter and the grandchildren. This maternal grandmother had undoubtedly acted as a buffer between David and his mother's psychotic influence and supplied him with care and protection. In spite of David's difficulties, he remained a relatively intact child. David's foster mother, a sensitive woman who had reared a large family of her own, applied for help for David when his nightmares persisted. Grandmother readily consented to this application.

For the first three or four months David's foster mother or a member of her family brought David regularly to his weekly sessions. However, when the nightmares subsided, and subsequently ceased, attendance became erratic.

In spite of the foster mother's verbal recognition that David still needed help, she reported that it had become a drain on her to bring David weekly and that others in the household needed her attention. As a consequence, a small grant was obtained to assist with David's transportation to and from therapy. A college student was employed to bring David each week, and the student was paid for his job by the therapist and in David's presence. After several weeks, David began to insist that his therapist pay him also—one nickel. The therapist demurred, intent on exploring with David what he really needed. These explorations were quite fruitful and David began to openly discuss his sense of deprivation, his envy of what others received, and his fear that he would never get what he wanted and needed. Despite the utility and importance of this material, the demand for the nickel did not subside but was repeated week after week with mounting urgency. This culminated in one session in which David brought a quarter to his hour and offered to give it to his therapist, saying angrily and triumphantly, "Now will you give me the nickel?!" When the therapist pointed out that David surely knew the difference between a quarter and a nickel and that this showed how the nickel really stood for all the things David longed for and could not get, the struggle over the nickel receded and was replaced by some evident sadness.

Another common technical "gratification" problem, closely related to the question of providing gifts and snacks, occurs when children ask or demand to take play materials home from the playroom. The issues involved in the management of such events are discussed in the cases of Terry and Peter (Chapter 5), and in the case of Jennifer (Chapter 6). The therapist's management of Peter's request to "borrow" something from the playroom as his therapy is coming to a close is a good illustration of the need to consider the risks and the benefits of agreeing to such a request.

For some children the request or demand to take something home will be a test of the consistency of the groundrules. Obviously, this situation requires a clear and unequivocal restatement of the rules. For others, the request will be an effort to extend the time and capture more of the therapist. Here the necessary approach is to learn to anticipate this "endgame" and begin the discussion before the last minutes of the hour. In still other cases, the request will be a reflection of the child's need for a transitional object to help relieve the anxiety of separating from the therapist. With such anxious children it can be useful to provide an appointment slip for the next meeting or some other paper token (a drawing, a calendar) which the child can take and may choose to bring back to the next appointment. For some children, the folder of their drawings, game scores and other mutual activities which remains in the office serves the same function. Young children may find it necessary or helpful to bring something from a parent into the playroom as a way of bridging worrisome separations.

The case of Larry Scott (Chapter 8) provides an interesting variation. Larry's demand is not for a tangible object, but rather for a report about him, promised by his therapist in the prior session.

A fairly common and most vexing problem which almost every child therapist encounters at one time or another is posed by the child who is difficult to engage. In extreme form this is the child who will not speak or engage in any activity. The following illustrates the problems in working with a silent child.

Raymond Singer was referred for treatment when he was eight years old, shortly after he and his mother moved to the area from St. Louis. He was the only child of divorced parents whose father remained in St. Louis and had erratic and limited contact with his son. Mr. Singer often disappointed Raymond by planning visits and activities which failed to materialize.

Shortly after Raymond and his mother settled in the new area, Raymond began to have lengthy nightly temper outbursts directed at his mother. Mystifying to Mrs. Singer, these seemed precipitated by the most minor frustrations. The temper outbursts did not occur at school where he was perceived as a good student, although his teachers complained about his failure to turn in homework assignments.

Mrs. Singer was unable to find a way to help Raymond control his temper. She could not explain the outbursts other than to report that when she asked Raymond why he was angry with her, he replied that he missed his friends in St. Louis. When not confronted with his temper, Mrs. Singer found Raymond to be a bright, pleasant, creative and interesting child.

Raymond's early development was uneventful. The Singer's marriage, however, was a rocky one from the start, ending in separation and divorce when Raymond was two-and-a-half. Mrs. Singer had returned to work part-time when Raymond was an infant and he'd been cared for by the same babysitter until he was ready to enter nursery school. The start of nursery school occurred shortly after his parents' divorce but was described as a smooth and pleasurable experience for Raymond. Raymond did well in nursery school and in the beginning of elementary school. Although Mr. Singer remained in St. Louis, the erratic pattern of his contact with his son began almost immediately after the parents' separation.

The move from St. Louis was prompted by a very good job offer which Mrs. Singer received. She was very pleased with her new position and with her life in the new city. Raymond's rages were the only discordant note for her.

From the onset, Raymond's male therapist found him difficult to engage. Although there were no temper outbursts in the office, Raymond would rarely play and even less frequently speak. He would arrive early or late without explanation and would often decide to leave the hour early, also without explanation. During the hour he would rush to occupy the therapist's chair and spin in it silently. Sometimes he would decide to call his mother at work and would simply pick up the phone without asking. Frequently he brought a book and spent the hour silently reading. On occasion he would turn the office lights on and off or he would play with the therapist's clock, changing the hours over and over. Sometimes Raymond drew his coat over his head and curled up in a ball inside the jacket. He frequently sat with his back to the therapist and occasionally barricaded himself behind several chairs. Once in a while he would complain that the move from St. Louis had separated him from his friends and his father. At other times he proclaimed that this did not bother him. Even when he complained, any effort on the therapist's part to explore his grievances was met with silence or occasional derisive sarcasm. Once he brought a water gun and squirted a variety of objects in the room, coming close to but just avoiding spraying the therapist.

The therapist's early interventions consisted of Herculean efforts to image out-loud the possible meanings of Raymond's behavior. Efforts to address the possible defensive meanings of Raymond's provocations and retreats were met with no response. Nor did efforts to label what Raymond might be feeling meet with any greater response or success. The therapist also made no effort to stop or limit Raymond's provocative behavior on the hopeful assumption that this would demonstrate that he did not intend to engage in a struggle of wills with Raymond and that his unconditional acceptance of the behavior would forge trust and build an alliance. Raymond provided no clues that these assumptions were warranted nor did he indicate whether the sessions were pleasing or frightening.

After many months, and despite some reports of slight improvement from Mrs. Singer, the therapist decided to try a different tack.

Reconsidering his rationale for the early strategies, the therapist began to consider the possibility that the unbridled sadistic and provocative behaviors were perhaps frightening to Raymond and that their acceptance was not useful. Slowly he introduced two new efforts. He began to limit Raymond's unexplained and provocative behaviors. For example, Raymond was told that his reasons for telephoning his mother were unknown and that, without some explanation, this could no longer take place. Raymond did not offer any explanation and the calls were then prohibited. Secondly, the therapist began to address the predicament in which the two of them found themselves. He could not guess what Raymond was thinking or feeling and Raymond didn't tell him. He remained interested in understanding but could not do this on his own. He added that he thought that some struggle was probably going on between them but that he could not know what this was about other than some mild protests about the limits placed upon Raymond.

These efforts produced no further contact or content from Raymond. However, Mrs. Singer reported a more dramatic improvement at home and at school. Although heartened by these reports, the therapist concluded reluctantly, and after several months of his new approach, that these strategies had not altered the therapeutic process any more than his original efforts. Nor could he assess with any certainty what had brought about the changes. Finally, he suggested that since things were much better and that they were not getting anywhere in the hours, perhaps it was time to stop. Mrs. Singer was pleased and relieved by this suggestion. Raymond, true to form, remained uncommunicative about whether he thought this was a good idea or not.

A review of Raymond's early history shows certain obvious stress points: the parents' separation and divorce which coincided with his entry into nursery school and the loss of his babysitter, followed by his father's erratic and disappointing contacts. Nevertheless, he remained symptom free and was apparently developing well until the move away from his familiar territory, friends, and his father. One can reason that Raymond held his mother responsible for these losses and that the unexplained temper outbursts were his way of expressing these feelings. It is less easy to understand his "withholding" behavior at school. Treatment seemed indicated and the necessary support for it from his mother was evident.

Throughout the one year of therapy both of Raymond's symptoms were manifest in the hours. The withholding of his homework was directly paralleled by his withholding words or other forms of engagement. His temper outbursts at home were more subtly displayed in his passively defiant and provocative behavior toward his therapist.

The first set of therapeutic strategies directed at unconditional acceptance and at efforts to guess or infer Raymond's state of mind, motivations or feelings led nowhere. The therapist's decision to change his approach seemed well conceived. To allow the unbridled expression of hostility and defiance does not promote safety or trust and implicitly gives permission for sadism and tyranny—however covert. However, the shift to limit some of Raymond's unexplained provocations, coupled with an effort to pose and discuss the therapeutic dilemma, were no more successful in changing the therapeutic climate than the original strategies. Although Raymond's behavior at home and at school improved markedly, coincident with the shift in therapeutic approach, it remained impossible to attribute, with any certainty, these changes to the new treatment strategy. It may be that Raymond shifted the areas of his anger from his mother to his therapist, who also stood in for his father, and that this shift accounted for some of the improvement. However, failing any confirmation from the patient himself, this can be only a reasonable and educated guess. Just as there are children whose failure to improve cannot be understood, there are others whose improvement remains inexplicable.*

It is important for therapists to make a concerted and sustained (sometimes even lengthy) effort to engage their child patients who are slow or fearful of making contact. The silence of a fearful child is palpably different from the silence of a hostile and withholding youngster, and this discrimination is of critical importance. The fearful child's silence will usually yield to time and patience. The silent resistance of many stubborn and withholding children will also yield to sustained contact and that indescribable quality of "being there" with the patient. The effort is worth making and should not be renounced too soon.

---

*Conversely and paradoxically, cases in which the gloomiest prognosis is made at the outset startle therapists by going well, attesting to the surprising resiliency of some children.

However, some children, like Raymond, can defeat even the best therapeutic efforts.

Many other commonly encountered problems are illustrated by the therapeutic work with the children throughout this book. The importance of stating some common understanding of why the child is coming to therapy is illustrated in the cases of Douglas (this chapter), Cornell (Chapter 6) and Steven (Chapter 2).

The difficult task of developing tolerance for unappealing and even disgusting behaviors is illustrated by the cases of Sherry (Chapter 5), Peter (Chapter 5), Carlos (Chapter 2), and Terry (Chapter 5).

The steadiness which is essential in confronting threatening behavior is well illustrated in the case of Larry Scott (Chapter 8). Larry is also instructive in providing exemplars of how a therapist can provide pertinent and relevant sexual information.

The problems of planning the scheduling and sequencing of appointments with various family members are illustrated in the cases of Gina (Chapter 7) and Monica (Chapter 7).

Numerous examples of some of the issues involved in working with parents are found throughout the book. Particular attention is drawn again to the case of Gina (Chapter 7), Jennifer (Chapter 6), Carlos (Chapter 2), Alicia (Chapter 7) and Monica (Chapter 7).

REFERENCES

1. Brody, S., Some aspects of transference and resistance in prepuberty. *Psychoanalytic Study of the Child*, 1961, Vol. 16: 251-274.
2. Chess, S., Selectivity of treatment modalities. *Canadian Journal of Psychiatry*, 1981, Vol. 26(5): 309-315.
3. Kay, P., Gifts and gratifications and frustrations in child analysis. In J. Glenn (Ed.), *Child Analysis and Therapy*. New York: Jason Aronson, 1978.
4. Lane, B., Some vicissitudes of the therapeutic alliance in child psychotherapy. In J. Mishne (Ed.), *Psychotherapy and Training in Clinical Social Work*. New York: Gardner Press, 1980.
5. Marcus, I., Countertransference and the psychoanalytic process in children and adolescents. *Psychoanalytic Study of the Child*, 1980, Vol. 35: 285-298.
6. Meeks, J., Children who cheat at games. *J. of Amer. Acad. of Child Psychiatry*, 1970, Vol. 9: 157-174.
7. McConvill, B. D., Opening moves and sequential strategies in child psychotherapy. *Canadian Psychiatric Assn. Journal*, 1976, Vol. 21: 295-301.

CHAPTER 5

Seriously Disturbed Children

Child therapists encounter a variety of children who are considered "seriously" disturbed although the level and nature of the disturbance vary over a fairly wide range. From a formal diagnostic perspective some of these children are deemed psychotic, while others are thought of as borderline, or as children with severe impulse disorders.* The cases of Sherry, Peter, and Terry, presented in this section, illustrate some aspects of the range of serious childhood pathology. In spite of their differences, they share certain common features and present their therapists with certain common technical problems.

Any casual observer would note Sherry's bizarre behavior and conclude immediately that she is seriously impaired. Peter's and Terry's difficulties are less immediately apparent, and become evident only with closer attention.

All three have great difficulties with self control, with the maintenance of clear boundaries, are prone to rapid and intense regression, are quickly overcome by emotions and intrusive fantasies, and are

---

*Current diagnostic nomenclature—e.g., DSM III—has shifted toward a more behaviorally descriptive taxonomy.

confused about body imagery and body functions. Each has difficulty with the demands of appropriate social interactions.

Similarly, each of these children confronts the therapist with major questions of and problems with therapeutic management and technique. These issues are not exclusive to the treatment of seriously disturbed children and can be found in almost any child therapy. However, the intensity of the pathology poses these questions and problems in more vivid and taxing forms. Because they appear in larger scale in these cases, such common issues as limit setting, the creation of therapeutic trust and safety, ways of responding to children's questions, the provision of treats and the giving of gifts, and what may or may not be taken from the playroom are addressed in some detail in the discussion.

The case of Sherry is presented in an overview with primary attention given to major themes. By contrast, the cases of Peter and Terry are presented in segmented, process accounts over time which permit a more microscopic examination of the therapeutic interventions.

The treatment of each of these children draws attention to certain general therapeutic principles: 1) Their treatment requires extensive investments of time, patience and resources.* 2) They tend to elicit strong positive and negative feelings in the therapist only some of which derive from countertransference. 3) Their families must be willing to allow someone else to enter the lives of their children in important and decisive ways and be willing to be active participants in the treatment process. 4) Children require much greater and earlier attention to techniques aimed at the promotion of stronger and more effective ego capacities before it becomes possible to turn therapeutic attention to conflict resolution. In fact, some conflicts do not become apparent until sufficient ego functions have developed. This is most evident in the case of Peter whose treatment takes a decided turn in the direction of conflict resolution, in contrast to the work with Sherry whose treatment, even after five years, remains centered around continuing "ego muscle" training.

Finally, it is worth noting that controversy persists about the precise etiology of severe childhood disturbances. There are still many who hold to an exclusively organic/genetic/biochemical explanation. Others insist on an exclusively environmental perspective, viewing the new-

---

*This is not to imply that the treatment of less disturbed children can always be accomplished rapidly. However, the treatment of seriously disturbed children is rarely a short affair.

born child as a blank slate on which the environment—usually a euphemism for the "mother" or the family—"inscribes the pathology." More and more, however, most workers in the field take a perspective which is, at the same time, richer, more complex and more difficult. This view recognizes the importance of innate—probably genetically determined—endowments and vulnerabilities in very complicated interplay with experience as the "etiology" of both pathology and strength. Such a perspective implies that treatment of seriously disturbed children is possible, but may have limits beyond which one cannot go and does not immunize the patient against life's vicissitudes for all time.

SHERRY TURNER

Sherry was referred to a psychiatric outpatient center at the age of eight-and-a-half by the staff of a special school and day care center for emotionally disturbed children which she attended since kindergarten. During her three-and-a-half years at the school, she had been seen in weekly psychotherapy by a therapist who was part of the school staff. When this therapy program was terminated, Sherry and her family were referred for further treatment with the understanding that Sherry would continue in the academic and activity programs at the school.

At the time of the referral Sherry was living with her 33-year-old divorced mother and her five-year-old brother. Her father, who lived close by, had remarried and visited with the children regularly.

Sherry was originally referred for treatment and special schooling by her nursery school teacher and the family pediatrician at about age five. The primary concern at that time was Sherry's delayed speech. She had a limited vocabulary and was echolalic. Originally, the pediatrician thought her delayed speech might be due to a hearing deficit secondary to numerous ear infections during the first three years of her life. Around age four, Sherry began a year of speech and hearing therapy. When little improvement occurred and Sherry appeared increasingly withdrawn and "anti-social" in the nursery school, referral for more extensive educational and emotional treatment was made.

The initial psychological evaluation brought many other problems to light which had not been stressed by the parents in their interchanges with the pediatrician. These included enuresis, oppositional behavior, intense attachments to articles of clothing, phobias, toilet rituals, bizarre grimacing and posturing, and destructive behavior.

Developmental History

Sherry was born after an uncomplicated pregnancy and delivery, weighing seven pounds, one ounce. She was described as colicky during the first six weeks, and then reported to be a quiet and content baby. Her motor development was within the normal range: she sat at five months, crawled at six months, stood unsupported at 11 months, and walked at 15 months. She spoke her first word—"Mama"—at nine months, but acquisition of further vocabulary was delayed. At about a year of age, she developed fierce attachments to articles of clothing and would scream uncontrollably at any efforts to remove these from her grasp. Her parents remembered that at age 16 months Sherry was withdrawn and unfriendly to people and unresponsive to loud noises. At around this time her paternal grandmother came to stay with the family, following her discharge from a psychiatric hospital for a "psychotic depression." She remained with the family for some four months.

Shortly before Sherry's mother returned to work, when Sherry was 28 months old, toilet training was accomplished, prompted by the need to place Sherry in day care. This transition to a day care center was reported as having gone smoothly. Four months later, Mrs. Turner became pregnant for the second time, which she experienced as a setback in her career plans.

Very shortly thereafter, Sherry had an extensive workup for the numerous ear infections which she had suffered since infancy. In the course of this workup, the pediatrician suggested that Sherry might be emotionally disturbed and Mrs. Turner remembered that she became so depressed that she even considered an abortion.

Mrs. Turner did acknowledge that she and Sherry's father "knew" that Sherry was unlike other children but they hoped that medical treatment of her hearing and speech problems would help her develop more normally. Sherry had a bilateral myringotomy and insertion of ear tubes. This resulted in a slight but undramatic improvement in her speech development.

Following the birth of her brother, Sherry (age three years, five months) regressed dramatically, demanding a bottle and once again becoming fiercely attached to particular articles of clothing. She also developed excessive and bizarre toilet and dressing rituals, insisting that clothing had to be put on in a certain order and that the toilet had to be flushed many times and in a prescribed way. Her parents complied with these demands in order to avoid severe temper tantrums.

Sherry was aggressive with her baby brother and often cut and destroyed books and other toys. At the day care center she required a great deal of attention and supervision by the staff, and always remained apart from the rest of the children.

Shortly after the birth of her son, Mrs. Turner again returned to work. There have been several babysitters in Sherry's life, to whom she has become very attached. Changes in these sitters, as any change in Sherry's life, lead to disruption and regressed behavior.

Family History

Mrs. Turner is an attractive woman who works hard, but feels burdened and unsupported. She has career aspirations which she feels unable to pursue because of her two children. Although she is bright and competent, she is frequently exhausted from hard work, childcare, and running a household, leading to her social isolation.

Her history is marked by separations from her family and much strife. Her parents divorced when she was six; her mother later remarried. She has a sister three years younger and two half-brothers, 10 and 13 years younger than herself. When Mrs. Turner was 13, she was sent to live in a boarding school.

Mrs. Turner's family has a history of psychiatric problems. Her father was alcoholic, her mother was described as "cold and business-like." One of her brothers had a psychotic episode during adolescence.

After high school, Mrs. Turner worked for a time and then began college at age 20. She met and began living with Mr. Turner in her first year and this arrangement continued throughout her years at college. When she became unexpectedly pregnant with Sherry during her senior year, she and Mr. Turner married.

Mr. Turner grew up in the east in a middle-class family. He was the second of two children with a sister three years older than himself. His parents divorced when he was eight. He was a shy, withdrawn child, who was described as having been rather sickly as a youngster. Despite his early illnesses, and his parents' divorce, he described his life as uncomplicated and untroubled.

Soon after Sherry's birth, the Turners moved west, where there was no family and where they made few friends.

Initial Psychiatric Evaluation and Treatment

The evaluation of Sherry at age five at the special school included a clinical assessment and a battery of psychological tests. In the play sessions Sherry's behavior suggested serious psychopathology with wide fluctuations between moments of almost age-appropriate functioning and eruptions of highly inappropriate affects, echolalic speech and ritualistic behavior. At times she used play materials properly, while on other occasions she created total chaos with piles of toys and torn paper and seemed oblivious of the therapist's presence. While her speech was markedly regressed, with frequent two-word phrases, she clearly comprehended far more than she could convey.

Psychological testing validated the clinical impression of the seriousness of Sherry's disturbance. Her test performance was extremely erratic, with errors plunging her into a state of frantic despair and agitation. She perceived and understood the world to be threatening, intrusive and thwarting. Despite the severe pathology, there were indications of better than average intellectual functioning.

Sherry's parents accepted the recommendation for special schooling combined with weekly psychotherapy for Sherry and weekly conjoint sessions with the parents. Shortly after this plan was implemented, the Turners' serious marital problems became evident, ultimately leading to their separation and divorce when Sherry was six. Mrs. Turner requested a referral for her own therapy which helped her to become more realistic and less guilty about Sherry's disturbance, although she continued to be understandably burdened and exhausted by Sherry's difficulties, the general demands of single parenthood and her increasing job responsibilities. She became a helpful and active participant in the therapeutic work with Sherry.

Following the divorce, Mr. Turner became much less involved in Sherry's treatment. He had only occasional contact with the therapist, though he continued to have Sherry and her brother with him regularly. Typically he would return the children to their mother when Sherry became more unmanageable than he was prepared to accept. Often this would be earlier than the planned end of his visit with his children. This pattern continued after he remarried when Sherry was eight.

Sherry's three-and-a-half years of work with her first therapist were described as slow moving and characterized by the following:

1) Sherry was able to remain at the special school and to make steady academic progress.
2) She developed a close relationship with the therapist.
3) Her speech improved markedly though speech content remained filled with regressed toilet talk and violence. There were many persistent confusions about body functions and gender differences.

4) Her play was erratic and frequently highly inappropriate and incomprehensible.
5) Much anger and hostility were displayed toward her brother, her schoolmates and, less often, her parents.
6) Sherry remained relatively friendless and, in the main, stayed on the periphery of the group at school and activities.
7) No changes occurred in her invariably messy appearance or in her enuresis.

Termination with this therapist occurred when the school lost the funding which had supported this phase of their program. Sherry experienced the loss of her therapist and the transfer to a new therapist and a new setting as bewildering and upsetting. After a time, Sherry was able to transfer her attachment to her new therapist who began seeing her twice weekly. The year-and-a-half of work with Sherry is reported by her second therapist as follows.

Current Situation

After five years of psychotherapy, and special schooling, Sherry's problems are still severe and multiple. She continues to have toilet rituals and phobias, occasional enuresis and excessive concern about all issues of bladder and bowel function. She speaks fluently and extensively, but with the inflection and articulation of a pre-schooler, despite a sophisticated, extensive vocabulary, including a host of medical terms. Echolalia has disappeared, but has been replaced by repetitive questions, toilet talk and breakthroughs of primary process.

Motorically Sherry is often clumsy and uncoordinated, at times showing stereotypical psychotic movements with arm and hand flailing when upset. Sherry has a number of disruptive, often disgusting habits, including nose picking, spitting, and public masturbation.

Intellectually Sherry is superior, with some interferences due to magical thinking and persistence of prelogical thought processes. Her affective disturbances include multiple fears, stranger anxiety, agitated behavior, and silliness used to ward off rage and depression. Socially, Sherry is often isolated, although she is making significant gains in her ability to relate to her peers. She also has a number of imaginary playmates. She is often oppositional, provocative, resistant to change, and whining.

Sherry's aggressive behavior toward her brother has diminished in recent months. Earlier, she was uncertain of her sexual identity, exhibitionistic and had poor control over her sexual impulses. Recently, however, she has established a more stable feminine identification, is less exhibitionistic, and shows more control over her sexual behavior.

Sherry's strengths are as extensive as her vulnerabilities. She is extremely bright, quick to learn, and has a remarkable memory. She is currently learning Spanish and German at school. In addition, despite a rigid and repetitive fantasy life, she can be very creative, using materials in an inventive fashion.

Sherry is acutely sensitive to environmental change, such as lighting and temperature, as well as to changes in people's physical appearance. She is also very sensual, often exploring her world with her kinesthetic and olfactory senses as well as visually. She is both a hedonist and an aesthetic, excited by good food, comfortable surroundings, pleasant smells and sensations. In general, she is intensely involved with her sensory world.

Despite her capacity for isolation, Sherry can be tremendously engaging, clever, and often very funny. Her most intriguing quality is her dramatic flux in ego states. She can enter a psychotic rage, be unable to respond or relate to others and be immersed in primary process, and within 30 minutes be able to reflect on the episode, evaluate her behavior, and think about the precipitants. On other occasions, she curls up in my lap, rocking like an infant, while discussing the causes and treatment of hemophilia, or the theory of gravity. Physical reassurance and being cuddled like an infant often appear to free up her most sophisticated, precocious cognitive function.

Course of Treatment

Sherry's treatment involves four major areas: 1) twice weekly meetings with Sherry focused on translating her uncontrolled primitive primary process thought into controlled verbally communicable secondary process thought; 2) collateral work with Mrs. Turner, exploring her reactions to Sherry, how she might best respond to Sherry's difficult and disruptive behaviors, and empathizing with her resentment and anger toward Sherry, while encouraging her to see the gains Sherry is making; 3) collateral work with Sherry's school, involving weekly phone calls with Sherry's teacher to discuss her behavior in school, and coordination of support services; 4) collateral work with Sherry's babysitters, who spend as much time with Sherry as does Mrs. Turner. These sitters need assistance in understanding Sherry, developing reasonable and consistent rules with her, and not allowing Sherry to pit them against Mrs. Turner, who is usually viewed as hostile and unloving by the babysitters.

Themes of treatment unfold in an interesting way. Sherry, like many psychotic children, has fantasies which become dominated by a conflict or fear, and she often spends months working through a theme before moving on. She has had a general improving course, despite temporary setbacks and regressions during times of disruptions, temporary losses and separations: school vacations, family vacations, illnesses, change of teachers and babysitters, and, most recently, her teacher's pregnancy.

There have been four overlapping conflicts with which Sherry has struggled throughout treatment, making important gains in each area:

Aggression

During Sherry's first months of treatment she was a ferocious tiger, rampaging in the office, attacking me, pretending to eat toys and puppets. After a while she began to grab supplies, hoarding them, concerned I might "steal" from her. After three months, Sherry was able, for the first time, to verbally express anger toward me at a treatment interruption, without attacking me physically. This ability to verbalize rather than physically act out all fantasies continued to improve. After I took a one-week vacation Sherry began discussing a dead big sister, revealing her rage and fear over our separation. Sibling rivalry between Sherry and her brother peaked seven months into Sherry's treatment when he went into therapy and also began making summer plans, while Sherry was to remain in school most of the summer. Sherry regressed with the intensity of her rage, expressed many homicidal fantasies, and attempted on several occasions to harm her brother. Soon after this, Sherry developed a long-lasting monster fixation, in which, week after week, monsters attacked her while her mother was off working. Sherry's anxiety about her own homicidal rage necessitated this primitive projection which literally dominated her for months. After a year in treatment, Sherry recognized her fears as internal forces, but in a fascinating way. She became obsessed with concerns about consuming poisons and germs that would attack her from within and kill her. For weeks she focused on diseases, poisons, and death.

With this shift from external to internal aggressors, Sherry made important progress. She became more verbal in treatment and with her peers, had increased concentration, and was more able to discuss her affects and fears. She openly discussed her jealousy of her brother and her ambivalent feelings of love and rage toward me.

When her teacher's pregnancy became noticeable Sherry became aggressive toward me, but was able to discuss her hatred and fear of babies. For two months she acted out the story of Sleeping Beauty, sometimes being the "prettiest baby in the land," and ordering me to kiss and compliment her; at other times she was the Wicked Fairy who tries to kill Sleeping Beauty; at still other times she was the Good Fairy who blocks the Wicked Fairy's attempts to harm the princess. Sherry's need to act out this story in 16 consecutive hours indicated the intensity of her conflict, as well as the restrictiveness of her fantasy life.

Loneliness and sociability

Initially, Sherry described her imaginary friends and siblings, often talking to them in our sessions. Later in treatment, she became attached to several of the puppets in the office, giving them permanent names and personalities. She often sets up the puppets around a table, including them in games. Only in the past six months has Sherry verbalized her desire for friends and begun to control her school behavior so that she is more popular and less isolated. A minor therapeutic triumph occurred recently when Sherry was invited to a girl's slumber party, behaved well throughout, and had a great time—despite having never entertained an overnight guest or spent a night at a friend's house. Actual rehearsal of slumber party behavior both at school and in therapy helped Sherry to successfully cope with this event.

For the first months of therapy, Sherry usually was a mess. She wore bizarre outfits and had uncombed hair, paint and dirt over most of her body and an array of distasteful habits. Recently she has become more concerned about her appearance, not wanting to alienate others by "looking stupid." She has become far more responsive to limit setting with her masturbation, toilet talk, nose picking, and other habits which alienate others.

Control issues

Sherry's treatment has always been dominated by control issues which overlap with her other conflict areas. Early in treatment Sherry

exhibited little control over her behavior. She was physically aggressive, "tantrumed" easily, was wildly exhibitionistic with her masturbation in the waiting room, and so forth. Only rarely, however, was
she truly out of control. Rather, her behavior appeared often to be
purposely provocative, inviting external controls.

As treatment progresses, Sherry is less aggressive, exhibitionistic
or wildly provocative. She is better able to verbally state her wish for
control and fear of losing control. In fact, of greater concern now is
Sherry's risk of becoming over-controlled. She employs a number of
obsessive-compulsive defenses, and has a tendency toward repetitious
action and verbalization when under stress. As some of Sherry's great-
est assets are her creativity and unique structuring of her world, such
excessive control would be at a high price.

Body image and sexual identification conflicts

Sherry has made her most visibly dramatic progress in the area of
her conflicts around body imagery and sexual identification. Early in
treatment Sherry said, "I'm a girl. What will I grow up to be? If I cut
my hair, am I still a girl?" On two occasions we went to a "funky lady"
clothes store where Sherry delighted in trying on old-fashioned clothes
and high heels. She asked, "Are these for ladies or big girls? I'm a little
girl, no, a big girl, no, a middle girl! Do middle girls become ladies?"

While struggling with the notion of gender being permanent, Sherry
became sexually very exhibitionistic. The receptionist summoned me
several times when Sherry was masturbating in the waiting room and
disturbing other patients. This issue quickly assumed a secondary
meaning as a control issue ensued. I forbade this behavior publicly and
Sherry became more sexually provocative in the office, causing me to
set further limits.

Sherry's concern about her sexuality and sexual identity was colored
by larger body image issues. For years Sherry has gone to a center for
the handicapped. In addition, Sherry's brother refers to her as handicapped, following the example of Mrs. Turner, who explained to her
son that Sherry is "emotionally handicapped." As a result, Sherry has
many fantasies and concerns about her handicaps. During the first
eight months of treatment with me, Sherry often entered the office on
her rear-end, claiming, "I can't walk." At other times, she played games
with her eyes closed stating, "I can't see." I interpreted Sherry's
"games" as her concern about being handicapped. She then confided
her true handicap: "I was born shy—not wanting to talk." This became

a jumping-off point for a discussion about Sherry's learning to use her non-verbalness to manipulate others. She heartily agreed that, by not talking, she made others try to get her to talk. She giggled when I suggested that this was gratifying and made her feel close to, instead of isolated from, others. Sherry played out far fewer handicap fantasies after this session.

Many months into treatment, Sherry slowly became more concerned about her appearance, wanting to look neat and feminine. One year into treatment, when she received some new clothes, she was careful and proud of these for a short period. As her teacher's pregnancy became visible, Sherry went on a fierce exercise binge, dieting, exercising, and encouraging me to do so also. She then brought in baby dolls, toward whom she was quite maternal, only later to wash out their eyes with Ajax.

Sherry was still unable to ask about pregnancies, but became far more concerned with her identity as a woman. She came in wearing a training bra one day—a present from her mother—which she wanted me to admire. She asked questions about menstruation. When I told Sherry that I knew her teacher was pregnant and noted that her behavior for the past two months had indicated she was wondering about this, she agreed but could not discuss why she was unable to broach the subject. She regressed for a brief period, reintroducing toilet talk. I interpreted her rage.

Her teacher's pregnancy stimulated two major lines of progress for Sherry. She became quite verbal about her hatred and fear of babies, quickly associating this to her jealous rage at the birth of her brother and how she still felt this way. Sherry became more willing to discuss her anger toward both the brother and her mother, and her feelings of being left out and cheated.

At the same time, Sherry appeared to cement her feminine identification. She became a leader in "Girl's Group" at school. She began to wear dresses, to comb her hair, and, at times, to wear perfume and nail polish. At school Sherry asked her teacher about pregnancy and babies. Her teacher took her to the library and the two read a book together, discussing Sherry's questions.

When her teacher was ill for a while, Sherry regressed, starting to use toilet talk again and not wanting to talk. When I interpreted her anger at once again feeling pushed aside for a baby, she was able to discuss this with me with some sadness. Shortly thereafter she had her first birthday party, with only girls invited, and was delighted to have a party where you could talk "girl talk."

Goals of Continued Treatment

1) To continue to help Sherry translate primary process thought into secondary communicative processes. A corollary of this goal will be to help Sherry continue to accurately label frightening feelings of rage, deprivation and isolation as well as to expand her experience of positive feelings and her vocabulary for expressing these.

2) To continue to assist Sherry to gain better control of impulses and inappropriate behavior. There is increasing evidence that she can manage these for longer periods of time.

3) To consolidate her feminine identification and begin to help her better understand ideas about menstruation, body changes, sexuality and pregnancy.

4) To further consolidate boundaries between inner and outer, fantasy and reality, and to continue the process of helping her become more self-observant.

5) To further expand Sherry's beginning efforts at making and retaining friends and entering a more normal social world. I have already begun to work with Sherry's teacher in connection with making arrangements for Sherry to spend an hour or two each day at a regular public school. Sherry is tolerating this well and, with considerable pride, is beginning to tell me of events that occur in this new classroom. In this connection I plan to continue collaborative work with all school personnel in order to insure that external stress is minimized and realistic opportunities for growth are promoted. This will be of particular importance as Sherry gradually makes the transition to a regular school, full-time.

6) Continued meetings with Mrs. Turner and Sherry's babysitters remain an integral part of the ongoing work.

Discussion

Psychotherapeutic work with children like Sherry involves extensive and Herculean effort. The account of the first five years of this effort attests to the importance of attending to all aspects of Sherry's life, including her physical world, educational setting, home environment, and social activities, in addition to the work in the therapy sessions. The work requires infinite patience, stamina, a capacity to tolerate many regressions and disruptions, and a willingness to measure progress on a "millimetric" scale.

Sherry is fortunate. Her mother is competent and willing to go to considerable lengths and expense to help Sherry. A fine special school is available and fully able and willing to collaborate in the therapeutic process and to provide a therapeutic-educational atmosphere. Mrs. Turner has made good babysitters available to supplement the school's day care program and these women have also been willing to participate in the therapeutic program and to learn how to understand and help Sherry.

Sherry's good fortune has also included two competent therapists who have been prepared to "hang in for the long haul." The report of Sherry's current therapist details the severity of Sherry's pathology but, even more importantly, distills every asset with which the therapist can ally herself in order to promote progress. The goals are clear and, in the main, realistically estimated. Perhaps one might quibble with the therapist's concern that Sherry's creativity not be impaired by a more compulsive defensive structure. The greater control and socialization gained from this development might be worth the price. Given the overall high quality of the therapeutic work, this is a very small quibble.

Parenthetically, it should be noted that the case report mentions that Sherry's brother also began psychotherapy during the course of Sherry's treatment. There is good evidence that the "normal" siblings of psychotic and otherwise severely impaired children do not escape the day-to-day impact of such situations. The toll which such events take on the other children may not be dramatically evident and, as such, is often overlooked. It is, however, not to be underestimated and warrants attention and possible intervention on behalf of these at-risk children. This is one further item in the extensive and expensive cost of an overall treatment approach in a case such as Sherry's. Many have asked whether such time consuming, resource exhausting and costly efforts are socially justified. This is a value decision that each therapist, each family, each agency and ultimately the society as a whole must grapple with and make. From another perspective, the technological question is easier to answer. Unless the resources exist and can be utilized, the technical task is, most likely, impossible.

PETER MARTIN

Developmental History

Peter is now almost 11, the only son of a bright, disorganized, and needy single woman. Ms. Martin gave birth to Peter when she was barely 17, and she has always cared for him while striving to put her own life in order. When Peter was about two, Ms. Martin met a man with whom she soon began to live. Peter became attached to this boyfriend, an attachment that was satisfying to all three members of this new family. Unhappily, this was not to last. When Peter was four, the boyfriend was killed in an auto accident. After a period of depression, Ms. Martin once again picked up the strands of her life. She continued her own education, worked part-time, and struggled to find another suitable relationship with a man.

It is not difficult to understand Peter's intense attachment to his mother, whom he has often had to protect and care for, in spite of her valiant efforts to be a good caretaker. Nor is it difficult to understand Peter's intense anxiety, warded off by braggadocio, impulsivity and failure to learn. He makes few friends, fearful that any deviance from his intense, albeit ambivalent, tie to his mother will be perceived as a betrayal of this primary attachment. Naturally, then, his treatment has been a stormy and difficult one, with the therapist expending as much energy and attention to Ms. Martin as towards Peter. These efforts to help Ms. Martin loosen the intense knot of her own symbiotic attachment to Peter, to help her provide a more stable and regulated environment, have paid off.

Initial Treatment

It is almost impossible to convey the mayhem Peter created in his early treatment hours. During the first months, when Peter was nine years old, his therapist was often left puzzled, and despairing at the end of sessions. At first tentatively and tenuously, Peter began to invest in his relationship with his therapist, to reduce the tempo of his seemingly aimless and destructive play, and to permit her to see the troubled and fearful themes which underlay his symptoms. Peter also began to demonstrate important gains in his real world. His chaotic school behavior receded, permitting him to use his superior intelligence to learn. Soon after Peter entered therapy, his therapist arranged for a more appropriate school for him. Therapist and teacher met regularly to assess Peter's progress and to enhance his learning and socializing.

Course of Treatment

Early in the second year of his twice weekly treatment, he arrives ten minutes early for his sessions. He can, with help, now wait for the session to begin—albeit reluctantly. As he is picked up, Ms. Martin informs the therapist proudly that Peter will be going on an overnight trip with his class—the first time he has been able to earn such a reward.

The therapist comments: "That's really neat!" In the playroom, Peter remarks: "You always say that dumb thing, '*neat*'," and bossily announces, while sorting through the play money, that he wants to play the robber game. He robs the therapist, commenting that the money he stole is counterfeit. The therapist states that Peter seems to be telling her that she has given him counterfeit money and counterfeit compliments. Peter laughs. Did the therapist see *King Kong*? She says: "A long time ago," and remembers that they'd once talked about how King Kong acted very scary when he was scared himself.

Peter begins to build a tower and topples it. The therapist asks: "Isn't that what King Kong did when he got scared?" Peter doesn't answer, but begins to rush about wildly, returning to earlier, more disruptive play.

The therapist notes that the "old Peter is back again" and adds: "Say, I forgot to ask you something." Peter quiets down. "I forgot to ask you if you *want* to go on the overnight?" Peter spells out his response loudly: "YENOS." The remainder of the hour is spent discussing his frightening and ambivalent feelings, his fear of being away from his mother, his concern that he will not be able to control his behavior on the overnight, his uncertainty that he has truly earned this reward, and his fear that his worry about the forest, a completely new experience, makes him a baby. Fortunately, there are two additional hours to work on these before the overnight.

The sequential elements of this encounter can be described as follows:

1) The mother's proud announcement in the waiting room;
2) The therapist's response to the mother and, only secondarily, to Peter;
3) Peter's derision of the therapist's response, followed by several play metaphors in which he conveys the improperly balanced therapeutic intervention as if to say: "Hey, therapist, you missed the other half of my feelings." These feelings are underscored by his mounting anxiety and regression to wilder behavior and earlier content, namely King Kong.
4) The therapist's alertness to these, and her recovery, framed in a deft, casual remark: "Say, I forgot to ask if *you want* to go on the overnight?"

5) This intervention is clearly effective, since Peter quiets down and produces a highly relevant response, thus permitting a return to important work about his frightening, ambivalent feelings in an immediate context—the overnight camping trip.

This work is excellent, yet, at the outset, not entirely on the mark. In fact, its excellence proceeds from a seeming error.

As his therapy progresses, Peter's orality and greediness become one of the prominent themes. They are played out in many ways, but most notably around the issue of his hourly treat. His manner of "dealing" with the treat has also served as one barometer to Peter's progress in treatment. In the first sessions he was voracious and constantly complained that it was never enough. Later, he denigrated his treat, wanting something different from what he'd asked for. Still later in therapy, he could not permit himself to eat the treat, but would inspect it to be sure it was still there. Even later, he could not decide which treat he wanted. More recently, he has been able to decide and enjoy his selection, often choosing a Top Ramen.

Peter arrives, asks for his treat, and begins to eat his Top Ramen, but stops at midpoint. He announces that he will save the rest to take home. The therapist inquires how he came to this decision. Peter replies that his mother will be coming home late tonight and the Top Ramen will help him wait. The therapist tells Peter that he has found a good and nourishing way to help him with waiting. She appreciates that waiting is hard, and notes that it used to be much harder. "Yup," he says, "waiting sure used to be lots harder."

One can see the shifts in this boy's increased capacity to take and enjoy nourishment, to tolerate delay and plan for ways of solacing himself during stressful times. He acknowledges that waiting was and is hard, and that he can do this better now. This increased capacity to wait is critical to ego development. To learn to wait helps children tolerate frustration, anticipate and "keep in mind" the outcome at the end of waiting; to differentiate and master an understanding of time—now, then, later—which, in turn, builds a firmer sense of reality.

Peter is now able to use the transitional Top Ramen from his hour with his therapist and connect it to his mother and waiting for her. Early in Peter's treatment, any attachment to anyone other than his mother was experienced as a frightening abandonment of her. In turn, such thoughts left him feeling totally alone and abandoned. Through his attachment to his therapist, he can now permit others into his world—a world once inhabited only by Peter and his mother, whose boundaries often merged. He has taken another step towards differentiation and growth.

Later, shortly after Peter reached his tenth birthday, he and a friend were caught on a school roof, aiming small pebbles at various windows. Peter's mother, now firmly allied with the therapist, phoned to inform her of Peter's transgression, and permitted the therapist to raise this with Peter. Moreover, she informed the therapist that this time Peter was upset, in contrast to his prior insistence that a similar incident a year ago was of no concern to him.

Peter's next hour takes place during a school holiday. He arrives almost two hours early, bringing another friend with him. He and his friend are permitted by the secretary to take two toys outdoors. When his therapist arrives, he introduces his friend and offers the therapist some of his candy. They agree to begin their session early. Parenthetically, it is important to note that Peter has, in recent hours, been making positive, but guarded, affectionate comments to his therapist. He takes his treat—now licorice, and leaves momentarily to share some of it with his waiting friend. When he returns, she comments on his being in a good mood today. "Yup," he assents, "I'm in a winning mood"—and asks her to save some of his licorice for next time. She comments that when Peter is in a winning mood, he can save some of the things he likes for later. "Good, strong feelings make a boy feel full—less hungry." In response to her question about his friend, Peter reports that his friend sees someone like her. Does Peter know why? No. She asks whether Peter knows why he comes to see *her* regularly? No, but after a pause and with an impish grin, he replies, "You are my playmate." The therapist agrees that they do indeed play games together. More seriously, he adds, "You are also my psychologist." Again, she agrees that she is there to help him understand and feel better about himself.

Peter commands her to play—they have by now set up a game of checkers and Peter is well ahead—having mastered the game ably as his capacity to concentrate has developed.

The therapist now asks about the escapade on the roof. Peter leaves the game and goes angrily to the cabinet, building two structures with the Legos as he mutters obscenities: "Bitch, Stupid, Weirdo." The structures are sturdily and well built, but each is destroyed as they are completed. The therapist sits quietly, until the obscenities disappear. She comments that Peter is disappointed in her—she hurt his strong, good feelings, he feels robbed of them, and now he has shut her out.

He stoutly denies that his feelings are hurt, and anyway the boy who came with him is not *that* friend. He wants his licorice, grabs and gobbles it. The therapist persists, commenting that Peter had come with very good, winning feelings and that she had reminded him of upset feelings. The obscenities and his building begin again. She again comments that he feels hurt, and now must play alone. He makes no response.

She watches quietly and then says that she has a thought. She is thinking that maybe Peter is playing against himself. One part, the strong, good-feeling Peter, is playing against the other part of Peter, the hurt, punishing Peter. Instantaneously, Peter responds, "Yeah, and the bad side wins." He bolts from the room. The therapist finds him standing by his friend and asks Peter to return since their time is not yet up. He protests, but comes readily. In the playroom, the therapist acknowledges that she is glad he returned. She knows that he is upset with her—that he may not have been ready today to talk about the punishing side of Peter. She wants to help him, so that side will not be the winner. They have time, time to play and time to figure and, although Peter isn't yet so sure about this, she is *not* a punisher. Peter leaves his partially standing structures in the middle of the playroom.

The sequence of this session can be understood as follows:

1) It is likely that Peter has brought his friend to see this place, where he feels safe and where he belongs. This is supported by his early arrival, his use of the center's toys, his care with them and his sharing of his treat with his friend—new skills for Peter. Peter also reveals that he surely knows what he and his therapist are about.
2) He is, by his own account, feeling like a winner today.
3) As the therapist and he begin a friendly, competitive game which he plays competently and without anxiety, the therapist approaches conflicted material. In earlier sessions, such confrontations would have led to explosive mayhem. Now, the wounded feelings are expressed in angry words, a need to gobble the remaining licorice and a play disruption. He plainly and firmly shuts her out.
4) Although Peter's vulnerability is clear, he engages now in a solitary game which includes building as well as destroying. Although the confrontation may have been a bit too quickly timed, the therapist permits his solitary efforts to repair and deftly shares responsibility by acknowledging that her observation may

have led to his disappointment in her, when he had been feeling so good. Imaginatively, she interprets the play as two parts of Peter: the good, strong Peter, and the punishing Peter.

5) Peter instantly validates the interpretation, but he cannot yet own or work with it; he must leave the room. Not so long ago, he would have asserted vehemently that he cared not one whit about his delinquent behavior. Instead, such acts would have been used to brag about his toughness and his daredevil accomplishments. It is probable that this once potentially dangerous behavior served a primitive, punitive conscience, which remained unconscious and totally unavailable—suggesting that Peter may once have been headed toward delinquency. Now, while Peter's conscience remains harsh and retaliative, it is available and can, in subsequent treatment, be modulated.

6) That such work is to come is supported by his easy return to the office—another recent achievement. The disconnection is temporary and reparable.

Recovery from regressions are now possible and more rapid. Peter, once locked into the frozen fortress of his isolation and fears, can now grow, learn, and enjoy—although more remains to be achieved.

Some months later Peter developed a friendship with the clinic switchboard operator. She is friendly and affectionate toward Peter, who correctly perceives that she has a special interest in him. This pleases him, but also makes him somewhat apprehensive.

On arrival for a session, Peter spends a brief time talking with his friend at the switchboard, but leaves quickly when his therapist approaches. He asks immediately for his Top Ramen, and begins to cook the noodles.

For the first time, he notices that this is "Top Ramen," while at home he usually has "Snack Ramen." The therapist comments that when he takes his time he notices a lot more. He absentmindedly pours too much water in the pan, and then says: "I forgot to make it stronger." The therapist replies that something kept him from concentrating. He reassures her that it will be OK, and begins to eat his noodles. He shows his therapist the comb which he's just been given by his friend at the switchboard. He runs outside and pretends to comb his hair in front of the switchboard operator. He returns to the playroom easily, but immediately announces that he must go to the bathroom. Rushing out again, he returns in less than ten seconds. The therapist inquires, "Did you go to the bathroom?" Peter says, "No, I just had to run around.

Watch!" He runs out again, up the stairs, and asks whether the therapist wants to see how he can jump over the banister down to the floor below.

The therapist tells Peter that he can't do that. He says, "Yes, I can." The therapist acknowledges that she knows he is *able* to do that, but that this is against the rules. But she understands that he likes to show her how strong he is, and the many things he can do.

He returns to the playroom, and continues to eat his Top Ramen, and begins to talk about Bruce Lee and his wish to learn karate. He wonders why he likes karate, but cannot offer any further ideas about that.

Peter begins to discuss a movie about two boys who rape women. The woman in the movie shoots the boys when they break into her house. Peter describes in some detail how they got shot. The therapist says that most boys have sexy feelings, but mostly they don't act on them like the boys in the movie. Peter is listening intently and the therapist adds that she knows some boys worry that they will be punished for having such feelings, even if they don't act on them.

Peter makes no direct response, but instead tells about another movie, in which a woman who got hurt "killed men by thought-power." The therapist asks if Peter believes that thoughts can cause things to happen. Peter says, "What do you think?" She says that she does have her own ideas about this, but it would be good to know his first. He says he knows it's a true story because he saw it on "That's Incredible." Again he asks whether the therapist believes it. She says she doesn't believe that thoughts by themselves cause things to happen, but she knows that children often worry about that. Peter asks: "Well, what if you had a thought and then something bad really did happen?" The therapist acknowledges that that is a very good and important question. She adds that if something bad really did happen, a boy would need someone to talk to, to figure it out.

Peter moves to the toys and begins a game of pick-up-sticks, which he begins to lose. The therapist notes that he usually wins at this game, and she wonders if something is on his mind that makes it hard for him to concentrate.

After a brief pause, Peter asks if his therapist sees four-year-olds. She says yes, but wonders why he asks. Peter responds with another question: "Why would you want to see a four-year-old?" The therapist replies that four-year-olds have ideas and feelings too, and that sometimes worrisome things happen to four-year-olds. Peter quickly says, "The only thing that happened to me when I was four was that David was killed." (This is the first reference that Peter has made to mother's boyfriend who lived with them when Peter was ages two to four.) His therapist says, "Yes, and I imagine you had many thoughts and feelings about that." Peter insists he had no feelings. The therapist tells him that this is just not true. His mom told her that Peter felt very sad and cried a lot. Peter denies it. The therapist says that his mom would remember that very well, and that it is curious that Peter would forget those feelings.

Peter now asks cautiously, "I was sad?" She assures him that his mother told her that he was very, very sad, just as his mom was. Peter becomes pensive for a moment, and then decides to get some paper and glue. The therapist remarks that four-year-old feelings can stay in a ten-year-old boy, and that it's never too late to figure them out. It's good to sort out four-year-old feelings from ten-year-old feelings. He does not reply, but notes instead that the glue won't come out of the bottle. He continues to try and without assistance he figures out how to get the glue from the bottle. The therapist says, "That bottle has been sitting around for a long time . . . people thought it didn't work . . . but it was only plugged up." Peter draws a happy face with the glue and says that he wants licorice next time. He wonders what he wanted for his treat when he first began to come here, and then remembers that he used to want cookies. The therapist agrees and reminds him that sometimes he didn't eat the cookies he wanted. Peter guesses that he must not have been hungry those times. The therapist suggests that maybe sometimes he didn't feel that it was OK to be hungry or to deserve cookies, or other good things. The hour ends with Peter wondering if she gives food to other kids. The therapist says that she needs time to think about that question because she isn't sure if Peter is asking more than one question. He leaves with a smile, saying, "See you Tuesday."

In this hour, the emphasis begins to shift away from issues of aggression which have been the primary focus for some time. The past work has had several major goals. These included slowing Peter down, creating an atmosphere of safety and consistency, developing a solid relationship which has had the effect of creating further separation and individuation, helping to reduce Peter's excessively punitive conscience, developing increasing ways for Peter to signal and control himself and validating this child's vulnerable self-esteem.

While none of these have been fully accomplished, enough developmental progress has been made to allow the work to focus on a new area: New material is emerging which has been obscured by the tenacity of Peter's preoccupation with his sense of himself as bad, angry and undeserving. This sense of himself and the primitive defenses he has struggled to erect to keep these feelings out of awareness have made it impossible for the therapist to know about other equally important issues. Tender, affectionate feelings and thoughts have for some time been present. However, more exciting sexual feelings have heretofore been repressed. These surface now, prompted by the unwittingly seductive relationship the switchboard operator has set in motion. Some of Peter's feelings toward the switchboard operator almost certainly are connected to the therapist as well as to his mother.

The understanding about Peter's psychodynamics now changes from a view primarily focused on fixation to one whose emphasis includes regressions and repressions. With this different perspective, there is a concomitant shift in psychotherapeutic technique.

With this in mind, the preceding hour can be thought about as follows: Peter enters the treatment room immediately after the most recent chapter in his "love affair." He is already excited and a bit worried. As he begins to get his treat, he makes an important distinction. The therapist praises his good powers of observation, which is a highly appropriate intervention to help Peter slow down, calm down, and take in. Paradoxically, this praise first distracts him and he dilutes his soup, commenting, "I forgot to make it stronger." While he tries to reassure himself and his therapist that all is well, his excitement mounts. He exhibits his gift of a new comb and runs from the room to use the comb in front of the switchboard operator. He runs in and out several times trying to offer some logical explanation, but quickly acknowledges that he just needs to run around. Peter's excitement and his need to discharge tension are overt and clear, and there is an abortive return to the previous braggadocio—but without its earlier intensity or fixity.

On return to the room, he reminds himself of his interest in karate, but this time wonders about his motives.   Now the emerging material spills out in his account of the movies. Here sexuality and aggression are interlocked. The therapist takes the opportunity to emphasize the distinction between thought and action, while acknowledging that thoughts can still be frightening. This is also an indirect observation about the heated climate in the clinic.

This permits Peter to explore further his fear and his confusion about the power of wishes and thoughts. In spite of several efforts to clarify that thoughts, in themselves, do no harm, Peter remains unsure.

Nevertheless he is considerably calmed by the therapist's "promise" that if something bad happened, she would be available to figure it out.

The therapist's support enables Peter to move toward a game both can play. However, he is not sufficiently calm to play with his usual skill. She notes again that something is on his mind. New material emerges. He approaches these concerns cautiously by asking whether the therapist sees four-year-olds. It seems clear that the discussion about bad happenings and their relationship to "thought power" has prompted this question. Very quickly, Peter reports the bad thing that happened when he was four, insisting that he had no feelings about the event. The therapist's gentle insistence that she and his mother know that he was very sad surprises him, helps him yield maladaptive denials and affords him some relief. Some repressed guilt about Peter's jealousy of David can be inferred from this interaction, supported more fully by the play that follows.

The old stuck glue is softened, and can, by his own efforts, be unplugged. It is used to display another affect—pleasure. Peter and his therapist spend the remaining time quietly reviewing their past history together.

This hour also illustrates a general technical problem faced by all child therapists: what to do with direct questions. This therapist uses a variety of responses to the many questions Peter asks:

1) A question about violating safety or the rules ("Do you want to see me jump over the banister?") is answered by firm, clear limit setting.
2) A question about the therapist's opinion in conflict-laden circumstances ("What do you think" about whether thoughts can cause bad things to happen) brings the reply that she will answer his question, but is interested in his ideas first.
3) The question persists, suggesting some mounting anxiety ("Do you believe it?") and this time is met with a direct answer, followed by an interpretation of children's worries.
4) The question of what the therapist does with other children ("Do you see four-year-olds?") is met with an affirmative reply and an inquiry about why Peter is asking. In this instance, the therapist has some hunch about the specific meaning of this question for Peter, and expects that her inquiry will prompt the worrisome material.
5) The question Peter asks at the very end, again referring to her

work with other children ("Do you give food to other kids?") receives a temporizing reflective response, to be dealt with in the
future.

These are not the only ways to deal with children's questions. There
are some guiding principles which can help the therapist select the
most appropriate responses. On one level, one can think about a therapist's responses along a gratification-frustration continuum. The therapist must have some capacity to understand how much frustration
the patient can tolerate, and how much gratification is necessary to
continue the work. No response to a question is maximum frustration.
Failing to respond to a child whose anxiety may be experienced as
unendurable cannot help the child to maintain an effective alliance
with the therapist. Very few children, particularly young ones, can
tolerate a total absence of response.

At the other extreme is a simple direct answer. This may be the
most gratifying response, but such gratification may close material off
and slow exploration. This excludes the simple limit-setting response
which attends first and foremost to safety and order.

Between the two extremes there are many variations, some of which
have been illustrated in the transcript of the last hour with Peter.
Other possible interventions can include such comments as:

"Why do you ask?"
"What brings that to mind?"
"Right now? Why do you ask now?"
"That's an interesting question, and I'd like to hear more about it."

Naturally the therapist's style and his or her knowledge of the question
and its context will influence the response.

Another principle that can guide responses rests on the therapist's
understanding of how best to enable a child's story to unfold, the wish
to enlist the child's curiosity, and the need to permit the expression of
heretofore forbidden ideas or fantasies. Needless to say, it is important
to be sure that the therapist understands the multiplicity of issues that
can be masked by a simple question. One needs to be sure that one is
answering the right question.

Still another principle to keep in mind is that answers and information offered without an understanding of the child's fantasy or worry
may throw good information after bad. It has been amply demonstrated
that the provision of correct information about sexual matters is useless

if the child is cognitively unready to receive it, or if conflict and fantasy are so enmeshed that it cannot be corrected by information alone. This principle holds for more than sexual questions.

Yet another way of thinking about responding to children's questions revolves around the importance on occasion of showing a child how the therapist thinks, reflects, and takes time to solve important problems. Here the therapist becomes a model for identification, showing new ways the child may be ready to try on.

Furthermore, some questions are best answered with an interpretation. Some children's questions about other patients relate to specific conflicts such as the wish to be special, rivalrous feelings and permission to be different, yet still acceptable. These are best answered with interpretations.

Finally, Peter's many questions illustrate the manner in which children's questions shift with changing developmental and therapeutic stages, altered by changes in him and his reality. At the same time, the questions have a unifying sameness in their thematic content. Persistently, some of the things he asks are: "Do I have a place with important people?" "Am I all right?" "Is it OK to have my own feelings and thoughts?" "Will I be cared for and protected?" "Do I deserve good things?"

Peter's case poses another generic question in child treatment. Should treats and gifts be used or avoided? Once again this issue is best addressed differentially and individually rather than by firm prohibitions or convictions. Children can, of course, be helped without these "aids" since therapists have better supplies to nourish personality than can be provided by a specific treat. On the other hand, some therapists argue that the concrete cognitive equipment of children makes the use of treats as important as the play equipment. It is a medium through which an alliance can evolve and grow, subject to use, change and interpretation.

In Peter's case, the treats were used ably in the treatment and served as a barometer for his progress. It is, nevertheless, very likely that the treatment of Peter could have proceeded without treats.

Whether to use treats or not can be considered with the following in mind:

1) What purposes might treats serve? In the main, the use of any modality should depend upon specific positive indicators, rather than on wholesale philosophies. Experience suggests that the more primitive

the child, the more likely one will tend to consider the use of a treat. Conversely, the child with more advanced development, who is capable of greater symbolic representation and able to tolerate greater frustration and delay, is less likely to need and use concrete forms of gratification. However, even the use of this principle of greater and lesser disturbance as a measure for decision must be tempered. A severely disturbed child who fears and mistrusts others may see the treat as dangerous, as a bribe or in some other misunderstood way.

2) One of the major risks in providing treats is the concern the child may feel about being angry or disappointed with someone who gives him things. For example, deeply disturbed Martin who has regularly received cookies found it difficult to imagine that his therapist would return after her vacation—an experience that his life, devoid of established constancy, made impossible for him to conceive. When she did return, he was at first confused and later overwhelmed with fury that she had temporarily deserted him. He reverted to turning his back on her, refusing any contact except to plead for more cookies than he usually received. After several hours of mounting struggle around these requests, Martin blurted, "If you give me more cookies, I promise I'll never be mad at you anymore." More cookies in exchange for exiling common human reactions is a bad bargain therapeutically and developmentally. It can be argued equally cogently that no treat is a substitute for true caring and human involvement.

3) Another risk in treat giving is the unwitting competition it may set in motion with the child's parents. Parents are already vulnerable to guilt and shame about the "failures" exposed by a troubled child. The therapist may be seen by them as a better parent than they, a stance which may enlarge the rift between parent and child. Competitiveness with a parent can derive from subtle wishes by the therapist to rescue the child from an inadequate parent, an over-identification with the child, an imperfect appreciation of the parents' subjective experiences and conflicts, or an array of other countertransference impulses in the therapist. If the parent experiences the child's therapist as a better parent or hungers for the treats given the child while the parent receives criticism instead, it will be difficult to enlist the parent's support of the active, allied connection which the therapist and child require for the most effective treatment environment.

In these nutrition-conscious days, some parents may complain about their child's receipt of sugar-loaded treats. These complaints may also be based on unconscious or preconscious perceptions that their children are receiving sugar-coated treatment. Such seemingly small matters and disputes can initiate treatment sabotage.

Some months later, a further shift occurs in Peter's treatment. No longer stressed by the switchboard operator's seductive overtures (she has left the agency), Peter begins to consolidate further the gains he has been making. He has continued to work on his fantasies about his mother's old boyfriend, recalling several rather brief, warm memories of him that are no longer shrouded in worried or walled-off feelings. He has been able to acknowledge that boisterous, daredevil acts or comments often mask fear, helplessness and a sense of being so little. He can read his "signals" much better now so that he can stop to think before rushing into action, telling his therapist that "mostly my brakes are in good working order."

Things have also changed in Peter's experience. His mother and her new boyfriend are soon to be married and the therapist has been introduced to the fiancé. They have met several times, with mother's consent, and Peter's soon-to-be stepfather has taken an increasing hand in the child rearing. A former college athlete, this man has engaged Peter in sports and won Peter's admiration. The school reports increasing progress, though the teacher would still like to see Peter exercise greater control over his occasional silliness and apply himself more fully to school work.

During this period of time, Peter has become increasingly interested in a Monopoly game. He seems totally absorbed in this game over several hours and in a brisk and task-oriented way, immediately sets up the board as he begins each of these hours. He plays in a well organized fashion, with sustained attention and concentration, eager to win but also clearly enjoying the game and the time he spends with his therapist.

Termination

The following three sessions suggest that Peter may well be in the terminating phase of his treatment.

In the first of these sessions Peter arrives ten minutes late as a result of a change in his class schedule. He asks his therapist to heat the water for his Top Ramen while he sets up the Monopoly board. When she returns, there are two packets of candy—one set out for her and one for Peter. She recalls that she used to give Peter sweets—now he has brought his own. He asks her to notice the name of the candy, "Now and Later," and that there are two pieces in each package. She can choose to eat both pieces in her pack now or save one for later as he plans to do. She agrees that his plan is a good one and she will follow suit.

As the play proceeds, Peter's therapist tells him that she has recently
visited his school. Is he interested to know what the teacher had to
say? He is. She reports that the teacher thinks Peter is very smart,
but that he occasionally behaves in a silly way. Can they figure out
why this is? Peter says, "Play—anyway, I don't like her very much."
The therapist replies that the teacher likes him a lot. Peter says,
"Hurry up, let's play!" The therapist responds, "If you took yourself as
seriously as this game . . ." Peter interrupts and loudly declares, "I'd
be terrific! Did you tell the teacher that?" She replies that she is sure
that his teacher already knows that.

By now, Peter is way ahead in the Monopoly game and has, on
several occasions, lent the therapist money so the game can continue.
The therapist begins to muse out loud about the unlikelihood of her
winning this game and her wondering if perhaps she should concede.
Peter encourages her to persevere, reminding her of how often in the
past she told him that he should keep trying and not quit. "You can't
tell what might happen," Peter reassures her.

As the hour draws to a close, Peter asks if they could possibly change
their meeting time so he does not miss the first ten minutes since he
now gets out of school later than he used to. Without pause, he goes
on to say that he wants to take with him a toy car that he found on
the steps of the clinic that day. He says that since he found it, it is his
and that he wants something to play with on the ride home. She responds that there isn't enough time left to plan a change of meeting
time, but that they will do that next session. Also she says that the
car is not really his since she recognizes it as part of the clinic's play
equipment and he may not take it with him. She acknowledges that
it's hard to leave something he wants. Peter accepts this without protest, although he's clearly disappointed.

In the next hour, while preparing to set up the Monopoly board,
Peter discovers a rocket ship built from Legos. Peter decides that it is
one that he made a long time ago and seems surprised that it is still
intact. The therapist notes his surprise and wonders if he is surprised
to find an "old thing" when he is now so different. This leads to an
extended discussion of things he has made during their work together
and the many things they have talked about. Peter says that he's more
grown up now but that he wants to build a duplicate of the old rocket.
He soon discovers that there are not enough pieces to complete the
copy. Without any distress, he changes plans and figures out something
else he can build with the available pieces. The therapist observes that
he could not have changed his plans so easily in the past. Peter grins

impishly and says, "I used to break things when that would happen." She agrees that he used to be very mean to himself that way and he didn't used to think he was smart enough to figure out another way. Peter replies with playful self-assuredness, "The teacher says I'm very smart."

Peter asks if the therapist has remembered to change his time so he won't lose the ten minutes and they work out a new schedule.

Peter then asks if he can take some of the play money with him so he can fool his friend, the bus driver, into thinking that Peter is rich. He promises to bring it back next time. The therapist asks if he could be rich in other ways and suggests that he would feel very bad if he forgot to bring the money back. He is sure he can remember and tells her that he was the one who remembered to check about changing the time. She decides to let him borrow some of the play money.

Indeed, in the next hour Peter returns the borrowed money. He has come to this session despite being obviously ill with a cold. He complains about his sore throat and together they prepare a warm gargle. He tells her that he wishes that Phil (his stepfather-to-be) could come and take him home today, instead of his having to go home on the bus. The therapist offers to call Phil and is able to arrange for Peter to be picked up. Hesitantly Peter says, "You know, I don't like to go on the bus when it's dark." She asks if he really means to say that he's afraid. He agrees that he really is afraid. The therapist tells him that lots of boys are afraid to go on the bus alone when it's dark and that she'll try to work it out with Phil and his mom to come and pick him up during these months when it gets dark early.

While it is difficult to predict how long this terminating phase of treatment will take, it is clear that the work is now centered on consolidating the gains which Peter has made. This is evident in:

1) His continuing attachment to his therapist, the importance to him of his time with her and his newly developed ability to request a change in the schedule in a forthright manner.
2) The development of a positive new attachment to his soon-to-be stepfather and his ability to admire this man and to use him as an ego-model and as a helper.
3) The continuation of his recovery of warm memories about a previous father-figure.
4) His appropriate awareness of his teacher's balanced view of his strengths and limitations and his ability to use humor to tolerate criticism.
5) Considerable evidence of the establishment of a solid latency:

age-appropriate games; ability to modify plans when frustrated; ability to seek and use adult help when he is ill; increasingly good working controls which he can assert and demonstrate; ability to acknowledge fears and feelings; a growing capacity to give and take good things.
6) An internalization of many of the therapist's interventions and interpretations which clearly reflect a new sense of himself.

The therapeutic approach has also taken a decidedly different tone. The therapist need not be so vigilant since Peter is now able to plan the hours and regulate and modulate feelings and defenses on his own. There is much order and routine in these sessions. Information from outside sources about progress and remaining difficulties is easily brought into the hours without risk of disruption or regression. Hidden feelings can be quickly uncovered and used to provide direct assistance.

A portion of almost every hour is used to review the therapeutic history. The therapist takes advantage of Peter's readiness to compare how he used to be with how he is now. This kind of review is a particular strategy for the terminating phase of the therapy. It begins to provide opportunities for both to make increasing coherence and completeness about Peter's experiences and about their extensive work together.

Of particular interest is the way in which the therapist manages Peter's two different "requests" to take something from the playroom. When he asserts that the car he has found is his and that he is going to take it home, she firmly says no, it isn't his, while acknowledging his wish and his disappointment. This is a brief return of old behavior which is responded to with a well-established intervention. However, Peter's reaction to the frustration shows his increasing capacity to tolerate limit-setting. In the second instance, Peter asks to "borrow" something for use in the developing relationship with his "friend," the bus driver. The therapist decides to take the risk of agreeing, after discussing the potential consequences with Peter. It is likely that she decides to do this because she wishes to support Peter's confidence in his ability to remember, to support his efforts to promote new relationships and to indicate her growing trust in Peter's abilities to behave responsibly. In addition, "borrowing" something from the therapy for use in the outside world is a metaphor-made-concrete for the entire course of psychotherapy. It is particularly appropriate and timely for work that is coming to a conclusion.

TERRY FRANK

Terry's mother brought him for treatment when he was ten. She could "no longer tolerate his infantile behavior" and her needing to tell him "over and over" what to do. Mr. Gibbons, the mother's long-term boyfriend, was distressed because Terry used "streams of dirty words" and seemed to do little else other than watch T.V. while masturbating openly. Repelled by this behavior, the stepfather spent as little time as possible with Terry.

In school, Terry often sat as if in a stupor, barely keeping up academically, despite everyone's impression that he was a very bright boy. He often stole other children's lunches, pencils, and other possessions, vigorously and angrily denying his culpability when caught.

Developmental History

Terry's mother married in her late teens and had a child within a year. Her husband drank heavily and was a poor provider. Although the marriage was constantly on the point of breaking up, the Franks remained together for some six years, during which time three more children were born. Terry and his twin sister were the youngest of the four. The twin was always considered the "good child." From his earliest months, Terry was considered difficult to manage, adding further burdens to an already troubled marriage. When the twins were three-and-one-half, their mother left her husband, taking the twins and leaving the two older children with their father. Within six months, she had a "nervous breakdown." Terry and his sister were returned to their father who, by then, was living with another woman. She was reportedly quite sadistic and locked Terry in the closet repeatedly for such infractions as sucking his thumb. Six months later, Terry and his sister returned to their mother, who had begun living with Mr. Gibbons. Within the next year, the two older children also joined Mrs. Frank. Since then, the family has had infrequent contact with Mr. Frank.

When Terry's therapist first met him, she observed that he was a tall, slender boy with large blue eyes and a handsome face capable, at times, of great expressiveness. However, more often he displayed enormous stubbornness and impassivity, was hard to engage and seemingly incapable of sustained play as he moved restlessly from one thing to another. In the treatment room, as at home, he was incredibly difficult to manage.

Course of Treatment

During the first year, the treatment was characterized by stormy, impulsive outbursts alternating with stubborn and angry silences. Initially, nothing was safe in the treatment room—neither toys, the therapist, nor Terry himself. At times, the sessions became so difficult that Terry's therapist resorted to inviting Terry's mother in to help him regain control. The therapist adopted this approach in keeping with Mrs. Gibbons' report that Terry would obey no one but his mother. At such times, Terry would quiet down immediately, but clearly these were his mother's controls at work. Troubled by the persistence of this pattern, the therapist sought consultation. Her consultant suggested a different strategy: When Terry begins to lose control make this plain quickly and firmly, and tell Terry that, while she believed he could manage his strong feelings, she would help him by closing the session if he seemed, temporarily, unable or unwilling to use his own "brakes." Terry began to demonstrate that he could, in fact, regain control if he was told by his therapist early enough when impulses were getting out of hand. A few sessions were terminated early, but gradually Terry demonstrated that he could regain control. This new strategy was based on the view that Terry would not learn self-regulation as long as the controls rested with his mother. It had an additional advantage as well: Each time the therapist called on the mother for help, she herself felt defeated, angry and helpless—much the same way Terry experienced his own outbursts; the new strategy helped alleviate the therapist's negative feelings. In part, his destructive behavior was a way of demonstrating and communicating such feelings by projecting them onto the therapist. This is an important issue as all patients do, in fact, frequently demonstrate what they are feeling themselves by evoking similar feelings in their therapists.

It was important for the therapy that the therapist not be rendered as helpless as her patient. Having a way of managing the treatment even when this occasionally shortened the hour provided the therapist with a sense of control, mastery and safety. Quickly, her own sureness mounted and conveyed itself to Terry, which accelerated the therapeutic safety. This further provided Terry with evidence that his therapist did not consider him an impossible monster.

The following hour occurred in the second year of the therapy, after Terry had made considerable progress. It followed an hour in which Terry asked to take some things home from the playroom. In particular, he wanted to take a large cardboard airstrip which he had made and played with for several sessions. The therapist responded by telling him that he could not take office things home, although she acknowledged that he wanted to take something nice from their sessions. Since it was at the end of the hour, she hoped Terry could help her understand better, next time, why taking some things home was so important to him.

Between these two hours, Terry's therapist reviewed her decision and recognized that Terry's own constructions were his and he could do with them what he chose, including taking them home—so long as these did not utilize basic playroom equipment. She remembered that Terry was a twin and that owning things is particularly complicated in a twinship. Terry's therapist reported the next hour as follows:

(As Terry enters the office, he goes to his private drawer and begins to rummage in it. I say that I have thought a lot about taking things home from the office. He picks up a ship he made in the previous hour and comments, "That's not my ship.")

Th: It is yours, but it might look different than you remembered it—you made a number of ships last week.

Terry: Oh, this is one of them?

(We are interrupted by a loud sound of banging—Terry bangs back and looks out of the office.)

Th: That intrusive noise spoiled your fun; it startled you and you answered back by making the same noise.

(I continue to talk about taking things home and make a distinction between the toys in the toy chest which are "community property" and things like his airstrip and his airplane, which are his.)

Terry: Fuck the other kids!!

Th: I understand that feeling. I know how hard it is for you to share, but *your* airstrip that you wanted to take home, I was wrong about that; you made it and used it here and you like it very much, it is 100 percent yours.

Terry: It's not yours?

Th: No, it's not mine. I can see where that could get confusing; you are free to take it home if you want, bring it back if you want, make another one if you want, lots of choices, Terry.

Terry: How did you figure it out?

Th: I thought about it.

Terry: Did you ask someone or read it in a book?

Th: No, I thought about it. I thought there is a difference between the planes that are part of community property, the starships that you build from the Legos that are community property and I save for you, and *your* airstrip. And when I understood the difference, I could say "no" to one part and "yes" to the other part.

Terry: Was it hard to say? (Smiling)

Th: Your smile tells me you are pleased. It took a while to think through. I'm not sure, though, what you meant by "hard to say?"

Terry: (Very frustrated) Nothing, forget it.

Th: I know it's hard for you when I don't understand right away. (He has begun building with the Legos.)

Th: I've got a hunch—maybe you wondered if it was hard to admit that I'd been wrong. It wasn't hard because I am much more interested in understanding with you than being right. Is it hard for you if you find out you are wrong?

Terry: (Nods—shows me how different parts of the starship fit on other parts.)

Th: One more part to my thinking—I want to find ways to help you take home the strong feelings, too—not just things.

Terry: What was that word? Intr? You know, the noise?

Th: Intrusive—do you know that word?

Terry: (Shakes head) No.

(I go for the dictionary as we have done before, and we discuss the word's meaning.)

Terry: Am I an intruder?

Th: No, you are welcome and invited.

Terry: Anytime?

Th: Anytime we make an appointment to meet.

Terry: You don't work on weekends?

Th: Sometimes you wish you could see me on the weekends?

Terry: This is a great traveler ship, the Christopher Columbus. Look, it's got 14 phasers and escape hatches; they are full of people who don't want to fight.

Th: What do they want to do?

Terry: They want to explore space. (He shows me how he has constructed the ship with special radar and removable fighter parts. Then he builds another equally elaborate starship and set of fighters: Darth Vadar's ship and the enemies. He has a great dialogue between the two sets of fighters in a very controlled way, using his fingers to take apart the little fighters as they are bombed. There are many repair missions and victories on both sides.) Am I making too much noise?

Th: No, but our time is about up for today.

Terry: Can I take the planes home?
Th: You know the answer, but we can save one.
Terry: (Rolls up his airstrip and carries it out of the room) See you!

Many important events and experiences are occurring in this session. Among them are:

1) What belongs to Terry and what does not—a vital issue in self-differentiation for this boy, not only because he is a twin, but because of his serious problems with all sorts of boundaries.
2) Difficulties in sharing—for similar reasons as those involved in his truly owning and respecting things, feelings and his own productions.
3) The ability to observe, reflect about and acknowledge when one is wrong which Terry worked on, in part, through modeling with his therapist. Terry's observing and reflecting capacities have, until now, been sharply limited by his difficulties with impulse control. Impulse and action have, until recently, been so wedded that no space remained for reflection, unless he withdrew into a stupor—hardly true reflection.
4) A growing ability to ask about what he does not know, as in the word "intrusive." To expose ignorance for this, heretofore, swaggering, whirling dervish, to avow curiosity and to permit his own learning are no small gains.
5) A growing capacity to tame and control contagious and easily triggered impulses. While he bangs back when he hears the noise outside the room a short time ago this would have triggered wild and uncontrollable behavior.
6) A demonstrable capacity for sustaining creative, complicated and controlled play. While this is self-regulated, he stops at one point to make a friendly check with his therapist by asking whether he is playing quietly enough.
7) An ability to explore space rather than to engage in a fighting game exclusively, occurring after he and his therapist have explored an important word together. This word leads him to test out his welcome and to assert his affection for his therapist.
8) And, at the end once again, testing what he may own and take, and a readiness to compromise with heretofore enormous greed, evolved out of unregulated need.

All these and many other significant themes are evident in the session. Moreover, the therapist's comment about owning and taking strong feelings with him heralds a series of important hours in which strong feelings are explored, uncovered and further managed. The culmination of those hours occurred several months later, at home, when Terry told his twin sister who was crying angrily, "You know, I think you should go and see my shrink—she needs to help you with all that angry blabbering."

At Christmas, Terry arrived with a gift for his therapist, paid for from his first paycheck as a newspaperboy. With it was a card inscribed, "to my friend." The present was a wall plaque that said, "Friendship is the best thing under the sun." As the therapist opened the gift and Terry watched her pleasure, he held his arms around himself and said, "I'm so happy."

There has been a concomitant improvement in Terry's life. School work and behavior have improved considerably. He can now enjoy activities with his stepfather, who formerly found him unmanageable and gave him a wide berth, and he has begun tentatively to make friends—an altogether new venture in his young life.

The following hour, some three months later, demonstrates that, in spite of the gains, many ups and downs still occur, especially in times of stress.

(Terry enters with a big smile that breaks out as soon as he sees me these days. A young woman has just left my office and has aroused Terry's interest.)

Terry: Who was she; why does she need therapy?

Th: I know you are curious, but who she is is confidential, like what happens in your sessions is private between you and me.

Terry: Who? Just tell me.

Th: Last week you were sad and mad when your sister wasn't private about your affairs. Maybe we could figure out something about that.

Terry: Shut up.

Th: I can wait until you're ready.

Terry: (He hides behind the drapery.) Can you see me?

Th: Sometimes you go behind the drape when there is a feeling you don't want to look at. (Hides deeper in the drape.)

Terry: My birthday is in two weeks and I'd like a really big Coke, the tall, thin one, 16 ounces, not the fat ones. I get my braces soon. First, they have to make them fit and then I can't eat candy, chewy stuff; I can't eat hard candy and no Cokes because it will rust, the braces aren't steel; I forget what they are made of. I can have orange. (He is very relaxed again.) (Suddenly, he threatens to spit on me.)

Th: I think you are telling me about your worry about the braces. I'd like to hear it, but not be spit on.

Terry: (spits on the floor)

Th: All this talk about braces and food rules makes you feel like spitting.

Terry: (goes to the toy cabinet and examines the door he damaged in anger last time) It's fixed; did you do it?

Th: Yes, I fixed the door.

Terry: Should I do it again?

Th: You were very angry last time and I don't know why yet. I think that breaking the door was your way of telling me you were angry. There might be other ways to tell me. Maybe we can figure out about your sister and her blabbing.

Terry: I have Legos at home, too, better than these. (shows me the size of the box at home, talks about vehicles he has built at home and in the office)

Th: You were planning to bring your train today.

Terry: How did you remember? I'll bring it next week.

Th: I try to remember what you say you want to do. I think to myself: Terry is excited about his train set and I'll look forward to seeing it. Terry wants me to see it.

Terry: Let's build something together. How did these get in here? Are you hiding them? Is your granny tall? Bet mine's taller than yours. Let's build a castle. (Terry builds and sings "Old McDonald" with the cumulative refrain.)

(Sometimes he stops to ask me what comes next but always remembers first—sings it with jazz intonations and hand-body clapping.)

Th: Your memory works better than mine on the song. Songs are easy for you. I wonder how come some things are hard for you to remember?

Terry: (While singing, he has built a big castle out of colored blocks. It is pretty sturdy, with a few precarious turrets and towers.) Now I'll bomb it. (He carefully bombs the castle, saying what will fall next.) This will topple it. Let's build it again.

(We hear the sound of a child screaming from another therapy room.)

Terry: Why is she screaming?

Th: I don't know, what do you think?

Terry: It's annoying (getting more agitated).

Th: Yes, it is annoying and it's spoiling your playing fun.

Terry: (makes louder and louder noises)

Th: You are answering her. (Terry's noise is covering my attempts to speak.)

Terry: Start, stop; start, stop.

(I get a piece of paper and begin writing. Terry comes over and watches me—as he quiets down. I wrote:

    1) A little girl screams.

    2) Terry wonders why.

    3) Terry answers back with noises.

    4) I wonder how come? I wonder if sometimes Terry's sister cries and screams and ruins his fun.)

Terry: (reads the paper, tears it) Let's play "hangman." (He goes for the dictionary to assist him. He has me guess "STUPID." I have him guess "FORTRESS." He has me guess "HISTRIONIC.")

Terry: I get up at six for my paper route. It's easy. I set the alarm.

(Terry reads the definition of histrionic aloud, gets excited, and announces that time is up, writes his name on the paper and the desk, slams the door, comes back and closes the door more quietly.)

In the hour prior to this, Terry had expressed considerable anger about his sister's "blabbing" that he was seeing a shrink. Her teasing had insulted him and assaulted his shaky self-esteem, leading to destructive behavior. These events carry over into the described hour. In addition, Terry has been struggling with concerns about his impending orthodonture and restrictions it will impose on what he may eat and drink. These concerns have been exaggerated and distorted, in keeping with his fears about body damage and integrity. These issues "frame" this session, which began with the additional stress of observing his therapist's other patient leaving, leading to his insistent questions about the other patient. The therapist attempts to deal with his curiosity by linking it to his concern about his sister's "blabbing" and simultaneously reassuring him about the confidentiality of their work. This does not relieve Terry's anxiety and his frustration remains evident. He regresses to old behavior, hiding behind the drapes. The therapist recalls that Terry often acted out his fears of looking and thinking about worries by hiding. This prompts a revelation about the stressful restrictions that are about to take place, which will interfere with his birthday wishes. He begins to relax, but only briefly, again giving evidence of the stressfulness of the orthodontic work, by threatening to spit at her. She interprets this behavior, which although it stops Terry from directing his aggression at the therapist, does not lead to his totally controlling his behavior.

He goes to the toy cabinet and discovers that the therapist has repaired the minor damage he inflicted last week. He threatens to break it again but is easily dissuaded. The therapist recalls that Terry had planned to bring his train and his pleasure about the therapist's keeping him in mind leads to a reinstitution of control, and he offers to build with the therapist. There is a period of sustained play and singing, which permits the therapist to work with Terry on what he recalls and what he forgets. While he bombs his own construction, it is done with careful control.

This sequence is disrupted by the sound of another child's screaming. He becomes more and more agitated, which the therapist cannot interrupt by verbal intervention. She resorts to a written account of the behavior, which enlists his interest and permits him to quiet down. Using the same mode as his therapist, he decides to engage in the word game "hangman," and the mutual play is resumed.

During this, Terry can report how he is more able to organize his activities at home. The hour ends with Terry's demonstrating still precarious controls as he slams the door, but returning to remedy the ending.

Over the next months, the therapist and Terry worked closely on the twinship, his growing capacity to control himself, his self-esteem and his sexual confusion. Terry made many additional gains during this period, which are manifested in his real world and in the therapy hours. His paper route is going well and school performance and behavior have improved remarkably. During this period, Terry's mother and Mr. Gibbons have married and are ecstatic about their changed boy. His obscenities and masturbatory behavior have disappeared. He has made a few friends, although these friendships are still tenuous.

In the therapy, Terry's destructiveness has receded markedly. Verbal interventions can usually calm him down, and Terry himself will often comment on how he "used to" behave. His play has been highly metaphoric and imaginative, involving an elaborated puppet fantasy which carries over from session to session. Earlier, the puppets did appear, but in fragmentary forms. Now the puppets are enduring characters, whose characteristics change and develop. In these recent weeks, Terry has been using the puppets to consolidate the gains of prior work and to herald a new stage in the treatment and his development.

The characters, all of whom are part-representations of Terry, are as follows: Rabbit is usually an intact artist who, on occasion, tricks people. Fox has traditionally been the crafty, smart but hungry character. Bear is basically a good soul but often, in his awkward bungling, destroys things unintentionally, sometimes steals when he has been victimized and most frequently represents Terry's most conscious grasp of self. Chicken, on the other hand, is voracious, eats everything in sight, often biting "cocks" capriciously and destructively.

The following hour illustrates the various ways in which Terry and his therapist work together in this new mode.

This hour follows one in which he and his therapist have worked on twosomes. Terry would draw something, ask his therapist to copy it and take both out to his mother to have her identify who had drawn what. His therapist utilized these drawings to make various interpretations about the twinship, self-differentiation, and boundaries.

Terry announces early in the session that he wants construction paper in order to make a backdrop for his puppet show. "Do you know about backdrops?" he asks, while he works diligently and carefully to tape four different pieces of paper together, each representing a separate home with separate details for each of his central characters: Fox, Rabbit, Bear and Chicken. Each house has some perspective drawing in it and Terry explains the details and the idea of perspective itself.

The home for Fox is very elaborately constructed, with a door that opens. This represents Terry's recent difficulties in staying out of the playroom closet and some work the therapist has done with him about separating out what Terry may safely explore and what is off limits as private property that belongs to others.

Now the puppet show is ready and takes the shape of a musical performance.

Rabbit begins by singing "Love Potion No. 9" and inquiring whether the therapist is knowledgeable about these songs from his mother's old records. Bear then sings, "Where Have All the Flowers Gone?" When the therapist applauds, Bear comments: "Thank you, friends!"

Fox is the next performer and he begins with several jokes. He is no longer crafty—and the therapist comments that Fox is developing a true sense of humor. Terry asks, "What shall I have Fox sing? He will be the finale." (He has glanced at the clock and sees time is growing short.)

The therapist comments: "Let him sing his favorite song." "Oh, all right. Let me think what is my favorite song," says Terry, as he takes on the personality of Fox. (Fox has never before taken any time to think things through, being heavily impulse laden in his crafty style.) Terry decides he will sing, "The Candy Man Can" and sings a variety of refrains, including: "getting childhood wishes—you can even eat the dishes—once the Candy Man's been there."

The time is very short now, and Terry asks to be permitted one more song. Chicken now enters and sings with great enthusiasm and fervor "Joy to the World."

The time is up, and Terry quickly but deftly puts away his puppet background and asks that it be saved in his private place. The therapist comments that the puppet show was wonderful—she enjoyed it very much.

This hour clearly documents Terry's ability to engage in constructive, sustained and imaginative play. He is able to plan and prepare what he needs for his own production. It is elaborate, detailed and differentiated. The negative attributes of each of Terry's characters have virtually disappeared, suggesting that useful repressions are taking place, appropriate to the latency period. While it might appear that such puppet play is more typical for a younger child, Terry's use of the puppets is at one and the same time a regression and a highly advanced progression. He is making up developmental work that one normally would see in a younger child. But Terry's severe ego deficits precluded organized fantasy play when he was at an age that it would normatively occur. At that time, Terry's primitiveness prevented latency development.

Although Terry uses a younger child's "equipment," he employs it in a developmentally advanced way. It is as though Terry is an adult artist-producer. His artistic work helps him with other important internal processes. For example, Terry's newly developed artistic skill in creating perspective matches his evolving emotional and cognitive capacity to distinguish boundaries between self and others, inside and outside, thoughts and actions, and between wishes and immediate gratification.

In concert with Terry's changed behavior, the therapeutic strategy has changed drastically. The therapist no longer need intervene as actively. She is now the audience who can appreciate and validate Terry's achievements. No longer the limiter, as Terry can manage this himself, the therapist can applaud and help Terry consolidate the various partial representations of himself into a more integrated Terry, who will not be at war with himself.

It is clear that Terry is in the final phase of his treatment.

In spite of Terry's seemingly intense pathology, this boy was able to make relatively rapid progress in treatment. Two factors may have been much in his favor: His innate endowment and significant ego resources were likely present, though masked by his difficulties. These were accessible and capable of being freed through the treatment, and the cooperative help of Terry's mother and Mr. Gibbons, whose attitudes and behaviors changed in response to Terry's progress. It is perhaps self-evident that the best diagnosis can be made at the end of a treatment.

REFERENCES

1. Anthony, E. J., and McGinnes, M., Counseling very disturbed parents. In E. L. Arnold (Ed.), *Helping parents help their children.* New York: Brunner/Mazel, 1978.
2. Bettleheim, B., *The empty fortress.* Chicago, IL: University of Chicago Press, 1967.
3. Chess, S., and Thomas, A., Part III, Heredity-environment interaction, *Annual progress in child psychiatry and child development.* New York: Brunner/Mazel, 1982, pp. 197-245.
4. Chess, S., and Hassibi, M., *Principles and practice of child psychiatry.* New York: Plenum Press, 1978, pp. 261-281.
5. Chethik, M., and Spindler, E., Techniques of treatment and management with the borderline child. In M. Mayer and A. C. C. Blum (Eds.), *Healing through living.* Springfield, IL: Charles C. Thomas, 1971, 176-189.
6. Fringling-Schreuder, E. C. M., Borderline states in children. *Psychoanalytic study of the child,* 1970, Vol. 24: 307-327.
7. Gratton, L., Object concept and object relations in childhood psychosis. *Canadian Psychiatric Assn. Journal,* 1971, Vol. 21: 229-237.
8. Kanner, L., *Child psychiatry.* Springfield, IL: Charles C. Thomas, 1972.
9. Mengot, S. W., "The impact of cumulative trauma in infancy: Some treatment techniques." *Clinical Social Work Journal,* 1982, Vol. 10(4): 265-274.
10. Ometz, C. M., and Ritvo, E. R., Syndrome of autism: A clinical review. *American J. of Psychiatry,* 1976, Vol. 133: 609-662.
11. Palumbo, J., Critical review of the concept of the borderline child. *Clinical Social Work Journal,* 1982, Vol. 10(4): 246-264.
12. Pire, F., On the concept of 'borderline' in children. *Psychoanalytic Study of the Child,* 1982, Vol. 29: 341-365.
13. Rutter, M., Childhood schizophrenia reconsidered. *J. of Autism and Child Schizophrenia,* 1972, Vol. 2: 315-337.

CHAPTER 6

Selectively Disturbed Children

Depression, anxiety, and aggression are not well-differentiated and separate entities within the spectrum of mental anguish; rather there is always a mixture of these emotions in which only the relative proportion may change. An anxious child is depressed by his awareness of his inability to cope with his environment and angered by his plight. An aggressive adolescent fears the ever-present possibility of retribution by society and his victims and is helpless in controlling his destiny. Fire setting, for example, is an aggressive and destructive act, but it may be the last desperate attempt of a deprived, abused child to bring attention to himself even though he risks being destroyed in the process (5, p. 120).

Efforts to distinguish clear, distinctive diagnostic categories among disturbed children have always plagued clinicians. Retrospective and reconstructive work with adults provided the first set of organized psychodynamic diagnostic perspectives. From this work a variety of theoretical systems evolved which included such familiar concepts as psychic structure, intra-psychic conflict and defensive processes, including symptom formation. Developmental notions were part of these early efforts and are clearly involved in such ideas as fixation, regression and progression. One early developmental framework centered around the successful progression through the Oedipal phase. This led to two major diagnostic categories which placed disturbed children who had achieved this developmental level into a neurotic category and children who had not into a psychotic category, later modified to include psychotic and borderline children.*

Subsequent diagnostic thinking modified, enriched and complicated these early systems. These derived from the direct treatment of children and from observations of their behavior. Defenses came to be understood as ubiquitous, serving not only to deflect conflict or deal with traumata but also as ways of coping, adapting and organizing the personality. The concept of subsequent developmental stages and the elaboration of developmental lines as well as the influence of culture, cognition and morality were additional refinements. The central importance of human relationships in development, which acknowledges the reciprocity between infant and caretaker and between temperament and environment, has been among the most recent contributions and complications to diagnostic thinking.

The quest for diagnostic precision persists and will, undoubtedly, continue to be refined. However, more and more contemporary clinicians recognize a continuum of disturbances rather than sharp demarcations of diagnostic categories. In this view, labels tend to be forfeited in favor of a more comprehensive understanding.

Although sharp demarcations of diagnosis have limited utility for the clinician, the children presented in this chapter *are* distinguishable from those in the prior chapter. Sherry, Peter, and Terry were seen to have disturbances which pervade almost all areas of important life functions. By contrast, Cornell, Ellen, and Jennifer have "selective" disturbances. Though these vary in intensity, quality and pervasiveness, all three of these children have areas of functioning which are intact and free from the interferences of their difficulties.

This is not to suggest that these children are not suffering. All are unhappy and fearful, and prevented from developing fully. Without

---

*Borderline here refers to the older concept of some intermediate territory between psychotic and neurotic rather than the more modern and highly elaborated ideas about borderline and narcissistic disorders.

help they are at risk of living impoverished and constricted lives, deprived of opportunities to use their potential, to have fulfilling and enduring relationships with others, and to experience themselves and their achievements as worthwhile and satisfying.

Each child is seen at a different stage in the treatment process, permitting a glimpse of beginning work (Cornell), the middle phase of psychotherapy (Ellen) and the completion of a therapy (Jennifer).

CORNELL WILSON

The workings of a fluent and well-developed ego are demonstrated by ten-year-old Cornell whose mother immediately called the local psychiatric center when Cornell's teacher reported that the boy had threatened to kill himself. Cornell's teachers consider him an appealing and competent student. He is a well-behaved but not overly compliant child, whose behavior has seemed to change in the past nine months. In these months Cornell has had two or three outbursts of crying, and has, at times, arrived at school atypically unkempt.

Developmental History

Cornell is the younger of two boys whose parents were divorced before he was born. The father, now located in another state, visits his sons about once a year. Mrs. Wilson is a 30-year-old woman who has worked on and off as a bank teller, intermittently attending college. She has been the main caretaker of her two sons though her own mother, who lives close by, has also been of help in raising the boys. When seen for the initial evaluation, Mrs. Wilson gave information coherently and thoughtfully. She is an attractive woman who expressed an appropriate amount of concern for Cornell, also noting that his behavior had changed in the past months. Only later in the hour could she connect this with the departure of a boyfriend who had come to live with the family when Cornell was four-and-a-half. They had parted amicably and Mrs. Wilson reflected that Cornell might be missing Richard, the boyfriend, since Cornell was clearly his favorite. Mrs. Wilson noted that Cornell now follows her around more closely, occasionally comes into her bed at night and more recently has expressed some deep concern over his small size. Her other son is tall, which may exaggerate Cornell's worries about his shortness, though doctors have assured Mrs. Wilson that, while Cornell is in the tenth percentile of the normal growth curve, he is in good health generally.

Mrs. Wilson can provide a clear picture of each of her sons, noting with pride that they are good boys, each with his own assets. She believes that she has given them both a good start, and is eager now to get on with improving her own life, believing the boys need her less now. She remained with Richard for some five years because he was good to the boys and helped to create a sense of family for all of them, but she knew for a long time that she would like to meet someone who would be more stimulating and serve as a fuller companion for herself. Mrs. Wilson planned to tell Cornell that she was bringing him to see someone who knew about kids and could be of help to them.

Course of Treatment

The following are the first three hours with Cornell, described by his therapist.

First session

I met Cornell and his mother in the waiting room. He was very neatly dressed and quite self-possessed. Throughout this first meeting he was extremely well-mannered and seemed like a little adult. He agreed readily that it would be OK if his mother remained in the waiting room while we went to my office. He sat down with his hands folded in his lap as though waiting for me to begin. After a moment, I asked what his mom had told him about coming here. He replied that she had said that I knew about kids. When I asked whether he had any ideas of his own about coming to see me, he said simply, "No." When I wondered whether this was how he imagined this place would be, he said that he hadn't imagined anything. He began to look around the room cautiously, and in a slightly hesitant but adult way he acknowledged that he had had some ideas about coming here. He said he thought it was about his growing and that he'd been to other doctors about this. When I asked further about it he assured me that he was not worried because he knew that he would grow. Suddenly he asked, "What's that noise?" I said I didn't know and he said that it sounded like his hamster. With some help from me he told me that he had gotten a hamster for Christmas and had named it "E.T.-Richard." He added that before the hamster, he had a dog, a cat, and fish but they all died. "Were you sad?", I asked. "No, except when it got to the last few fish."

Again he sat, listening, for a moment and asked about other noises he heard. I commented that he had good ears and that he heard a lot of things. He said it sounded like a bus outside. I asked if he would like to get to know this place and invited him to look around and to ask any questions he might have. He said he wanted to go back to the waiting room to get a magazine he'd seen there. I said that his mom was in the waiting room and wondered if he was worried that she was still there. "No." I noted that it was kind of different to be here, to which he agreed by an affirmative nod. He then asked, "Why *am* I here?" Once again, I wondered what his mother had told him and he gave the same response—that I knew about kids. I told him that was so and that I was interested in kids' worries and that his mother had some worries about him. I let him know that we could talk or play with the many toys in the cabinet. He noticed some of my professional books and asked what those were. I said that they were about all different kinds of things.

Once again, I invited him to look around and see if any of the toys might interest him. He went to the toys and pulled out a man doll whom he said he had seen on *Sesame Street*. "Who is he?", Cornell asked. I replied that he could be whoever Cornell wanted him to be. He put the doll away, returned to his chair and asked, "Who are you?" I said that I thought he had lots of questions and that it was good to be curious. I told him that I had questions, too, so that we could get to know each other, and that he must be wondering what kind of a person I really was. He asked how I knew what he was thinking but did not wait for an answer. Instead, he went back to the toys and examined the microscope and the stethoscope, which he tried on. He said he couldn't hear his own heart. He took the man doll again, found a baby doll and, linking their arms, announced that the father was picking the baby up at nursery school. He set them aside quickly and found the kaleidoscope and, peering through it, said, "It makes aliens. I wish it would make a star." Then he found some cars and said that they were like some he had at home. Finding the silly putty he asked, "Who put gum in this?" I asked if it smelled like gum to him. He decided that he'd rather not touch it.

When he found the Tinker Toys, he told me that he hadn't played with these since he was a kid but that he was going to build a diesel truck. He measured each piece for size and kept saying that various pieces were too small. When I noted that it was hard, but important, to find the right sizes, he decided instead that he would make a boat. "I'll just make it up as I go along," he said. He did not reply when I asked if he liked to do things that way. Instead he seemed very preoccupied with the boat building, talking to himself about finding the right-sized pieces. For the first time, he seemed to be enjoying himself. I told him that we had to stop for today, explaining that he could continue his project next time. I said he could draw a picture of it or memorize it as far as he had gone so he could remember it next week. No response. Instead, he pulled the construction apart and, carefully, put everything away in the cabinet. When we walked out to the waiting room, we found his mother asleep.

Second session

Cornell came with me readily and once again sat down in the same chair. This time he looked around more easily and noticed a plant on the bookshelf. He told me that his grandmother had plants and they were big like mine. He wondered if I watered them regularly. I nodded and asked if he liked plants. He said, "Yes, I have seven plants I'm growing from beans. It's an experiment for school. They'll die if I don't take care of them." He told me that his hamster had run away and they looked all over the house before they finally found it. In the course of this he described the layout of the rooms in the house. Once again, he looked around the office and I said that looking around was a good way to get to know a place. He asked again about a noise outside. I said I didn't know what the noise was, just like I didn't know about the noise the last time. I noted again that he had very good hearing. He said, "Why am I here?" I told him that his mother had some worries about his saying, at school, that he wanted to kill himself. She thought that, maybe, he'd like to talk to someone about this. Cornell shook his head "no" and again asked about the books on the shelf. I said that mostly they were about people.

He sat quietly for a bit, and I said that it seemed to me that he wasn't sure what to do here and was waiting for me to tell him. He said, "Yup, how did you know that?" I told him that this was a place where he could play and talk and that he could choose what to do. He went to the cabinet and got the Tinker Toys. He began to put some of them together but soon put them away in favor of two dolls. He told me they were twin sisters; "They hug each other because they're glad to see each other." Then a boy doll goes for a walk with the sisters. Soon, one of the sisters' husband comes along and hugs his wife, saying, "I'm glad to see you." Cornell put the dolls away and began a more thorough search through all the toys. I said he was getting to know what's in the cabinet and he examined many items, putting each back neatly.

He hesitated a moment with the checkers but did not ask to play. He found a box of toy soldiers and animals and placed one soldier on top of the cabinet saying, "He's in a war and just got shot." As the soldier fell from the cabinet, a kangaroo puppet came and caught him. Cornell explained that the kangaroo saved the soldier from falling into a fire.

This ushered in a game of soldiers and animals fighting against one another. Cornell said that all the people who are fighting are "Santa's helpers" but they all want to be Santa. At one point a lion went crying home to his mother who was a polar bear. She sent him to his room and soon he felt better. At the end of the war, Santa made an agreement that the soldiers and animals must stop fighting. The polar bear joined Santa on top of the cabinet and, following the fighting, they all had a feast. Cornell put all the toys away, and I told him that in a few minutes we'd have to stop for today. He took some animal finger puppets and told me that all the animals he'd gotten were gifts from Richard. At the end of the hour he left and then immediately re-opened the door and asked if he should turn the sign around so that "office in use" would not be visible. I said that since our time was up, the office was not in use and that he could turn it around.

Third session

Cornell, once again, headed for the same chair. He asked what people do in the other offices: "Are they psychiatrists?" I asked if he was wondering if they did the same kinds of things that we did. He nodded. I asked what he thought psychiatrists did. He didn't know but he'd seen them on TV and they listened to people and talked to them. "Then the people get sick and the psychiatrist just sits with them." I said, "So sick people go to see psychiatrists?" "No. Are you a psychiatrist?" "I'm someone who is interested in helping kids with their worries." Cornell looked again at my books and I said that I noticed that he was very interested in the books. Would he like to take a look at them? He asked me what they were about and I told him that they were about people, how to understand them and how people help themselves. He said, "I guess I will take a look." He took down Freud's *Lectures on Psychoanalysis* and thumbed through it. I asked if there was something in particular that I could help him understand in the book. He said, "Have you read it?" "Yes." He read a sentence out loud and then put the book away. Then he found a book on child psychiatry and said, "I didn't see this one before." He looked through the table of contents and again I offered to help him understand anything in it that inter-

ested him. He seemed pleased when he found some drawings and car-
toons in the book but said nothing. He found the telephone switchbox
and the wire running along the baseboard and asked where it went.
He said, "I guess it goes to the waiting room." I said that I had noticed
that his mother wasn't in the waiting room when he began today. He
said, "I think she's going to meet me here later."

He noticed the ashtray and asked, "Do you see grownups?" I said
that sometimes I did and he asked me how late I stayed here. I asked
him what he would consider late and he replied, "Eight o'clock." I said
that he still had a lot of questions about this place and how things
work here. He responded, "You have a clock and I have one just like
it, and I have an ashtray, too. I have teddy bears, not exactly like
yours, but sort of." I said maybe asking questions about this place
helped him feel less strange. He told me he has five teddy bears all
named "Teddy." He liked to play with them. "Sometimes I scare my
hamster with them when I hold them up to the hamster. I got my
favorite teddy bear five years ago when I was in the hospital but I don't
remember what for. My mother gave him to me. He's the oldest. My
hamster doesn't like him. I'm careful not to put my hand in the hamster's cage because sometimes he bites my finger. He might have a
disease like rabies and might die." I commented that he's worried that
he might lose the hamster like his other pets that died. He agreed and
reminded me that he had a cat, a dog and a goldfish that all died. I
said it was sad to lose important pets and people, and this time he
agreed. I added, "You've lost a lot of things you cared about. That's a
very sad feeling." Again he silently agreed.

He began to play with many of the puppets and I greeted each one.
He emphasized how the cat puppet cleaned itself and he pretended to
have it lick milk from my ashtray. When he found two frog puppets
he told me a story about them. They were twins who fought over a
pizza. While they fought, their baby brother ate the pizza. When I
asked about this he told me that the twins should have reached an
agreement. Next came a skunk puppet who sprayed the beaver. He
told me that the skunk's secret weapon is the spray and then moved
the skunk up to his ear. Cornell said that the skunk was telling him
a secret that Cornell was not supposed to tell me. Then he put the
skunk to my ear and had the skunk whisper something to me but in
"skunk language" so I couldn't understand it. I said that I understood
that the skunk had a secret and wasn't sure if he wanted me to know
it. Maybe someday he could tell me the secret in "human" language.
Our time was up and Cornell turned the office sign around again as

we left. His mother was still not in the waiting room. Without apparent anxiety Cornell informed me that his mother had said that, if she wasn't there, he should go home by himself, that it was nearby and he knew the way.

Discussion

In spite of the fact that Cornell is being evaluated because of a worrisome statement of his distress (a threat to kill himself) and some deterioration of his care of his own person, there is considerable evidence that he is a neurotic child.* His difficulties are of recent onset and seem clearly related to the loss of an important figure. Cornell continues to be able to function well at school and in his social network. His many areas of competence have not deteriorated to any significant degree. His development, other than his physical growth, has been slightly precocious. He has an obviously good relationship with his mother who has been an able, consistent, and loving parent who can differentiate clearly between her two sons and take pride in each boy's assets.

Cornell's behavior in the first three sessions is further confirmation that he is an intact and well-functioning child. He can separate readily from his mother and despite some evident separation concerns, he can remain with the therapist without needing to act on the wish to check on his mother's presence in the waiting room. By the third session, he can manage coming to the hour and going home on his own. He develops a good working relationship with the therapist, but at his own pace. He regulates what and how much he will tell and generally shows an appropriate capacity to develop a relationship with a new person.

A review of these three hours reveals the unfolding of a variety of themes, conflicts, and coping mechanisms:

1) From a stolid, rather constrained beginning his play and behaviors become more spontaneous, imaginative and revealing.
2) He is alert and concerned about possible dangers (the noises—whose precise meanings and significance are unclear). However, this self-protective alertness does not interfere with his ability to at-

---

*Although a suicidal threat is always to be taken seriously, it should be viewed in the context of its persistence, its precipitants, its intensity and the presence and/or history of self-destructive behaviors. In any event suicidal thoughts or impulses are not necessarily correlated with a type of psychopathology or the degree of internal disorganization.

tend to what is going on in the room, with his curiosity about the place or with his ability to tell his story.

3) Despite his caution the themes and conflicts emerge quickly and easily. He conveys his concern about size and growth directly, in the Tinker Toy play and again in the discussion of what growing plants need. Issues of loss are clearly portrayed in his stories about his pets who are connected to Richard. Aggressive themes appear in several sequences which are, however, modulated and do not end in mayhem. They include the important notion that peace agreements are always preferable to warfare. The fighting is about who will replace the leader (Santa) and who will get the goodies (pizza). These stories suggest some conflicts about aggression as well as efforts to cope with Oedipal and dependency strivings.

4) He uses many materials, some age-appropriate, some surprisingly more typical of younger children (dolls and puppets) and some precocious (Freud's *Lectures on Psychoanalysis*).

5) He is curious and persistent in his efforts to find out why he is there, who the therapist is and what goes on in this place. Some greater degree of comfort about and awareness of the "culture" of therapy is evidenced by his request to turn over the "office in use" sign.

6) He can acknowledge affects, particularly sadness, after some initial denial.

7) The "skunk language" reveals that there are secrets to come when Cornell feels more comfortable and trusting.

Methodologically the three hours are handled generally well. The therapist permits Cornell to tell his story in his own way and in his own time. He defines himself as a person who is interested in kids and their worries, and he offers to help Cornell understand anything he has questions about. He makes several appropriate efforts to link content and affect (particularly sadness) and on the second or third try this is effective. He promotes the idea that they can be curious together and learn together.

While these three hours are technically competent, there are a few areas which could be polished a bit. The therapist pushes Cornell to play with toys more than is necessary, particularly since Cornell seems ready and able to talk. Whether this gentle pressure to play is a factor in some of the play appearing surprisingly immature cannot be determined with certainty, but also cannot be ruled out. Secondly, the therapist is more cautious than he needs to be in telling Cornell clearly and directly what he knows about the presenting problems. This sort of excessive caution tends to mystify the therapeutic process for children who usually know that their parents and the therapist have talked about the problems. Finally, the therapist tends to use certain standard and frequently useful technical strategies in places where they may not belong. The best example of this gratuitous error is his effort to "help" Cornell remember his Tinker Toy construction by drawing a picture of it or memorizing it when there is no evidence that Cornell is either interested in doing so or concerned about it.

ELLEN HODGES

Ellen Hodges, an eight-and-a-half-year-old child, is brought for treatment because she's doing poorly at school, despite her very obvious intelligence. Her teachers and her mother describe her as lethargic and given to much daydreaming. She believes that no one likes her and, in fact, has few friends. When scolded, she withdraws petulantly. She seems uninterested in things, activities or people. Her mother reports that Ellen either clings to her excessively or "there is a wall between" them.

Ellen's current family consists of her mother, a sister five years older, and Ms. Hodges' boyfriend. Ellen's father died suddenly of a heart attack when she was five. Ellen was, reportedly, her father's favorite. The impact of his unexpected death was compounded by his separation from the rest of the family who were, at the time, on vacation and awaiting his arrival.

Ms. Hodges dates the onset of Ellen's clinging and unhappy behavior to the time of the father's death, adding that she, herself, was severely depressed for several years thereafter. She comments that only in the past year-and-a-half has she begun to pull herself together, and expresses some considerable guilt for being relatively unavailable to her daughters during her intense grief. She remains perplexed, however, that Ellen seems to be suffering so much more keenly than her older sister. Prior to her father's death, Ellen's development progressed normally, uneventfully, and somewhat precociously.

Once-a-week treatment sessions were arranged for Ellen and bimonthly meetings with Ms. Hodges, who quickly learned to inform the therapist by phone of important events which occurred between their meetings.

After the first few sessions, characterized by Ellen's compliance, caution and superficial cordiality, the early therapy hours were filled with petulance, aggressive puppet play with themes of "eating-up," biting and stinging, and greedy wishes for playroom supplies which were conveyed covertly. Ellen's curiosity was intense but directed entirely outward in the form of continual questions about her therapist: What does he do? Who else does he see? Who made that drawing and which does he like best? When he suggested that Ellen was curious about him, she vigorously denied it. Another prominent theme was Ellen's complaints that whatever her mother gave her wasn't good enough. The food her mother prepared was cold, the clothes her mother picked for her were "gross," in contrast to the things her older sister got which were far better.

Notable by its absence was any direct mention of her father or her mother's boyfriend. When the therapist tried to talk about either, she ignored him or proclaimed, "I don't want to think about that."

Drawings and crafts which Ellen produced were immediately denigrated. Again and again she hinted that there were many dangerous secrets which neither she nor the therapist might know about.

As the alliance with her therapist became more sturdy and stable, her play became more imaginative, revealing a rich fantasy life which had been kept carefully concealed. She reported a dream of a big cave in which many things were hidden. Ellen and the therapist were able to make use of this dream to develop a descriptive metaphor about her imagination. With a mixture of interest and anxiety, Ellen gradually permitted an exploration of what was hidden in the cave of her imagination. There she stored questions which were too dangerous to ask about. "They are stupid. You'll think they're stupid." Stored there, as well, were her many wishes which were either "too personal" or "not nice to ask . . . it's like begging." Still more frightening were her many worries. "The cave is very dark and maybe a monster lives there."

This early work reveals major neurotic conflicts about knowing and not knowing; about secret, greedy feelings; about intense jealousy and envy of others. Her defensive efforts to cope have led to constriction and an inability to take pleasure in things and achievements, as well as her failure to learn and her withdrawal from closeness with family and friends. The history suggests that these conflictual difficulties may well have been organized around the trauma of her father's death and her mother's subsequent depression. It is important to note that these events occurred at the time she entered school—a normative crisis for many children.

Typical of the beginning of many therapies, the early interventions were aimed at providing an ever-increasingly safe relationship. Repeatedly, the therapist expressed his interest in her wishes, efforts, productions and concerns. Again and again, he would observe Ellen's mood and wonder aloud about her feelings and thoughts. When Ellen retreated from these observations and speculations, he would not push further, announcing instead that he could wait for Ellen to tell him whatever she wanted to, whenever she was ready. As more of her greediness emerged, the therapist acknowledged the acceptability of wishes and wants in both verbal and non-verbal ways. For example, when Ellen conveyed her wish for more paper, he offered to let her have a pad for herself. Ellen's curiosity was accepted, but neither overly solicited nor invariably gratified. But the wish to know and the value of knowing were steadfastly supported.

In fact, many of the early techniques of alliance building are accomplished by what is not done as much as by what is. Ellen's petulance and her many complaints were simply accepted with calm and interested silence. The therapist's intent was to repeatedly demonstrate that he wished to understand and could tolerate qualities other than superficial niceness. His interest in her did not waiver, whether she was nice or petulant. Such behavior allowed Ellen to feel increasingly safe about the expression of all sides of herself, while also presenting a model for her of how to be curious without being intrusive or distant. The "accuracy" of this therapeutic stance was validated by Ellen's fuller attachment to her therapist and her gradual disclosure of fantasies about yearnings, and worrisome dreams in which she often faced dangers alone.

In the twentieth week of the therapy, her therapist announced that he would shortly be going on vacation for three weeks. Ellen became more resistant, her play became less imaginative and more solitary, and angry feelings emerged. Since she was sure that he would not tell her where or with whom he was going she wouldn't ask any questions. When he wondered about this, Ellen replied that she didn't want to know and "anyway, I'd scream if you wouldn't tell me." Several pre-vacation hours were spent on the therapist's efforts to interpret Ellen's worry that he would not return and her worry that he would be going with someone whom Ellen thought was more special than she. He could appreciate her worries and her anger about his leaving. Ellen appeared to hear this, but made little response to these remarks.

In the first session following his vacation, Ellen says that she couldn't remember that the therapist had a beard. As she announces this, she begins to draw two balloons with hearts in each. The therapist comments that the two of them are once again meeting together and that he is glad to see her. Ellen can now acknowledge that she was not sure that he would come back. The therapist responds that that may have been a hard idea and hard ideas could crowd out the picture that she had of him in her mind. He continues that "forgetting" is sometimes a protection against worried or hurt feelings but it "is a sad protection." Ellen asks, "Why is that?" He assures her that it is good to want to know how things work, and he's glad to tell her. "It's a sad protection because the worried feelings are still there but the protection makes people not know. Knowing is good."

Ellen continues to draw bigger and bigger hearts. Shielding one of her drawings from his view, she writes, "I like you." She leaves it folded on his desk as she departs, taking all the other drawings with her.

The following hour, reported directly by the therapist, occurs four sessions later:

I went to the waiting room and nodded to Ellen, who was seated alone. She had evidently just finished taking a sip from a plastic bottle. She glanced sideways at me with a sly, pleased smile, as if she had happily expected me to catch her in the act. She followed me into the office and took the seat at my desk, setting the plastic bottle down at her elbow. She had never brought food into the office before. She asked if we could cut out snowflakes. We had been doing this for about a month. She collected paper and scissors, began to fold and cut a piece of paper into a snowflake, and then rather formally took a break from the work to have a sip from the bottle. She smiled again at me, and went back to her snowflake. Soon, she sipped again and gave me the same sideways glance to see if I was looking, accompanied by the same smile.

"Look at that smile," I exclaimed.

She giggled, set the bottle down, and went back to her work on the snowflake, unsuccessfully trying to suppress her smile.

"That is really some smile. You must get a big, nice feeling from that punch," I said.

She told me her mother buys two packs of this punch each week. When it's gone, she goes out and buys more. She had put the punch in her lunch that she made today. In response to my interest in this, she detailed what else she had put into her lunch: an apple, a tuna fish sandwich, potato chips, and punch.

"Does the same thing happen when you eat the tuna fish sandwich or the potato chips or the apple as when you drink the punch; I mean do you eat them and get this nice, warm, full feeling and the smile?"

She explained that she only got this feeling from the punch. I was interested in knowing all about this feeling, but she said she couldn't put it into words.

"Besides," she said, "it's embarrassing." Then, with a tone of dismissal, she said she really didn't know anything about it.

"Oh, you know lots of things that you pretend you don't know. I bet you're just saying you don't know so you can keep this big, nice feeling a secret."*

"Mmmmm," she acknowledged. Then she asked, "How big were you when you were my age?"

I didn't answer.

"Did you have this feeling about anything when you were my age?"

"I'm sure I did," I said. "That looks like a terrific, secret punch feeling."

All the while we talked, she was cutting snowflakes. Occasionally, through this discussion and the remainder of the hour, she would interrupt to deflect my curiosity by handing me the scissors or a piece of paper or a finished snowflake, and asking, "Do you want this one?" or "Do you think this is OK?" I accepted her snowflake, but added that I thought she probably wanted to know if her secret punch feeling was also OK. She insisted she was only asking about the snowflakes. I said, "Well, maybe you were embarrassed about the secret punch feeling and wanted to change the subject."

She asked if I had any brothers or sisters. I asked what her imagination told her about that. She said I had one older brother and one younger sister. She asked if I thought about growing up a lot when I was her age, and did I want to grow up.

"I thought a lot about it. How about you?"

"Sometimes I want to grow up just like that, right away. I wonder what I'll look like when I grow up."

She then asked how tall I was when I was nine.

"About your size," I said. I asked what she imagined she would look like when she grew up, but she didn't answer.

She stopped cutting to take another sip of the punch. I watched and

---

*This intervention has been made many times before—sometimes yielding productive material, other times not. Despite the fact that it is not invariably successful, it can, with many variations, be used repeatedly, since it is so central to Ellen's conflicts and has been validated by many observations in the clinical encounters. Beginning therapists occasionally fail to persist in intervening in a conflict.

waited. She smiled and giggled. I commented, "There it is again. That's a powerful secret punch feeling."

"Just one sip gives me the feeling," she said a bit teasingly; "I bet if I drank the whole bottle at once I would have the feeling for the rest of my life."

"I'll bet that sounds wonderful to you," I said.

"Do you think grown-ups ever get this feeling?" she said.

"Well," I considered, "let me see. It's an exciting, fun, warm, full feeling. Right?"

"Right."

"It sounds like being in love."

"Noooo," she giggled.

"Yes, I think so. I'm almost sure of it."

"Maybe," she conceded.

Ellen continued to cut snowflakes. I was still very interested in this feeling, and thought about it out loud.

"That certainly must give a girl a special happy feeling about herself. Almost," I ventured, "like when a girl gets something special from someone she likes, like when you got a whole tablet of paper from me."

Ellen was listening carefully, began to smile, and turned away toward the desk, so that I couldn't see. "Maybe," she said.

At one point in moving around, she knocked over the bottle, and spilled some punch on the chair.

"Oh, no! I spilled some of my good feelings," she said.

We blotted it up with Kleenex, and I asked her if she wanted to save these. "No," she giggled. As we were blotting it up, she said softly that she had worried I would be angry with her.

She went back to cutting, and I was silent for a while. Then I told her that I had been thinking about her idea that if she drank this whole bottle of punch all at once she would have that good, warm, secret punch feeling for the rest of her life. I said, "Some girls worry that they will get that secret punch feeling that's so good, and then it will just melt away like a snowflake."

She said nothing in response, but turned to look at me. She put down the scissors and reached out and touched my beard. "It feels good."

She suddenly asked me a whole series of questions: "Do you shave?" "Where do you shave?" "Did you think you would have this beard when you were a kid?" "Did you want to have this beard when you were a kid?"

I was reminded of her saying that I looked different when I came into the waiting room right after my vacation because she hadn't remembered my having a beard. I asked her if she knew anyone else with a beard.

She looked down at her snowflake and said, "Yes. My father." She was very still for a minute and then said, "Well, he didn't really have a beard; he had a moustache. He had an orange moustache."

I wondered what else she remembered about her father.

She didn't answer, but asked if I ever got food in my moustache and how, when it happened, did I get it out? She picked up her bottle and, ceremoniously, took the last sip of punch.

"Wait!" she said, very excited. She went to the drinking fountain with the bottle, filled it partially with water, came back, shut the door, sat down, and showed it to me.

"I wonder," she said, "if the good feelings come from the punch."

"You think maybe they come from something else?"

"Maybe."

"You mean you're going to do an experiment?"

"Yes!" She put the bottle to her lips, and drank. She put the bottle down and the punch smile came.

"I get it from the water, too."

"You think it's the bottle?" I asked.

"Yes," she said, and put the mouth of the bottle in her mouth without drinking, and just held it there, looking at me. She hummed and smiled.

"You think it's from having the bottle in your mouth?"

"No," she said. "I think it's from the ideas I have when I put the bottle in my mouth."

"Oh! You put the bottle in your mouth, and then you get ideas—and then you get that special secret punch feeling?"

She put the bottle in her mouth, and nodded, "Yes."

"What could those ideas be?"

Turning toward me with the bottle in her mouth, she stroked her cheek with the palm of her hand.

"Do you think about your father when you have the bottle in your mouth?"

Humming into the bottle, she made a "maybe" sound.

"You put the bottle in your mouth, and the good feelings come from the ideas about special people."

She shook her head, no, and looked sad for a moment. Then she said, "Maybe," very softly.

I said, "I have the thought that the ideas about special people are about your father and also about me. And I think the good feelings are also a little sad."

She smiled and turned her eyes away and, looking embarrassed, hummed a final "maybe" into her bottle. She looked at the clock and said she had to go.

Discussion

Disruptions in treatment can create opportunities as well as difficulties. In Ellen's case, the therapist's vacation is a loss of a person who has become important to her. Simultaneously, this separation evokes memories of conflicts about the loss of her father and the consequent unavailability of her mother. The father's death was sudden and totally unexpected; the therapist's vacation was planned, anticipated and discussed. The reunion with the therapist is a partial repair of Ellen's now internalized fear that important people will disappear and disappoint. This partial repair helps Ellen reveal her worry that any separation is permanent and helps to bring her father into the treatment directly. This emerges first in the form of a love affair with the therapist, whose return has prompted a shift in the focus of Ellen's intense attachment to him from a more infantile, "needy-greedy" level to a more affectionate-romantic one. The availability of these feelings helps surface the "presence" of her father and helps begin the shift of her curiosity toward her own inner life.

In the first post-vacation hour, the therapist's major effort is directed toward an interpretation of the defensive nature of Ellen's forgetting. Expressing his pleasure at their reunion permits Ellen to avow her separation worry. He begins to detail how her efforts to protect herself from that worry are costly. This serves to further engage her curiosity: "Why is that?" In this way, the therapist is informed that he may proceed to help Ellen begin to understand the detailed structure of her defense and its impact on her learning. Ellen can now "know," know about and express her affection in a more direct, though not yet totally overt, fashion. Her "billet doux" is a harbinger of things to come, seen in full flower in the session reported four weeks later.

The tone of this later hour is markedly different from the early sessions. It is filled with coy affection, seductive teasing, experimenting, and curiosity about Ellen and the therapist.

An examination of this hour reveals the following details of dynamics and technique. The first clue to Ellen's mood appears in the waiting room, where the therapist notices her "sly, pleased smile." This continues in the treatment room and, when the therapist makes note of this, Ellen attempts to suppress the smile—but not altogether successfully.

The therapist persists with his observation of Ellen's affect, but this time links it to the punch she is drinking, which may give her those "nice big feelings." Given the "distance" of the punch, as metaphor, Ellen can elaborate about all sorts of other oral pleasures—an emerging capacity in this inhibited child. Together, the therapist and Ellen playfully differentiate that special pleasures come only from the punch. The playful tone of the interaction parallels the pleasurable content. Form and content are now congruent.

The therapist makes a further attempt to reach directly for the affect. Ellen is not ready for this and backs away three steps: She can't put it into words; it's embarrassing; and she really doesn't know anything about it. The latter is a return to the familiar defense about not knowing, but the preceding statements demonstrate the loosening of this resistance.

The therapist immediately confronts the not knowing, which Ellen acknowledges.

Ellen counters with a pair of questions about the therapist. The first question seems to be a departure from the content. When not answered, Ellen quickly returns to the content of her good feelings. By acknowledging that he, too, has had such good feelings, Ellen is permitted to have these, to reduce her embarrassment about them and to continue the exploration with him.

Ellen asks in a slightly shifted style whether the therapist will accept her snowflake. The therapist interprets her offer of the snowflake as a question about the acceptability of Ellen's feelings. Over her denial, he suggests that her embarrassment about her feelings may have led her to want to change the subject.

The appropriate timing for persisting with an interpretation in the face of defensive resistance is a matter of finely-honed technical judgment. In this instance, the therapist is relying upon the maintenance of Ellen's playful mood, her continued productivity with the snowflakes and the content, the absence of any accelerated anxiety and the continued congruence of the form and content.

Once again, Ellen seems to veer toward other issues—questions about the therapist, particularly when he was her age. It is likely that Ellen is creating greater safety for herself, by establishing that she and the therapist have enough in common to proceed.

This seems to permit her to return to a discussion of the feelings which she signals with a sip of punch, another smile and a giggle. Together, they can then elucidate the qualities of this good feeling, which earlier Ellen could not put into words. While the therapist assists with the wording, Ellen validates that he has understood her very well.

The validation permits the therapist to link the description of the feeling with its possible derivation and meaning: "It sounds like being in love." He is aware that he is stating her likely feelings about himself, as well as other significant people. She denies it. He persists, and she is able to give a qualified acknowledgement. This allows him to go a step further in interpreting the feeling as one more directly related to him. At the same time, he can underscore how the feeling enhances her self-esteem, and permits her to enjoy getting things from the people she cares for.

The spilled punch seems to further validate the correctness of the intervention, which is accompanied by a slight increase in Ellen's anxiety. A playful interchange once again diminishes the anxiety and permits Ellen again to check the acceptability of her feelings, even if they are spilled in larger quantities. The therapist can now approach another side of this complicated interchange, the dynamics of which include conflicts about affectionate and probably sexual feelings and, in a more general way, all sorts of powerful affects, how these arise and may be lost, and issues about growing up and growing "effectance" and autonomy.

He now intervenes from the side of Ellen's fear of losing good feelings. In response to this, Ellen reaches up to touch the therapist's beard and asks further questions about it. The intimacy in the room mounts. It is probable that the therapist's next remark is an intuitive leap, linking what is occurring in the moment to Ellen's anxiety about loss during his vacation and about another loss in the more remote past.

There is immediate confirmation in Ellen's very first reference to her father. This is a more serious interchange, but Ellen can take it no further.

The playfulness reemerges in the experiment with the punch bottle which leads to an important clarification: The good feelings come from the ideas she has. It is quickly established that the ideas are about her father and her therapist, and that the good feelings can be accompanied by sad feelings.

Ellen has taken important steps forward in this session. She has taken these strides without inordinate anxiety or attendant regression and seems ready and able to master these conflicts with greater control over her inner life, similar to her control of the ending of the session. The therapist's skillful and playful use of the transference has enabled Ellen to progress.

JENNIFER PARSONS

Jennifer Parsons, nearly six years old, is a black girl who had been seen by two different therapists during the past year-and-a-half. She lives with her mother, her cousin Gwen, age four-and-a-half, and her eight-month-old baby brother. Mr. Parsons, who is a merchant seaman, is home for only various periods of time and away for lengthy intervals.

In addition, Jennifer has a 12-year-old half-brother, who was born when Mrs. Parsons was 15, and who lives mostly with his paternal grandparents who are close by. Periodically he spends time in the Parsons' household.

Jennifer's cousin Gwen has lived with the family since infancy and calls Mrs. Parsons "Mama"; she and Jennifer refer to one another as sisters.

Jennifer has recently begun kindergarten and attends day care before and after school. Mrs. Parsons is a cook whose work hours change from time to time.

Presenting Problems

Mrs. Parsons brought Jennifer for evaluation and treatment when Jennifer was four years, three months. Mrs. Parsons had noted a pronounced change in Jennifer during the preceding year. At home Jennifer had become obstinate, uncooperative, and "bratty." Mrs. Parsons' morning schedule was an extremely tight and demanding one. Jennifer's stubbornness, whining, complaints of imaginary stomachaches, and refusal to dress and "get going" were becoming increasingly exasperating to Mrs. Parsons. In addition, the staff at Jennifer's day care center reported that Jennifer was becoming increasingly sullen, hitting and biting other children, disrupting the group and throwing temper tantrums.

The day care staff called Mrs. Parsons frequently, complaining that Jennifer was extremely difficult to manage and urging her to discipline the child more firmly. Mrs. Parsons experienced these calls as humiliating and as unwelcome intrusions and burdens in her already busy life. Mr. Parsons was away so much and few relatives could be called to give Mrs. Parsons any respite. Mrs. Parsons said that she could not get Jennifer to tell her what was bothering her, that she thought Jennifer deliberately misbehaved and "tried to make people like her." She summed up her concern and irritation with the comment that

"Jennifer is becoming the kind of child that I wouldn't like, if she weren't my own." In a guarded way Mrs. Parsons indicated that she felt unable to find solutions to the well-established and ineffective struggles in which she and Jennifer engaged.

Although Mrs. Parsons reported that similar behaviors had occurred from time to time in the past, Jennifer's difficulties had become more pronounced and pervasive, beginning with the time that Mrs. Parsons' work schedule had changed from afternoons to an early morning shift. This required that Mrs. Parsons take Jennifer and Gwen to a friend's house at 6:30 in the morning in order to get to her own job by 7:00 a.m. The friend would then take the two girls to the day care center.

Developmental History

Pregnancy and delivery were uncomplicated. Mrs. Parsons smilingly remembered that the nurses informed her that Jennifer had one of the most lusty cries they could recall. Unfortunately, Jennifer's diarrhea kept her at the hospital several days beyond Mrs. Parsons' discharge. Mr. Parsons was away when Jennifer was born. Developmental milestones were reported to be precocious, although Mrs. Parsons, in giving this information, seemed not to know how advanced her baby had been. Mrs. Parsons returned to work when Jennifer was six weeks of age, leaving Jennifer with a friend who cared for several children in her home. This arrangement continued until Jennifer was about six months of age, at which time she began day care.

At age one, Jennifer was hospitalized for several days for croup. At age two, a second hospitalization occurred for surgical correction of strabismus. Just before this hospitalization, Mrs. Parsons' youngest sister and her nine-month-old baby Gwen had moved into the home. Shortly after Jennifer's return from the hospital, her aunt, who felt unable to care for her baby, left. During the next few months, Mrs. Parsons' sister returned unexpectedly several times. Finally, Mrs. Parsons confronted her sister with this "irresponsible behavior" and the two sisters arranged for Mrs. Parsons to have permanent guardianship of Gwen.

Six months later, when the day care center, which both children attended, terminated its infant program, Jennifer and Gwen were moved to a new day care program. Initially, Mrs. Parsons minimized any effect upon Jennifer of these changes. Later, as she became more trusting of the therapist, she recalled that Jennifer had shown some jealousy of Gwen and had greater trouble separating from her mother in the new day care center. Despite this, Jennifer did well at the new center and some teachers remarked on her precocity, intelligence and leadership.

Mrs. Parsons

Mrs. Parsons is a fiercely independent and competent woman. She is an intensely private person whose trust is given slowly. In the transfer summary, Jennifer's first therapist remarked: "Do not be fooled by Mrs. Parsons' initially stolid, depressed and slightly hostile presentation. It is only a protective cover. She is waiting for criticism, to be patronized or lectured to. When she experiences the therapist's respect and empathy, she blossoms and uses collateral work better than any parent in my experience."

Description of Jennifer

Jennifer is a thin, almost spidery girl whose skin is clear and luminescent and whose hair is always neatly braided. Initially, she wore a serious expression, concealing her true feelings. But this gives way to a range of expressions when Jennifer begins to feel more trust. Jennifer is very bright, precocious and, on occasion, appealingly provocative. She has an exceptional vocabulary and attention span, and a wide range of skills and interests. She speaks clearly, with no infantile articulation, but will attempt to disguise her abilities by playing dumb.

The following is a report by Jennifer's first therapist of her first two hours with Jennifer, followed by a summary of her six month's work with the child and Mrs. Parsons.

Session I

When I greeted Jennifer and her mother in the waiting room, Jennifer ignored me and looked only at her mother. I invited both of them into my office. Jennifer immediately but covertly scanned the room and seated herself in the small chair, staring ahead stiffly. Again, she ignored my greeting and my first efforts at finding out why she thought she was here. I told her that I had toys that she could play with and that we could talk and play. Suddenly, she looked at her mother, who was smiling at me nervously, and said angrily, "Stop that. Don't do that." Mrs. Parsons asked what she was doing, to which Jennifer replied, "You're laughing at me." Mrs. Parsons explained that she was not laughing at Jennifer but smiling at the doctor. In a softer tone she added, "Come here, honey." Jennifer went immediately to her mother and climbed onto her lap. She then permitted herself to look around more thoroughly, with obvious attention to the open toy cabinet. She climbed down and began to play with the set of nesting eggs. After a few minutes, I suggested that perhaps her mother could wait in the waiting room. Mrs. Parsons hesitated a moment, as if uncertain how Jennifer would manage her leaving. Jennifer made no obvious protest but, soon after her mother left, told me that she had to go to the bathroom. We went together and when we returned Jennifer relaxed, the serious and worried expression left her face, and she began a careful review of the toys, which she named and showed to me.

When she found the baby doll, she cuddled it briefly, then turned to an airplane and a knife. Then she began to build a block tower, and told me that it hadn't fallen. She added a few more blocks and smilingly watched the tower fall. Undaunted, she returned to the baby doll and asked why I didn't have a bottle for it. With a good deal of concentration, she wrapped the doll in a blanket and put a bonnet on its head. Setting it aside, she found the Snoopy puppet which gradually approached the baby and suddenly bit the baby's leg. Finding two other puppets, she had the frog bite her own arm and the dragon bite mine. When I asked why this was happening, she said, with wide eyes, "He's mad!" When I inquired, Jennifer said she did not know why the puppet was mad and set it aside. Instead, she took the doctor's kit, found the syringe and gave me two shots which, she assured me, were "very little shots," although she had been to a doctor who gave her "big shots."

When I told her it was time to stop, she rummaged rapidly through the doctor's bag and insisted on taking a Band-aid with her.

Session II

This time, Jennifer readily came with me without needing her mother's presence. She headed immediately for the doctor's kit, looking, she said, for the Band-aids. Finding none, she had the dog puppet bite her gently. I said I thought that the puppet was mad and asked why. She did not know. Then I said I thought that sometimes people got mad and didn't know why either. No response.

She found the baby doll again and seemed pleased to discover some used Band-aids on the blanket. She played doctor with the doll, examining it several times and giving it shots, explaining that the doll was "very sick and needed a hard shot." When I asked how the doll was sick, Jennifer told me that its "stomach hurt because it ate something very hard." She continued to play with the doll and then with a flashlight which was complicated and had several buttons. Some of the buttons are hard to manipulate and, occasionally, she asked for help. Once she stated simply that there was something wrong with this flashlight.

Toward the end of the hour, she found the scissors and wanted to cut. Noting that one point of the scissors was shorter than the other, she commented that that blade "was broken." Then she told me that she has a sister. When it was time to leave she stopped to look at everything with which she had been playing and then asked, "Do you stay here forever?"

Discussion

Although Mrs. Parsons' pride and sense of privacy tend to make her a somewhat guarded historian, she does provide important and relevant information about Jennifer's current difficulties and her earlier development. Central to the understanding of Jennifer's problems are the following:

1) Mrs. Parsons' demanding work schedule has necessitated the involvement of other caretakers with Jennifer since she was six weeks old.
2) Mr. Parsons is away a good deal of the time, adding to the burden falling on Mrs. Parsons' shoulders.
3) Jennifer was separated from her mother during the two hospitalizations at ages one and two.
4) Coincident with the second hospitalization, two new people were added to the household and the baby cousin/sister became a permanent resident.
5) A change in day care centers followed very shortly thereafter.
6) When Mrs. Parsons' work schedule changed, another major alteration in routine was required which appeared to be the acute precipitant of Jennifer's difficulties, although her vulnerability to anxieties about separation, constancy and sibling rivalry have been present for some time.
7) Her half-brother's appearances and departures to live elsewhere likely rouse further concerns about possible abandonment.
8) Isolation from family and a social network has been another

important element in this family's ecology, locking them further into disturbing and frustrating transactional patterns.

The symptom picture presented at home and at the day care center validates further that Jennifer's conflicts revolve around separation anxiety and sibling rivalry—displaced to her peers at the day care center. Some significant depression obviously underlies the behavior disorders. The first two sessions with her therapist are further confirmation of the basic conflicts and simultaneously offer a picture of a child with very good ego strengths. From the very first moment, she finds the right size chair and surveys the territory. She can express anger at her mother—albeit, with displaced content—but this does not prevent her from accepting comfort from Mrs. Parsons. Despite her anxiety, she can permit her mother to leave the room without becoming overwhelmed. Though she must leave the room temporarily, she can return and engage with the therapist and with the toys. She is curious and can ask questions and request help. She can play ably and imaginatively. Her aggressiveness (the tower, the biting puppets, "he's mad") is regulated and not out of control. She remembers from the first hour to the second and picks up the threads of previous material. Most notably, she readily conveys the table of contents of her problems.

The biting puppets and the baby with the stomachache are direct translations of some of her own symptoms. The play with the doll clearly conveys her ambivalence about a smaller child whom she cares for and aggresses against. The doctor kit play may be a reference to her own traumatic medical experiences and to her wish to discover what kind of doctor's office she is in. The identification of the smaller scissors blade as broken seems to suggest that little is bad and is immediately associated with her "sister." Her parting question in the second session sums up her concerns about object constancy.

The therapist can feel quite confident after this initial period of evaluation that Jennifer is an intact child, struggling with neurotic conflicts, and quite amenable to treatment.

In addition to the understanding of Jennifer's intrapsychic conflicts, the therapist also has an initial view of the established transactional patterns between Jennifer and her mother, and the contribution these make to Jennifer's internalized view of herself. Simultaneously, this view adds to the understanding of Mrs. Parsons' sense of herself as enraged, bewildered and helpless to alter the situation. It is in this sense that the child is a significant part of the environment for the parent and the parent is, for the child, an important element of her inner and outer realities.

The following is a summary by Jennifer's first therapist of her six months' work with the child and Mrs. Parsons.

Summary of First Six Months of Treatment

Work with Mrs. Parsons

As we came to know one another, Mrs. Parsons and I developed a true partnership in assisting Jennifer. Our work together could be characterized as part parent education, part exploration of how Mrs. Parsons' own conflicts interfered with her good parenting, and part pride and pleasure in Jennifer's abilities and progress.

Initially, Mrs. Parsons was very worried, embarrassed, and guilty about Jennifer's difficulties. She was concerned that Jennifer might be a severely troubled child. Later it became clear that this worry was, in part, related to the serious problems which some of her own siblings had had. When reassured about Jennifer's strengths and given a more balanced picture of Jennifer's unusual talents, as well as the meaning of Jennifer's circumscribed conflicts, Mrs. Parsons' guilt diminished and her pride in her daughter increased.

Our work focused on understanding Jennifer's difficulties in terms of separation anxiety and sibling rivalry. I tried to explain in a normalizing, non-blaming way how Jennifer probably developed these concerns as an outgrowth of her life experiences. Together we worked on figuring out ways that Mrs. Parsons might help Jennifer, within the limits of her time and energy. For example, she offered Jennifer a locket of hers to wear to school as a constant token of her presence. Jennifer treated the locket as a great treasure and shortly thereafter, her dawdling in the morning decreased considerably. Mrs. Parsons' delighted recognition of the effect added to her conviction about the value of such interventions.

Perhaps the most important area of our work concerned giving Mrs. Parsons permission to feel differently about Jennifer and Gwen. Out of her guilt about Gwen's plight, revealed to be consistent with Mrs. Parsons' rivalry with Gwen's mother, she had "bent over backwards" to treat Gwen with extra care and affection. As she understood this, she was able to acknowledge, without guilt, the special love she felt for Jennifer and to be less quick to side with Gwen or accuse Jennifer. She has become more protective of Jennifer generally and, in particular, in defending Jennifer against the sometimes unjust criticism of the day care staff. She and I also worked to clarify Jennifer's confusion about Gwen being a cousin and not a sister.

In the third month of our work together, Mrs. Parsons informed me that she was pregnant. She had mixed feelings about this, concerned for her own already hectic life and also concerned about how much she might have available to give to all the children and the rivalry this would stir up for Jennifer.

Work with Jennifer

Through the medium of much imaginative play, Jennifer and I worked over and over on her fears that she might be abandoned by important people in her life. She revealed her fear that her mother might not come for her after school or might send her away. This theme was interwoven with her concerns about her father's and her big brother's comings and goings. In connection with her mother's gift of the locket, I was able to talk with her about what a wonderful thing her memory is and how she could carry in her memory all the pictures of important people in her life.

We have reviewed, many times, how Jennifer acts most provocatively and babyishly when she is most worried and most wants her mother's attention. She could agree with my interpretation that it is a big test to try to be sure that her mom will stay, no matter how Jennifer acts. As this became more firmly integrated, Jennifer began to tell me about and show me her more mature achievements and abilities—none of which Gwen shared.

These developments in the therapy sessions were accompanied by more mature behavior at home and at the day center. There were some occasional regressions, but generally the movement was progressive.

My work with Jennifer around sibling rivalry themes focused on two issues. First, we talked about how hard it is to share—especially a mother. Secondly, we discussed the confusion about whether Gwen is a cousin or a sister, and how many different feelings Jennifer has about Gwen. Sometimes Jennifer loves her, sometimes she hates her. Related to this was a continuous process of helping Jennifer differentiate herself from Gwen and value her own talents and achievements.

Jennifer's considerable progress in all areas and her marked symptomatic improvement led to my considering, seriously, the possibility that she could discontinue treatment as I was leaving the clinic. Mrs. Parsons was less certain, in light of a new baby coming into the picture, and we agreed that continuing with a new therapist was, on balance, the better plan.

Discussion

The therapist began her work with a particular point of view. She perceived the situation as one in which four people shared a common painful predicament, which each experienced in his or her own way. A more traditional perspective might focus more singly on the child's suffering, with the concomitant view that the parents are the "cause" of Jennifer's pain. Typically, this perspective tends to view the parents as culprits, leading to a "therapeutic search" for their unconscious conflicts and the roots of these conflicts in their earlier experiences. Thus, the search will be on for the parental psychopathology. At times, even the most empathic and seemingly neutral therapist may, in this process, wittingly or unwittingly join with the parents' self-blame and guilt.

Jennifer's therapist started with another view. She was there to learn about the family's situation and to engage them in a collaborative enterprise to observe with her the here-and-now of their daily experience. Of course, she kept in mind the importance of the past history of this family. Nor did she overlook Jennifer's unique place in this process, given her current developmental phase and the clear evidence of intrapsychic distress. Her focus at the outset was directed toward helping Jennifer and her mother change the reality of their transactions while simultaneously working with Jennifer to alter her subjective and unconscious distortions and feelings about herself. This starting point rested on the assumption that changes in the reality can change experience and ultimately alter attitudes and perceptions of another. She understood that this would be an ongoing process, with each level of change influencing changes at the other levels. Toni Morrison put this more poetically:

> They slipped in and out of the box of peeling grey, making not a stir in the neighborhood, no sound in the labor force and no wave in the mayor's office. Each member of the family, in his own cell of consciousness, each making his own patchwork quilt of reality—collecting fragments of experience here, pieces of information there. From the tiny impressions gleaned from one another, they created a sense of belonging and tried to make do with the way they found each other. (10, p. 31)

This therapeutic stance will not always suffice. The therapist was mindful that she might need to modify her plan should she discover that Mrs. Parsons was so locked into her behavior by the persistence of the past-in-the-present, projected onto and "played out" with her daughter, that changed behaviors would not register. Such a discovery would lead the therapist to shift to a focus on individual parental difficulties as central to the work. However, she tried a simpler beginning—doing the most with the least.

Given this choice, a particular technical approach was devised and applied. The therapist saw herself as ally to each, inviting them to join her in careful observation of their day-to-day transactions. She became translator and messenger, sharing with all of them her own careful observations and experiences as well as her understanding of the needs and wishes of all parties.

She avowed the importance of Mrs. Parsons to Jennifer and Jennifer's selective importance to her. She conveyed her respect for their struggle as an effort to cope and adapt. She noted the struggle as their mutual, enduring effort to retain their relatedness to one another. She proposed a series of new experiments and improvisations based upon careful, detailed observations. These were tested and validated and, through these efforts, a new set of transactions were negotiated and experienced by the family.

Nor was the work limited to interventions with Jennifer and Mrs. Parsons. Careful collaborative work with the day care staff helped them develop a more balanced and tolerant view of Jennifer's abilities and difficulties.

Second Phase of Treatment

Jennifer's new therapist summarized the first four months of their work together as follows:

The work with Jennifer and her mother continues to go well. After an initial period of mourning and questions about her first therapist, Jennifer made a firm attachment to me. We have been working on themes of Jennifer's "getting enough," her continued but diminished rivalry with Gwen and her questions about her mother's pregnancy and the recent birth of her baby brother. Jennifer ably explored with me her fantasies and worries about the birth and her brother's arrival. She continues to be concerned about being displaced by the new baby. What has recently emerged is more curiosity about where babies come from and about her own anatomy. Mrs. Parsons and I meet regularly. She uses the time to keep me abreast of current information and to seek advice and clarification about ways of helping all the children. I have had an opportunity to meet with Mr. Parsons, who has been at home somewhat more regularly. He is a regular part of all parental sessions whenever he is not at sea, and makes special attempts to spend time with Jennifer alone.

Jennifer made the transition to kindergarten and is very proud to be "in a learning school."

Eight weeks after her baby brother was born, the therapist informed Jennifer of her upcoming vacation. The two hours just prior to the vacation are reported in detail.

Attempting to engage Jennifer in exploring her feelings about this impending separation, I began to help Jennifer make a calendar to mark the times when we would not meet. Jennifer soon insisted that she wanted to make her own calendar. Bossily she asked, "How many lines do I draw?" When I said that Jennifer might have many other questions and feelings about my vacation, I was told firmly, "Count the lines." Jennifer's proficient lettering became quite sloppy and, in a whiney voice, she asked many questions about her lettering.

I remarked that, at first, Jennifer knew how to write the numbers, but then got mixed-up and unsure—maybe there were other things she was confused about? "Will you leave tomorrow?" "No, we will still have another time together."

Angrily Jennifer crumpled her calendar: "It's no good—it's all messed up." I noted Jennifer's anger and linked it to my vacation. Jennifer moved about aimlessly and sadly. "Are you going to Disneyland?" she asked. I replied that perhaps Jennifer would like to think that I would be going to a place where Jennifer had been. Jennifer agreed, as she began to work competently on a second calendar.

I said that people go away for different reasons. Some go on vacation; some go for other reasons. Her mom recently went away for a few days. "Are you going to have a baby?" Jennifer asked curiously. I replied that Jennifer might wonder if I would come back with a baby like her mom did—lots of questions about people going away and about babies. Jennifer insisted, "You're *not* going to have a baby. You *are* going to Disneyland."

As she worked on her calendar and came closer to the dates of my departure, once again Jennifer began to write backwards and messily. In a babyish voice she asked, "Is this right? Is it right now?"

I said that Jennifer seemed worried about doing "what's right." "I think you have so many feelings about my vacation; it's making big worries." Jennifer scribbled all over her page and turned to the toy phone. "I'm calling you!" she said peremptorily and, "I want your real home number and *now*." I interpreted Jennifer's upset wish to know how to be in touch with me, when I was going away soon.

Leaving this play, Jennifer began to scribble rapidly on one sheet of paper after another. I said that perhaps Jennifer needed a lot of paper because we would soon miss our time together for awhile. Jennifer ceased to scribble and announced that she would make pretty stars for her mommy, daddy, Gwen and her brothers. "They will all get pretty stars, but you get an ugly star." I acknowledged that I would get an ugly star "because I'm the one who's going away." Jennifer promised, "you'll get a pretty star when you come back." I commented that Jennifer did know something about people going away and people coming back and "that being angry doesn't mean forever." Jennifer looked up lovingly and proposed, "Let's feed the baby." The brief remaining time was spent on jointly feeding and diapering the baby doll.

In the final hour before the vacation, Jennifer, atypically, left her mother reluctantly. She repeated the sequence about the pretty stars for her own family and an ugly star for me, alternately scribbling stars and the number five on lots of paper. I asked, "Tell me about the number five." Jennifer said she was five years old. I agreed and added that five is also the date on which I would return from my vacation. Jennifer circled the date on the desk calendar with a red magic marker and put the calendar in a drawer.

Then we played cards, with Jennifer asking questions about the rules and my vacation. I suggested that perhaps Jennifer really knew the answers, but felt confused, maybe a bit sad and mad. Sadly Jennifer asked, "Why do you have to go on vacation?" Jennifer's ideas were invited. She didn't know. Did she remember other people who went away? "Yes. No. Yes. No." I said that it was hard to be sure, when you are worried. "Do you need a rest?" asked Jennifer. Not waiting for a reply, Jennifer ran to the cupboard and began to shoot a lion puppet. "Shoot him if he acts stupid," she asserted angrily. I said, "Why, look how angry you get at yourself when you think my vacation has something to do with you." Jennifer replied sadly, "I think you need a rest from me." I said that could be a big worry and inquired further about Jennifer's worried ideas. Silence. I suggested, "Sometimes children worry that when people go away it's because of something they did." Jennifer replied that her mother gets tired. I said, "Yes. Mommies do get tired sometimes. Grown-ups, children, everyone gets tired and need a rest sometimes. But you worry that it has something to do with *you*."

Jennifer asked whether I would see other children when I went away. "I understand, you wonder whether I'll see other children but not you. You worry about being left out." Insistently, "WILL YOU?" "No, Jennifer, when I go on vacation, I don't come to work at all. That's what a vacation is." Jennifer smiled. When I announced that we would have to stop, Jennifer insisted that she did not want to leave and wanted to take some jacks with her. Acknowledging how hard it was to say good-bye, I interpreted Jennifer's wish to have something of mine while we were not meeting. Jennifer became alternately sad, whiney, and demanding about taking the jacks. I commented that Jennifer was having a hard time with her "missing feelings"—particularly since her mom had gone away for a while not so long ago. Jennifer burst into tears and cried, "I don't want you to go," but allowed herself to be comforted. I spoke to her about how sad it was to say good-bye, and about how we would think of one another, reminding Jennifer that we would be together again in two weeks. Jennifer calmed down within minutes and left.

Discussion

The therapist's impending vacation allows Jennifer to portray the conflicts and worries which brought her into treatment in the first place. It is very apparent that she is struggling with concerns and fantasies about separation, about causing important others to leave and about fears that other children will get more than she. These conflicts lead to sadness and anger which are directed toward herself (shooting the lion—a self-representation) and toward the therapist who will get an ugly star. All of this reduces Jennifer's competence and her capacity to play and enjoy the therapy hours. These are costly adaptational efforts, but it is possible to note other more effective coping devices which Jennifer institutes. She tries to place the therapist in familiar territory (Disneyland) and to secure for herself partial representations of the therapist (jacks and telephone number). The therapist assists Jennifer's efforts by enabling her to express her concerns and her wishes, by providing real comfort, by clarifying the real cause of the separation, by linking her vacation with the more important recent temporary loss of her mother, by acknowledging and accepting the affects as appropriate and not dangerous and, finally, by affirming that she will return and that, while she is away, they will remember each other and that Jennifer will remember good things about her as well as being sad and angry at her leaving.

The material in these two hours is characteristic of patients struggling with the processes of separation and individuation and with the as yet incomplete attainment of internal object constancy. The therapist's efforts serve to promote this progression and the development of a firmer internalized representation of important others who can be held in mind with good and bad affects and qualities intact.

When the therapist returned from her vacation, Jennifer was able to resume their work together without any evident regression. In fact, the therapist's return "sans baby" provided Jennifer with an opportunity to consider and acknowledge that some separations could be without bad consequences. The therapist summarized the final five months of work as follows:

With far greater consciousness, and in verbal as well as play sequences, Jennifer continued to work through issues of rivalry, the better management of aggression and some anxieties about her own body. She showed marked symptomatic improvement at home and at school. In fact, consultation with her teachers disclosed that Jennifer was an excellent student. Jennifer became more and more proud of her achievements and competencies, spoke of the many friends she was making at school and acknowledged her recognition of some of the advantages of being the biggest and oldest girl in her family. She continued to make excellent use of the toys and in the last few months showed an interest in more structured games, suggesting her beginning movement into latency. In the final six weeks, we worked together on bringing the treatment to a close. Mrs. Parsons participated actively in the process. Unbeknownst to me, Mrs. Parsons arranged to have Jennifer's photograph given to me in our final therapy session. Jennifer brought it with great pride. In that last hour Jennifer decided that we would draw pictures of each other to keep. I asked for instructions about how Jennifer would like me to proceed with the drawing of her. Jennifer instructed me, "Make me look pretty and put two good things in my hands. Put an apple in one hand and a big basket in the other." She then dictated the following story to go with my drawing.

"Once upon a time there was a little girl walking to her doctor, and she walked inside and she went up some creepy, squeaky steps, and she opened the door and she saw some *more* steps and she walked up those steps. Then she went into the office. . . . They played together because they wanted to. They played and played and played, week after week, and one day her doctor said to the little girl: 'You're gonna have to leave in three weeks!' The girl felt *sad* and *mad*—and *glad* to have a good-bye party to celebrate *being big* and *just right.*"

This simple story is as fine a closing summary of a complete therapy as one is likely to see.

REFERENCES

1. Adams, P. L., Psychoneurosis. In J. Noshpitz (Ed.), *Basic handbook of child psychiatry II*. New York: Basic Books, 1979.
2. Arnold, E., *Helping parents help their children.* New York: Brunner/Mazel, 1978.
3. Bachrach, H., Diagnosis as strategic understanding. *Bulletin of the Menninger Clinic*, 1974, Vol. 38: 390-405.
4. Chandler, L. A., and Ludahl, W. T., Empirical classification of emotional adjustment reactions. *American J. of Orthopsychiatry*, 1983, Vol. 53(3): 460-467.
5. Chess, S., and Hassibi, M., *Principles and practice of child psychiatry.* New York: Plenum Press, 1978.
6. Freud, A., *The ego and the mechanisms of defense.* New York: International Universities Press, 1936.
7. Hollingsworth, C. E., Tanguay, P. E., Grossman, L., and Pabst, P., Long term outcome of obsessive-compulsive disorder in childhood. *J. of Amer. Acad. of Child Psychiatry*, 1980, Vol. 19: 134-144.
8. Kovaks, M., and Beck, A. T., An empirical clinical approach toward a definition of childhood depression. In J. G. Schulterbrandt, and A. Raskin (Eds.), *Depression in childhood: Diagnosis, treatment and conceptual models.* New York: Raven Press, 1977.
9. Malmguest, C. P., Major depression in childhood: Why don't we know more? *American J. of Orthopsychiatry*, 1983, Vol. 53(2): 262-268.
10. Morrison, T., *The bluest eye.* New York: Washington Square Press, 1970.
11. Minde, K. K., and Minde, R., Psychiatric intervention in infancy: A review. *J. of Amer. Acad. of Child Psychiatry*, 1981, Vol. 20(2): 217-238.
12. Murphy, L. B., and Moriarity, A. E., *Vulnerability, coping and growth from infancy to adolescence.* New York: Yale University Press, 1976.
13. Thomas, A., and Chess, S., *Temperament and development.* New York: Brunner/Mazel, 1979.

CHAPTER 7

Crisis Intervention

Increasingly, patients in crisis are seen by mental health professionals. This is likely a reflection of increased stress in American family life* and leads to a probable absolute increase in the number and kinds of crises people experience. In addition, contemporary societal values give somewhat more sanction to the exposure of crises outside the family and to the seeking of assistance from health and mental health professionals, in contrast to past tendencies to seek help within the extended family, from the clergy or from specially designated community leaders.

The organization of the mental health treatment system has paralleled this societal development through the evolution of more services oriented toward crisis intervention and resolution. These organizational changes have been accompanied by the gradual evolution of a body of concepts about crisis work.

The following is excerpted from *A Night in Crisis* by Herbert G. Lau and Shirley Cooper (11) and serves as a general overview of some of the principles underlying crisis intervention as a therapeutic modality.

Crisis theory has attempted to delineate the similarities and differences between this work and its more leisurely counterpart, outpatient treatment. While responding to the psychodynamic

---

*See Chapter 8 on "Adolescence" for a more detailed description.

principles which govern all human behavior, crisis interventions have been conceptualized to include specific attention to the following: 1) current precipitating life concerns; 2) selected patterned genetic experiences and the compromises and limits these place on present and future adaptive functioning; 3) interpersonal transactions both within and without the treatment encounter including transference concerns; 4) a manageable, tentative, cognitive, and affective formulation, with blocked and partially aware connections pulled together with and for the patient's consideration and action; 5) concern for the patient's current motivation, goals, expectations, and reality considerations; and 6) rapid, active involvement between therapist, patient, and those in the environment who can offer support and care. . . .

Such work requires a high degree of synthesis between theory and practice, an orientation which discriminatingly selects and neglects facets of what the patient reports, and an organizational structure which can facilitate crisis treatment. . . .

People in acute distress . . . cannot easily wait. The pressure of their difficulties, whether physical or psychological, makes delay difficult or impossible. Provision of immediate help dilutes intensive anxiety, helping some patients past overwhelming flooding of affect or ideation so that they can continue along lines of prior adaptation. For others, the service enables them to arrange or reestablish more continuous care.

For some, the mobilization of environmental resources is critical in reducing agitation and insuring adequate care.

Crisis work can be divided into two major components; the first, an inquiry which elucidates the precipitating stresses and helps to bring order into the therapist's awareness. Here the psychological interventions are not only diagnostic but also serve to mobilize the patient's attention and recuperative potential. . . .

The second major component revolves around active experiential working through. . . .

There has been considerable discussion in the literature about crisis theory and practice and its difference from more traditional psychotherapy. Patients and their dynamics do not alter simply because they appear at a crisis service; the same psychodynamic principles apply. . . .

Yet, it is important not to obscure the real differences. For example, crisis patients more typically come with an urgency which makes delay difficult—for both the patient and the therapist.

The now of their lives is their primary concern and must be the therapist's, at least for the moment. Yet what therapists do must in some way connect to both the patient's immediate needs and his more long-term future. In order to create continuity, we need clues from the past, though in our search for these we must often use coarser scales than those we typically attend to in more leisurely work. Crisis work demands a compact and compressed three-dimensional model—one plane being an altered priority in the relevant information that is obtained, a second being the use of selective diagnostic concepts that guide inquiry toward specific priorities, and the third being the focal use made of the configurations which evolve from the psychotherapeutic interaction. In fact, crisis intervention requires precision inquiry into a psychological field of uncertain and distorted fragments which the patient presents with little associational cohesion. . . .

Another difference is the necessity to make formulations rapidly. Hypotheses generated from the patient's material in more traditional work can be tested at a slower pace, after much more information has been accumulated and understood. In contrast, we test hypotheses with crisis patients serially, tentatively, and in accelerated motion. Further, the crisis patient's capacity to distinguish the experiential from the observing ego is impaired. This creates alterations in the range, scope, and quality of transference reactions. The same selective use must be made of transference phenomena as is required in the process of inquiry.

In addition, the therapist has available to him a variety of concrete services, which at times he must use. The use he makes of these important in-vivo supports for the patient helps to promote the real relation between the patient and therapist.

Crisis work compounds the pressure upon therapists to make dispositions. All therapists face this pressure. In crisis work, dispositions must often be arrived at more quickly, must be based on less information, and affect the patient's life in immediate, often critical ways. Of necessity, then, a disposition must not be simply "disposing of the patient." (11, pp. 26-36)

Under the pressure of the crisis, psychotherapy has a different rhythm than a more conventional outpatient treatment. Frequently the work takes longer blocks of time than the traditional 50-minute hour. Since it requires the rapid, active involvement of the therapist, the patient and the others in the patient's immediate environment, the work takes on an intense and condensed quality. Often hidden meanings can be quickly elicited by "the moment of openness" created by the crisis event.

The following cases illustrate how these principles were applied in a variety of crises facing some children, their families and their therapists.

THE LINDQUIST FAMILY

Gina is a 14-year-old who was admitted to the hospital on a Sunday evening for ingestion of aspirin. Gina was asymptomatic by the time she reached the medical center but was hospitalized for observation and evaluation. The following account was provided by the hospital social worker who met with Gina and her family.

I learned from her medical chart that Gina lives with her parents and her 11-year-old sister, Sonia. Mrs. Lindquist is 41 years old. Both parents work, Mr. Lindquist has two jobs. Gina attends junior high school and is in the eighth grade.

On Sunday afternoon while her parents and sister were watching TV, Gina ingested 16-18 aspirins. Later, when she began to feel dizzy and had abdominal pains, she informed her parents that she had taken a lot of aspirin and said she was sorry. Her parents brought her immediately to the Emergency Room.

Session I

I saw Gina first in her hospital room. Gina is a tall, large girl with huge, watchful brown eyes, long brown hair and olive skin. She is a sensitive, talkative, street-wise girl who was quite articulate about her problems.

The first interview proceeded as follows:

Th: I know that you've been asked many questions by several different people since you came here yesterday. And here I am having more questions I'd like to ask and talk about with you.

Gina: Yeah—It's OK (smile), I don't mind talking.

Th: I'd like to know what happened yesterday.

Gina: (sigh) Well, I took some aspirin. I'm sorry I did it now; I was sorry right away but I just wasn't thinking. . . .

Th: I wonder how you were feeling before you took the aspirin, what was on your mind?

Gina: I was really upset. You see, well, I guess it all started last week. I was having trouble with the neighbors who used to be my friends. But, things went bad with them last summer when they didn't want me babysitting anymore or seeing their kids, even. They thought I was into smoking and hanging out. I did hang out sometimes with kids who did smoke, but not much.

Th: What do you mean by smoking?

Gina: Oh, just regular cigarettes, I wasn't really doing the stuff they said I was doing. Anyway, since then things haven't been good with the neighbors and this week things got really terrible. It all upset me so much I didn't know what to do. I really didn't *mean* to kill myself, I just didn't know what to do.

Th: Sounds like you felt very helpless and upset. What really upset you?

Gina: Well, on Tuesday I found out that the neighbor's girl, my used-to-be-friend, Mary, and another girl were saying I spread rumors about them. People at school were telling me what they said about me and some girls came to the house saying they heard I was saying Mary was cheap 'n stuff and that she wanted to fight. That really made me mad. I didn't say anything. I don't know why she's spreading stuff about me. So I just marched over to her house to tell her to stop spreading lies and have her friends lay off. . . .

(Gina describes at length and with much emotion the incident in which Mary's mother, who answered the door, had two of her sons hold Gina down while she scolded Gina and called her names. ["I was really mad."] Upon hearing her story, her parents called the police.)

Gina: She shouldn't have pulled my hair and I had a bruise where one of those guys held me down. The police couldn't do much 'cause I was on their property and I didn't have any real bad bruises. . . . Anyway this all happened Tuesday and I just couldn't take it. Not being believed. All those things they said weren't true. Everybody seemed against me—all my old friends were saying stuff.

Th: Sounds like you were feeling very alone. (pause—Gina looks tearful) Old friends seemed against you. Was there anyone who felt like a friend who you were able to talk to?

Gina: My boyfriend—Tommy. I guess no one else really. I just don't get along with those kids at school anymore. They say things about me and about others that aren't true. They say I've been spreading rumors when it's them. Everything is so messed up. I don't know what to do.

Th: You've been feeling lonely and as though you can't fix the mess. When did you first begin to think of suicide?

Gina: On Tuesday after that stuff happened. Things at school weren't good. I haven't been going too much. My parents aren't around much. They don't like me to have boyfriends. I couldn't even tell my dad about Tommy. He's hard to talk to and just gets mad a lot. I thought about taking aspirin that week off and on, I guess. Things have been bad at home. I've really made a mess of things.

Th: How do you feel you've made a mess of things?

Gina: I've just ruined everything—none of my friends like me anymore. I'm lousy at school. Everything's going wrong.

Th: That's a terrible feeling to have—that everything's going wrong, that you've messed things up and you're not sure how to fix them. Sounds like you've been feeling hopeless about your life—with friends, at school and at home.

Gina: Yeah, hopeless. Nothing seems right.

Th: Is that how you were feeling yesterday? Tell me what led up to taking the aspirin.

Gina: I don't know. (pause) I guess I was feeling hopeless, like nothing was gonna change. I was in my room feeling bad. My mother and father were watching TV. My sister was there too. I was just sitting there, walking around. I just couldn't cope with things. So I found a lot of aspirin and just took them.

Th: Did anything happen between you and your parents or sister that morning or the night before?

Gina: No, just the usual. My mom gets upset easy and yells. She doesn't listen. That's not new. All they do is watch TV lately. The more I thought about the mess, the worse I felt.

Th: What happened after you took the aspirin?

Gina: (explains sequence of events as described in the chart) I didn't really mean to kill myself. I guess I never thought of dying—just of not being around—not having to cope with it. In a way, maybe I was punishing myself . . . you know?

Th: How come you might want to punish yourself?

Gina: I don't know exactly, just for making such a mess. I think I wanted to hurt myself a little, not really to die, just to hurt myself. I don't know really.

Th: This business of trying to hurt yourself a little—but not too much. That's serious—to try to hurt yourself because you're feeling so lonely, confused, angry and upset with yourself and others.

Gina: Yeah. Boy, I'll never do that again! Everybody got *more* upset and I see now that I could've really hurt myself.

Th: Yes, you could have. Part of you wanted to die—or to not be around; the other part of you wanted to live to have things be better—this time the part that wanted to live won.

Gina: I guess so. Boy, I'll never try that again. I really could have hurt myself forever.

Th: Yes! I wonder if maybe you were sending out an S.O.S. to someone? Do you know what I mean?

Gina: Yeah, like who did I want to really help me out of this mess?

Th: Yes, that's it. Do you have any ideas what you were trying to tell someone?

Gina: I don't know. (shrugs)

Th: I have some ideas. You said before that your mother gets upset and doesn't listen, your dad doesn't either. You were home feeling very upset, angry with yourself, perhaps upset and angry with others. Maybe this was a way of saying to your parents, "Help me."

Gina: (pauses, looking at me) Yeah. They never seem to listen to me. (pause) I couldn't just tell them. They wouldn't understand. My mom's impossible to talk to. She gets mad too easy. (pause) I guess I take after her. (She glances sharply at me.)

Th: How do you take after your mother?

Gina: Oh, I get mad too easily and stuff. That's how I was to the neighbor. Somebody makes me mad; I start mouthing off, cussing, you know. I can't help it. My mom and I just start yelling.

Th: So it's hard to talk to your mother about important feelings and thoughts. You both get mad easily. What about your dad—can you talk to him?

Gina: Not really. He doesn't get mad. Really, he's hardly ever around, anyway. Since he has two jobs I *barely* see him. Things aren't the same and he's not so easy to talk to.

Th: When did he start working two jobs?

Gina: Around six months ago.

Th: Let's see, your father's not around much; he keeps to himself; your mother gets upset, and you get easily upset with her. You felt you couldn't really get the help you needed from your parents. It was hard even to let them know you were hurting inside. I wonder what a message might be to your family through all this? (Gina is listening intently.)

Gina: I guess I wanted them to know, but here I am telling them in the wrong way. My mom was so upset after I told her about the aspirin. I don't like to see her so upset. I feel like I've messed things up even more. (She looks away, teary.) I don't know why I did this.

Th: You've been having serious, sad and *confusing* feelings about yourself, your friends who are no longer friends, your school, and your home. Somehow it all added up to feeling extra confused, sad and angry and you wanted to stop things. So you took some aspirin. Is that how it felt?

Gina: Yeah.

Th: I wonder what might happen in the future.

Gina: I don't think I'll do this again. Next time I'll tell someone, or I'm not sure but maybe I'll be less confused and stuff. I never really wanted to die. It scares me that I could've really hurt myself. The one thing I'm worried about changing is my school. I used to do OK, then last year sometime I just wasn't interested and now it's all a mess. I've missed a lot of school this year 'cause I just don't go.

Th: It's very important for you to have things go alright in school and it bothers you that you've been missing so much. (She interrupts me saying—Yeah. She knows one reason is that all these friends that don't like her are at school and that's where she has arguments with them and they bug her a lot.) You've told me a lot of important things today and I get the idea that you *are* trying to figure things out and get out of "the messes." (I tell her that if she is interested I can help her find someone who can figure with her, like we've done this morning. She is clearly interested and asks if I'll talk to her family about this.)

At this point, Mrs. Lindquist enters Gina's room. She says hello to her daughter and then asks if I'm the social worker. I let her know that I am, and that I have just been talking with Gina. Could she and I meet soon and would Mr. Lindquist be able to join us? She says yes, he and Sonia will be here soon. I tell her that I'm glad she and Mr. Lindquist will be able to meet with me. She agrees to let Gina and me finish our talk and we arrange for me to meet with them in 15 minutes.

Session II (Mr. and Mrs. Lindquist)

Mrs. Lindquist is a short, stocky woman who speaks with an accent. Mr. Lindquist is a tall, heavy, fair-skinned man of Scandinavian origin. He seemed uncomfortable and said very little at first, in marked contrast to Mrs. Lindquist's loud, rapid speech. Both parents were visibly upset. Mr. Lindquist made little eye contact, but his face was set and grim. Mrs. Lindquist sighed repeatedly and sat on the edge of her chair.

I explained to Mr. and Mrs. Lindquist who I am and that I speak with most of the parents of children or teenagers who are on the ward. I told them that I talked to Gina that morning and that I imagined this was a very difficult time, a real crisis for the family. I let them know that I would like to meet with them briefly together, and I was interested in their feelings and ideas about what happened. Then I would like to meet with Gina and Mr. and Mrs. Lindquist and Sonia. The parents agreed to this plan.

I asked them what happened yesterday. Mr. Lindquist looked as though he would begin to speak, then withdrew. Mrs. Lindquist engaged quickly, describing how she was still so shocked and upset. She was "beside herself" when Gina told her that she had taken aspirin. She was still upset and confused about why Gina couldn't say something first, though she was relieved that Gina was physically OK. She was worried about this happening again and didn't know what to do. She looked at me pleadingly. I commented that I, too, was concerned about the future and that perhaps, if together we could understand more about what happened, it need not happen again.

Mrs. Lindquist said she didn't know why Gina was so upset. She thought the difficulties with the neighbors during the past week upset Gina tremendously, and she was also concerned about her daughter's recent isolation from other kids who were once her friends. Also, Gina had been doing very badly in school the last two semesters. "But then," she said, "I don't understand why she's done this." Mrs. Lindquist was tearful as she recounted Sunday's events and expressed her shock and disbelief.

I asked Mr. Lindquist what he thought might have been going on with Gina. He said the family was just watching TV, then Gina told them what she'd done. They rushed her to the hospital. He was very upset and concerned that Gina would feel so bad and he took this "very seriously." He guessed that Gina felt badly about neighborhood troubles as well as her poor school performance and sporadic attendance.

Mrs. Lindquist interrupted, adding comments on Gina's school attendance and her concerns that she never knew whether Gina would go to school or not. After a brief pause, she asked if she could be confidential? Mr. Lindquist tensed up, squirming in his chair. Mrs. Lindquist looked directly at her husband and stated that the "real problem is his drinking—it's been pulling the family apart." He appeared angry, scoffing silently at his wife, then shrugged his shoulders and listened to what she was saying. She continued that they worked long hours and when the family is together, "it's not good time." They couldn't talk anymore, he's rarely at home and Gina needs more attention. Mr. Lindquist appeared embarrassed and angry at his wife for exposing his drinking. He said, "Yeah I drink, but it hasn't been the problem." I told him that he seemed to me to be somewhat angry at his wife for bringing up his drinking. "I haven't been drinking since January or so," he said, "and yeah it bugs me that she brings this up now. I'm concerned mostly about Gina trying to kill herself. Our troubles are another story."

I said that their daughter was feeling isolated, upset and desperate. Yet, from what each of them was saying now, they, too, were feeling the weight of some problems at home. Could they tell me a little about how things have been in their marriage?

Mr. Lindquist sighed. I asked if he would begin. In spite of my request, Mrs. Lindquist interrupted to repeat her accusation about his drinking. He got a furious look on his face but said nothing while she spoke. I let Mrs. Lindquist know that I understood that she had many important feelings and thoughts that she wanted to talk about. Some things we would not have time to discuss, though I would make sure, as much as possible, that she was heard. Could Mr. Lindquist begin? He explained that he and his wife have had troubles. "She interrupts me, like here, and is on my back all the time. Things used to be better, but now I can hardly stand to be at home." I asked him when things seemed to change and how it used to be. He said they used to just get along better. He thought that since January, when he began holding down two jobs, there's been more tension. He hardly has time now for the family. He took a night job because they had so little money for spending on fun, which really bothered him. He hates when the kids ask for simple things that he can't afford. He's working hard now to have those things but he and his wife are getting along worse. She doesn't realize how hard it is for him to be responsible for so much. He paused. "I've been very unhappy lately," he said. I said that since January, Mr. Lindquist has been very busy trying to provide more for the family. He feels that Mrs. Lindquist doesn't understand or appreciate this extra burden. In a different way he feels isolated and not cared for, just like Gina.

I turned to Mrs. Lindquist and asked how things have been for her. She sighed and said drinking is still the real problem. Mr. Lindquist used to drink a lot, and not come home. Once he came home with a bloody nose from fighting while he was drunk. His drinking is really ruining things, and they almost broke up two years ago because of it. Mr. Lindquist interrupted. He thought things have been better since then. She said maybe, but it seemed the same to her. I asked if Mr. Lindquist thought that his drinking has been a problem? Quietly he said, "Yes, I drink too much sometimes." He used to go out with friends at a neighborhood bar a lot, but he doesn't anymore and he's not drinking much now. I said that the drinking has been a sore issue between them for some time. They agreed. Mrs. Lindquist added that things have been bad at home for a while; she doesn't know what to do. In addition to his drinking, they hardly see the kids. She drives him to his second job six nights a week and is barely home. I asked if the two of them ever have time together lately? Both of them looked at each other and he said, "no." He's been working six days a week lately and is tired on Sundays. Mrs. Lindquist said that there have been no real good times lately—either with them or with the girls. She wished there were. "You have been so busy, each of you," I said, "taking care of the family, making ends meet that there has been too little fun." I wondered how the problems that the parents have been facing affected Gina?

Mr. Lindquist said that Gina must feel out of sorts at home—no one is there to be with her. Then she's losing all her neighborhood friends—"I can see how she feels so bad." Mrs. Lindquist added that her husband should be paying more attention to Gina. She herself has little control over her daughter and they argue a lot. She couldn't understand why Gina had to do this.

I asked them for some background information, and learned that they met in Italy. They have been married for 15 years and came to California before Gina was born. Few relatives live in California. Mrs. Lindquist's family remains in Europe. They also have few friends. They used to frequently get together with the father's brother who lives nearby, but don't see him much anymore.

I asked them if there were any questions they'd like to ask me before the girls joined us. They asked what would happen next—how long Gina would need to be in the hospital, and who decides the length of her stay. I told them that the medical team, which includes me, will discuss this in the afternoon. I asked them what they thought about Gina leaving the hospital. Both parents agreed that they would like Gina to come home today, but were concerned if she would do this again. I said that they care a lot about Gina and are rightfully concerned about what this suicide attempt means and how this may be prevented from happening again. I suggested that Gina and Sonia join us now.

Session III (Gina, Sonia, Mr. and Mrs. Lindquist)

Younger sister, Sonia, is fair-skinned and slender. Sonia is jittery, smiling shyly, but appeared pleased to be included. The two girls entered the room tentatively and Gina headed for an empty chair between her parents.

Mrs. Lindquist sighed repeatedly and said, "It's been quite a night."

I agreed and added that it's been a trying time for everyone and maybe talking together now can be of some help. Surprisingly, Mr. Lindquist began by saying that Gina was feeling like the whole world was against her. He knows what that's like. "I've been there before." Gina nodded her head with some surprise that her dad understood so well how awful she felt. Mr. Lindquist described the trouble with the neighbors and then the accusation that Gina had been the one who stole some money from another neighbor several months ago. Gina chimed in that she was real mad about that "cause now that they don't like me, they're blaming old things on me unfairly." Mr. Lindquist admitted that he, too, was upset about the problems with the neighbors.

I asked Sonia what she thought. She thought her sister felt very sad about school and the fight and "a lot of things." Maybe, that's why she thought of killing herself. I wondered what it was like for Sonia when she found out that her sister had tried to end her life. She shrugged, smiled shyly, and said she was scared. She was afraid Gina wouldn't ever come home from the hospital. "That's a *very* scary feeling," I said. "You were worried about your sister. Gina was feeling so bad that her strong feelings got in the way of her thinking." Gina quickly stated that she never really meant to kill herself. She didn't really think it through. She just couldn't stand the way things were going.

Mrs. Lindquist said she can't understand why Gina couldn't tell them first—why did she do this? "Why didn't you talk to me?" Gina replied that she couldn't tell them. "You're hard to talk to and you never listen to me anyway." Mrs. Lindquist shrugged her shoulders, looked at me and then told Gina she should have told her own mother. She had no idea Gina was so upset. How could she know?

I asked how people in the family knew when someone was upset. Mrs. Lindquist said she could tell if someone told her or when Gina is mad and yelling. Gina said she's not sure how she knows. Mostly people are unhappy if they're not saying much. I said that it can be confusing how to know if someone is upset—some people talk about it, some people are quiet.

I asked Gina how she showed her family she was upset before she took the aspirin. She replied that she talked to her sister, but didn't say anything to her parents. Mrs. Lindquist asked why not. Gina looked pointedly at her mother and blurted out, "You don't listen, you just talk back and fight and then we both fight." Gina said she doesn't think her mother really wants to know what's going on with her. Mrs. Lindquist sighed and threw up her arms, looking at me, then at her daughter: "That's not true, Gina." The mother explained that she has high blood pressure and gets upset with Gina easily. Things have been tough lately. If Mr. Lindquist didn't drink and paid more attention to the family, it would be better. Mr. Lindquist shook his head, and looked downward but said nothing. I commented that everyone thinks things have been difficult. Gina was saying that it's hard for her to talk to either parent. Somehow Gina had the feeling that no one cares and no one understands. Gina agreed that she felt that way a lot. Mrs. Lindquist sighed again. Gina said, "It's true you don't really understand. You get so upset when I tell you things, then I get mad, too." "So when you talk to each other," I said, "instead of feeling understood, you both end up feeling confused, upset and angry. I wonder how that happens?" Gina said she and her mom both have hot tempers and start each other off. Mr. Lindquist softly agreed that they both needed to watch their tempers and listen to each other more. Sonia nodded her head vigorously. I asked her if she had some ideas about this. She smiled, face downward and stated that Gina and Mom should just stop arguing, stop talking if they're mad. I told her yes, both her mother and sister want very much to stop arguing and aren't sure how. These are things that will take time to change.

Gina began to talk more about the things that bother her about her parents. She likes her sister a lot, they're good friends, she said. But, she thinks her parents pay more attention to Sonia. They must like her better because they hardly get mad at her at all. But they're always saying no to her (Gina) and getting on her back. Father intervened to insist that Gina is loved just as much as her sister, but she's older and maybe they expect more of her. Gina said, "You're always on my case." Like about her boyfriend. Why can't he visit? Sonia can have a friend in her room. Mr. Lindquist said Tommy shouldn't be in Gina's room with the door closed. "Where else will we have privacy?" Gina asked in a belligerent tone. "The TV's always going. What are you afraid of—that I'll get pregnant or something? I don't do that stuff." Mrs. Lindquist said that it's always been OK for Tommy to visit but there have to be some rules; Gina is still young. Gina scoffed at her mom. I asked Gina what she thought might be a reasonable rule. She wasn't sure—"I guess I could leave the door partly open." Mr. Lindquist said, "It'll stay open, period."

Gina was in a huff and she looked at me for the solution. I commented that they were each looking toward me to judge what is fair. Yet, I thought the family might have some good ideas about how to work things out even though they may not always agree. Gina reluctantly agreed that it wouldn't be unfair to have her bedroom door mostly open when Tommy visits, even though her folks should know that they can trust her. I wondered if, at home, they were able to discuss differences and come up with some solutions, as they did just now. "No!" Gina declared. " 'Cause we're never together. Usually Sonia and I are home alone or Mom's home for a little while. Dad's never home."

Mrs. Lindquist said she can't control the girls. Gina refuses to go to school sometimes and just doesn't go. Gina said that she hates that school. She's been telling them for a long time that she wants to transfer. She has no friends at school; she's messed things up. Mrs. Lindquist said she called about the transfer last week and will call again to make an appointment with the school counselor. Gina looked relieved. I commented that Gina was also saying that she misses having both her parents at home. Having Dad there to help the family make decisions together seemed important to both mother and the girls. "Yeah," Gina said. "Since Dad has two jobs things have been bad at home." Mr. Lindquist explained why he must, financially, keep his second job. I commented that, according to dad, the family needs the money, but they want dad home more—this puts him and them in a bind.

I said that we had talked today about some of the ways they each felt alone, upset and angry, and that they talked about what Gina has been feeling that contributed to her taking a drastic action yesterday. I asked each of them what things they felt needed to change in the family so that things could get better.

Gina said she wasn't sure. Mostly she wanted to feel better about a lot of things. If she could talk more to her parents it would help. She wanted them to not be so mad at her. She thought her mother needed to change by being less jumpy. She smiled and said, "Me, too, I guess. Dad has to listen more, too." She thought that if they all spent more time together, like before, it would be better. "You know, going places, bowling 'n stuff on Sundays—anything. That's all I can think of."

Mr. Lindquist took his turn next. His wife listened and didn't interrupt with gestures or words. He said that he, also, would like them to spend more time together. He wished he had the money to do things for them, but he didn't. Gina interrupted to tell her dad that it didn't have to cost money to be together. I commented that father felt so responsible for having extra money. Was it possible, for now, to have a good time with his family without spending money? Both girls immediately listed things they could do without money. Sonia said, "Picnics like we used to." Gina volunteered that they could play all kinds of games without watching TV. Mr. Lindquist said, yes, he'd like that. He also felt that he and his wife needed to get along better. That would be enough changes, he concluded. I said that thinking about what you want to change was a good beginning.

I asked Mrs. Lindquist what she would like to see change. She said that her husband had to stop drinking. That was the biggest problem. Maybe this all wouldn't have happened if he'd paid more attention to the girls and to Gina. It was really up to him. Mr. Lindquist said nothing. I commented that Mrs. Lindquist was very angry with Mr. Lindquist and felt that it was up to dad to do the changing. Yet one of the things he had said today is that he felt too responsible for everything. I asked Mrs. Lindquist if she could name some specific things the whole family could do to change things for the better. She wasn't sure but thought that maybe on Sundays they could plan to see Dad's relatives. That would be good. With some hesitation, she added that she'd also like to argue less with Gina.

Sonia said, "What about me?" She wanted to see her cousins and spend time together with everybody. She was thoughtful for a moment and after a few seconds said that everyone should fight less. It bothered her when her parents fought and her mother got so upset. I said that all the changes mentioned were important but that change took time and effort. What was clear to me was that they had been able to talk together today about very important things. This was a hard, sad way for them to come together. How did the family feel about Gina going home? Fortunately, Gina is physically well. How would it be for Gina to go home?

Mrs. Lindquist thought that if Gina was telling the truth, that she wouldn't try this again, then she should come home today. Gina interjected that she wouldn't make another attempt. She didn't realize what could have happened. Mrs. Lindquist asked about counseling. "We need some help. My husband needs help and what if Gina gets upset again? This worries me," mother said.

I told them that, after consultation with the doctors, I would know if Gina could go home today and would let them know. I added that counseling for the family and for Gina might be the best way to begin working out some of the problems and changes we'd talked about. How did they feel about continuing to see a therapist, someone like me, together? Everyone agreed. Mrs. Lindquist was especially certain that this was the best plan. Mr. Lindquist was willing to take work-time off, if that was necessary, for a weekly session. We discussed the day's plan. I would inquire about a therapy referral for them by discharge time or at least the following day. Mr. and Mrs. Lindquist thanked me.

Later that day, Mr. Lindquist caught me in the hall to find out about discharge and wanted to know more about therapy. He told me he's had experience with AA counselors which wasn't very helpful. He said our session was OK. Would it be like that? Everyone seen together? I told him that just as I worked with families, the therapist that I recommended would work with them in the ways that seem most useful. I encouraged him to bring up any such questions or preferences with this therapist.

A therapy appointment was arranged for the Lindquists and Gina was discharged later in the day. I subsequently heard that the family kept their appointment and that the work was underway.

Discussion

This case report is illustrative of crisis work in a hospital setting with an adolescent and her family.

A suicide attempt can never be taken lightly, even when it appears to be a "minor gesture." Rapid intervention is always essential in order to assess the risk of repetition, the meaning of the attempt, and the impact upon other important people, and in order to arrive at a reasonable plan for further and future assistance.

In this instance, the first interventions are, properly, medical and will, to some extent, set the tone for the subsequent psychological work. Not the least of this is that a hospital setting affords little privacy, and often promotes passivity and regression.

First session

The therapist begins her contact with the patient armed with the information from the medical record. It is particularly important in crisis to gather as much information as possible in the shortest possible time. The therapist's first direct effort with Gina is aimed at establishing a relationship which she quickly sets in motion by acknowledging that Gina has already talked with many other people and by implicitly asking Gina's permission to engage in yet another conversation "with more questions." Guided by Gina's assent, the therapist moves promptly to the critical event and inquires, directly, about Gina's thoughts regarding the suicide attempt and the immediate pressures and stresses which may have led to the act. This elicits an account which includes facts and feelings. Repeatedly, Gina asserts the stupidity of her action, her regret about it, and the sense of helplessness which led to the ingestion. The therapist regards these reflections and Gina's judgments about her suicide gesture as good signs and takes these as permission to identify and label the varied feelings which Gina had been experiencing. In this way, Gina is helped to make more sense of her immediate predicament. Gina is now ready to consider alternatives to her behavior and the therapist begins to inquire about who was available to Gina when she had felt so overwhelmed. A shift occurs in Gina's reflections from an external focus ("Everything is so messed up") to an internal focus ("I've really made a mess of things"). The therapist has now learned two very important additional pieces of information: something about the nature of Gina's support system and about Gina's capacity to think psychologically.

The therapist now moves, deliberately, from how Gina had been feeling generally in the recent past to a specific inquiry about how she was feeling just before she took the aspirin. Again, important new material surfaces about Gina's perception of and relationships with her parents and sister leading her to another possible meaning for her action ("Maybe I was punishing myself").

With several important links established and permitted by the deepening rapport in the therapeutic contact, the therapist moves to underscore the seriousness of Gina's action. Gina appears to understand, acknowledging that her feelings crowded out thought, and asserts more firmly that she will not repeat this self-destructive behavior. This provides the therapist with another important piece of diagnostic and prognostic information. She can feel more confident that Gina's suicidal potential has diminished markedly. This confidence allows the therapist to deepen her therapeutic work through further exploration of other possible meanings of Gina's act (the SOS metaphor). Once again new material is uncovered about Gina's difficulties in communicating with her parents. Conflicts and identifications in the family begin to emerge. In addition, Gina's ability to reflect about and take distance from, as well as take responsibility for, her behavior becomes more clear.

Shifting focus once again, the therapist begins to bring the interview to a close with a discussion of the future and, specifically, further therapy.

Mrs. Lindquist's arrival brings this first session to a close and permits the immediate scheduling of the next phase of the crisis intervention: work with the family.

Second session

Quite properly, the session with the parents begins with the therapist stating who she is and with an acknowledgment of the Lindquists' anguish and concern.

Briefly suggesting the format of their work, she focuses immediately on obtaining the parents' version of Gina's suicide attempt. Mrs. Lindquist's initial remarks center on her own distress and confusion and herald an important family issue with her comment, "Why couldn't Gina say something first?"

Quickly another preoccupying worry appears about possible repetition. The therapist recognizes the validity of this concern but brings the focus back to the need to understand what happened as a possible way of averting recurrence.

Mrs. Lindquist takes the lead in describing her version of what Gina's troubles may be. In this account, two observations are of particular interest. The account is bracketed by the mother's insistence at the beginning and end of her statements that she doesn't understand what she clearly seems to understand very well. Secondly, her version of what may be troubling Gina is an exact replica in content and in sequence of Gina's account: 1) neighborhood squabbles; 2) isolation from friends; 3) school problems; 4) the events on Sunday. Gina's perception of how much she and her mother are alike seems indeed accurate.

Noticing the father's silence, the therapist moves to engage him. Mr. Lindquist's account is at first more reticent but he is able to describe his upset and his recognition of the seriousness of what Gina has done. He agrees with his wife about the possible "causes" of Gina's distress; however, it is notable that he omits mention of Gina's isolation, which later becomes evident as an important personal issue.

Mrs. Lindquist interrupts her husband ostensibly to expand upon his description of Gina's poor school attendance. It is evident, however, that this agreement reflects her helplessness about controlling her daughter. This expression of her helplessness appears to lead her to another problem about which she feels no control. Mrs. Lindquist introduces this new issue by asking if she can be "confidential." Her husband is instantly uncomfortably alert to what he knows is coming. An extensive interaction takes place between the parents about the father's drinking. Mrs. Lindquist takes the role of the accuser and blamer, and Mr. Lindquist attempts to fend off the attack and to silently suppress his mounting fury. In this interaction, Mrs. Lindquist hints at her own needs as well as Gina's ("Gina needs more attention"). Mr. Lindquist makes strenuous efforts to minimize the importance of his drinking and to separate it from Gina's problems. During this interchange, the therapist intervenes to help Mr. Lindquist acknowledge his anger with his wife more directly. This is an effort to support him as he is under attack. He responds to the support and is able to tolerate the therapist's gentle dispute with his idea that the marital problems are separate from Gina's problems. Her "dispute" is presented tactfully and without blame. She addresses the parents' difficulties and asks if they will tell her more about their marriage.

Recognizing that Mrs. Lindquist is on the attack and that Mr. Lindquist is in need of more support, she asks that he begin. When the mother cannot remain silent, the therapist intervenes again to assure Mrs. Lindquist that she will be heard, but stands firm in her request that the father give his version of how things are first.

This is a very carefully modulated intervention since it simultaneously takes into account the differing needs of each parent. Mr. Lindquist can now speak and uses the opportunity to tell the therapist that she has just seen what some of his troubles are: "She's on my back all the time. Things used to be better." The therapist chooses to respond to the second part of his statement. This choice has several purposes. It temporarily sidesteps the more heated aspect of their exchange and turns their attention to how things became difficult. This reduces tension and allows for development of some important recent history. Mr. Lindquist takes the lead in informing the therapist of the financial burdens which compelled him to take a second job in order to better provide for the family, and his awareness that this has contributed to strife between himself and his wife. Mr. Lindquist has now moved a considerable distance from his earlier taciturn and beleaguered position to one in which he more openly reveals his inner feelings.

Then it is Mrs. Lindquist's turn, and she continues to insist that the father's drinking is the major problem. With the therapist's help, Mr. Lindquist can finally acknowledge that his drinking *has* been a problem.

At that juncture, it becomes possible for both parents to agree that a current problem is how little time they all spend together and how few good times there are for anyone in the family. Even though it appears that Mrs. Lindquist has missed her husband's appeal for some understanding, they have found some common ground.

The therapist can now try to make a link between the parents' problems and the immediate issue of Gina's distress. This must be the focus of her work in this crisis situation. She has developed sufficient information to place Gina's "crisis" into the context of the family's more long-standing troubles.

The parents work along with her and begin to make some connections between Gina's "act" and their circumstances. They add some further important history about the family's isolation. Once these connections have been made verbally, it is possible to have Gina and her sister join them. However, before doing so, the therapist invites their questions and provides important information about how the decision will be made for Gina's return home.

Third session

The session with all four family members present begins again with an acknowledgment of how trying the past 24 hours have been. The therapist reaffirms the importance of their beginning to talk together.

Surprisingly, Mr. Lindquist takes the lead with an empathic statement of what Gina must be feeling. Gina is surprised by her father's understanding. Their mutual discussion of the fight with the neighbors serves to cement this empathic interaction. Parenthetically, it is revealing that the father also lost neighborhood friends when he ceased going to neighborhood bars and took on a second job. While it is tempting to speculate whether the second job has been taken to help with the drinking problem as well as to increase family resources, these considerations are beyond the immediate scope of the crisis work.

Since Sonia is the only person who has not yet been heard from, the therapist invites Sonia's participation. Sonia's response is also an empathic one. She also takes the invitation to speak as an opportunity to express her own fears and her fears for Gina. The therapist uses Sonia's remarks to convey to Gina that others in her family care about her. She does this while explaining Gina's behavior to the family and indirectly re-interpreting the meaning of Gina's behavior to Gina.

Gina's response demonstrates that the therapist's comments are falling on receptive ears. Although Mrs. Lindquist restates her continuing bewilderment and helplessness, she moves the discussion to a major theme: the inability of the family to talk together. This enables the therapist to open the wider question of how the Lindquists tell one another of their distress. Despite Mrs. Lindquist's return to a defensive and blaming stance, the family has an extended discussion and are engaged in the experience of sharing their common and separate grievances. Much is revealed in this lively interchange about styles of relating, identifications within the family, the defensive patterns employed by the various members, family rules and a demonstration of the family's ability to use this process to approach a compromise as a way of problem-solving.

Each has an opportunity to say how things might be better. Although the therapist encourages this process, she reminds them that there may be conflicting interests between family members, as well as internal conflicts which create binds. As the session proceeds, it seems clear that each is listening as well as talking, although Mrs. Lindquist is finding it hardest to relinquish her "single-cause-culprit" perspective. Despite this, they can all agree that it is safe and desirable for Gina to return home and that further family therapy will be in their interest.

This brief "crisis intervention" has certainly addressed and temporarily resolved the crisis. It has also provided the Lindquist family with an experience of therapy and left them with a sense that further work of this kind will be productive and helpful. Perhaps the most telling evidence that this is so is Mr. Lindquist's offer to take time off from work for weekly sessions.

This day's effort illustrates crisis work with an adolescent and her family. The work reveals the interplay between the internal psychodynamics of the identified patient and the longer-standing troubled family interactions. As with all "crisis" treatment, the therapist is obliged to discriminate, as rapidly as possible, what factors are important and what will be selected for therapeutic focus. Whatever the focus, it is essential to engage the significant figures in an active experience which brings order and meaning to a seemingly chaotic and incomprehensible set of events.

What to select and what to "neglect" becomes a matter of fine therapeutic discrimination. For example, in the case of the Lindquists, the therapist brought some of the major components in the marital strife to the surface, but chose to set these aside after they were sufficiently developed to connect these issues to Gina's suicide attempt. Further work on the marital problems remains a task of subsequent therapy. This piece of the work connects to the family's immediate needs and sets a hopeful stage for some more definitive resolution of the more chronic problems.

ANTHONY WILKINS

Seven months after beginning therapy, a critical event occurred in the life of Anthony, an eight-and-a-half-year-old boy.

When Anthony was eight, his mother was advised by the family pediatrician that psychotherapy might be a useful approach for the treatment of Anthony's encopresis which had persisted since Anthony was five. Anthony had been soiling his pants two to three times a week since shortly after starting kindergarten. Anthony and his mother were both embarrassed by the soiling. Sometimes Anthony would cry about it. Often, he would hide his soiled underwear in his closet. Teased by other children at school about being "stinky," Anthony would try to ignore their taunts by withdrawing from social contact. He was becoming increasingly isolated from his peers. This isolation, along with the continuing encopresis, led to the referral for therapy after an extensive medical workup failed to show any "organic" basis for his poor bowel control.

Anthony lives with his divorced working mother and a brother who is four-and-a-half years older. His mother, Ms. Wilkins, is a bright, attractive 35-year-old woman. She has tried "everything" to stop Anthony's soiling: promises of rewards; punishments including spanking; threats; efforts to understand what he might be worried about; medical inquiries; and finding a "big brother" for Anthony on the earlier advice of the pediatrician, all to no avail. This left her feeling humiliated and defeated, which is particularly bothersome since she has high expectations and ambitions for herself and her sons. The older brother fulfills many of these expectations. He is a model student, a highly competent and responsible youngster who is a source of great pride to Ms. Wilkins.

Ms. Wilkins separated from Anthony's father when Anthony was one year old. The father now lives in another part of the country and visits rarely, although he contributes to the support of the children. Despite the family disruption, Anthony's development was reported as uneventful in the early years. He walked and talked at appropriate times and was toilet trained shortly after his second birthday. Ms. Wilkins could remember little detail about his toilet training, but generally recalled that it proceeded without difficulty. Ms. Wilkins began working shortly after separating from her husband. Anthony and his brother were cared for by a neighbor whom Anthony continues to visit frequently, although his older brother now assumes much of Anthony's after-school supervision.

When Anthony was about three-and-a-half, Ms. Wilkins's boyfriend began to live with her and the two boys. This household arrangement lasted about one-and-a-half years, with increasing tension and quarrels beginning when Anthony was about four-and-a-half. During this period of increased strain, Anthony also underwent unsuccessful surgery to repair an undescended testicle. Four months after the surgery, Anthony and his brother spent most of that summer visiting the maternal grandmother who lived in another state. While they were there, Ms. Wilkins's boyfriend moved out of the house. Both boys were surprised to discover this when they returned. Anthony, in particular, had become quite attached to the boyfriend and asked about him frequently. Ms. Wilkins, who was somewhat depressed at that time, did not invite or encourage these inquiries and Anthony soon stopped asking. Shortly thereafter, Anthony began kindergarten and within a few weeks his encopretic symptoms appeared. Despite this symptom, Anthony has done reasonably well academically, and was described by his mother as a good and obedient child.

When first seen in treatment, Anthony impressed his therapist as a quiet, almost somber child who talked little and avoided all inquiry about his symptom. He came regularly to the sessions with his male therapist whom he seemed to like. His shyness and constriction resulted in therapy hours which were verbally sparse and slow-moving. His play was somewhat more revealing, although it took him some time before he could explore the playroom and use the toys in more than a very hesitant and tentative manner. Gradually, however, Anthony's play began to portray many of his concerns. Two armies, in continuous warfare, was a repetitively played out theme. However, who the armies were and why they were at war was never explained. Again and again the soldiers were bombed and shot without any apparent cause or explanation. Broken toys were quickly discarded and efforts to engage Anthony in repairing them were ignored. He would occasionally play darts with some "accidental" hard throws which would miss the target. These "accidents" were usually followed by an abandonment of the game. All efforts by the therapist to discuss the dart game and its disruptions were met by silence. On the few occasions when he would talk with his therapist, there were some clues about concerns that he was less preferred than his brother and also some worries about body intactness.

Anthony used a particular airplane with folding wings in almost every session. The warfare frequently revolved around this special plane and Anthony diligently searched for it when it was not immediately visible. Four months into the treatment, Anthony's therapist gave him a similar plane as a Christmas present. In the sessions that followed, Anthony began to express some curiosity about other patients who used the toys, especially wondering who else liked his favorite airplane. His play took on some greater animation and there was some indication that Anthony was becoming more willing and able to stay longer with a verbal discussion of his interests, curiosity and concerns.

As this was developing, Anthony and his therapist learned that a second surgical attempt to repair the undescended testicle was to be scheduled for the immediate future. Ms. Wilkins was understandably anxious about this in light of the previous unsuccessful surgery, and enlisted the therapist's help in obtaining a second medical opinion. Since both surgeons agreed that the surgery needed to be done now, she proceeded to arrange for it somewhat sooner than the therapist would have hoped. As a consequence, the therapist had less time than would be desirable to help Anthony prepare for this event. He was able to elicit some of Anthony's questions and confusions and to provide some useful information. He and Anthony prepared a calendar showing when Anthony would be in the hospital and when he would likely return home. There was insufficient time to explore Anthony's fears fully though these were acknowledged. Finally, the therapist arranged to see Anthony when he was in the hospital. Anthony was clearly pleased by this arrangement.

During the hospital visit, the therapist brought a building set which involved many magnets which could connect one part to another. Anthony played eagerly with the magnets and he and his therapist discussed how powerful these small magnets were in holding things together and how useful they could be in making new things.

Fortunately, the surgery was successful and Anthony's recovery was rapid. Shortly after discharge, Anthony returned for his first, post-hospital therapy session.

He greeted the therapist warmly and seemed more pleased than usual to see him. He searched through the toys purposefully until he found the playroom magnets, while explaining that, by following the directions which came with the building set, he had made many things with the magnets in the hospital. He spoke of trying to make the see-saw "like one of the pictures on the box," but it kept falling apart. He tried to make a comparable one with the playroom magnets and worked diligently at keeping it in balance, fixing it over and over again when it fell down.

The therapist commented that lots of things can be fixed. It is good to know that toys can be fixed and also that the doctors fixed what was wrong with Anthony. Anthony began to report some of the events of the hospitalization, though he seemed somewhat confused about how long he had been in the hospital. The therapist said that "some things are hard to understand—like the operation." Anthony replied that he cried when they took the stitches out. He cried so hard that they left one stitch in. In a confused way, he said that his mother would take that one out, but that other stitches underneath would stay in. His mother told him that those stitches are made of catgut.

Again the therapist commented about puzzling and hard-to-understand things and wondered what Anthony understood about the stitches and the catgut. Anthony did not answer, but instead began to talk about his cat "Blackie" who was killed by a car some months ago. Sometimes Blackie popped into his mind. Sometimes his brother would tease Blackie and Blackie would scratch, but Blackie never scratched him. The therapist acknowledged Anthony's missing Blackie and confirmed that thoughts do pop into people's minds, about pets and people who are gone. Anthony nodded and talked about having gone recently with his mother to the ASPCA to get another cat. He wanted a female so it could have babies and hoped one would be a boy, but his mom didn't want a female cat and anyway there wasn't a good one at the ASPCA.

The therapist asked Anthony if he'd ever seen a cat have babies. He said no, but he had seen a dog with puppies. The puppies crawled all over him, but the mother dog was angry and growled at him. The therapist wondered why Anthony thought that might be, and when Anthony remained silent, suggested that perhaps the puppies' mother wanted to protect the puppies and was unsure that Anthony wouldn't hurt them. Mothers do want to protect their children, but they can't always be sure that their kids are not hurt—like Anthony's mother couldn't protect Anthony's being hurt in the hospital.

Anthony listened intently, and then said that he hadn't seen the puppies being born, but he had watched the puppies being nursed. The therapist asked if Anthony knew how they were born. Anthony commented that someone must take the mother to a hospital—dogs, and people, too—to cut the stomach so the babies could come out.

The therapist inquired further about these ideas, but Anthony seemed unable to elaborate. In an effort to reassure Anthony, the therapist told Anthony that this is not the way babies are usually born and provided Anthony with a more correct account. Anthony listened and seemed to be a bit puzzled. After a slight pause, he told the therapist that when he was in the hospital, a friend had borrowed the airplane the therapist had given him for Christmas and it had been broken. Anthony seemed angry as he reported this. He then found the playroom airplane and spent the final minutes of the hour folding and unfolding the wings.

Discussion

It is not uncommon, in the course of therapy, to encounter critical and traumatic events. These new events are filtered through the prior experiences of the child and influence the child's development and the therapy. When such an event recapitulates past traumas, its impact may be even more profound with the potential for intensifying pathology on the one hand, while presenting an opportunity for a more effective resolution of past and present conflicted situations on the other. This situation poses particular technical problems which require modifications in the treatment strategy to address the crisis event while simultaneously insuring that the "crisis intervention" is not out of harmony with the overall treatment approach. Anthony's therapist faced this set of therapeutic problems.

A review of Anthony's circumstances, up to the moment of the crisis event, reveals a child whose many conflicts have been expressed in a specific symptom and in an emerging personality marked by constriction, sadness and isolation. His early history is filled with the loss of important people who leave at critical moments in his development and in ways that are largely incomprehensible. For example, Anthony could not understand the disappearance of his mother's boyfriend, to whom he had become attached, which occurred while he and his brother were away from the home. His efforts to find out why and what had happened were unsuccessful. This baffling loss occurred shortly after the first surgery. No four-year-old child can truly comprehend the meaning of a surgery. For Anthony this, very likely, was made even more confusing in view of the strained relationship between his mother and her boyfriend. In Anthony's understanding, these events were probably compressed in time, their sequence confused and jumbled together and probably surrounded by many emotions including loss, guilt, anger and punishment. In rapid order, and at a time when new developmental demands confronted him, Anthony experienced the surgery, separation from his mother, the loss of the boyfriend and the start of school. The appearance of his symptom is understandable, embodying the entire constellation of rage, aggression, loss, regression, helplessness, body control and body damage. The symptom has further consequences for Anthony leading to social isolation, struggles with his mother, intensified sibling rivalry and additional shame and loss of self-esteem.

The early months of the therapy proceeded very slowly. Anthony was withholding, cautious, slow to engage with and trust his therapist. His play revealed small glimpses of his conflicts, seen in the repetitive but incomprehensible warfare, the clear avoidance of any broken toy, the "accidently" misdirected darts and the preoccupation with the airplane with movable parts. The therapist's choice of a similar plane for a Christmas gift seems to have enhanced the rapport and the subsequent therapeutic work showed evidence of some opening up.

The somewhat too precipitously arranged second surgery, occurring at that juncture, unfortunately recapitulated prior perplexing experiences. The therapist was not able to intervene forcefully enough to insist upon a delay of adequate duration for the elective surgery. A sufficient postponement may well have permitted more effective preparation and an opportunity for Anthony to master an event partly through anticipation and planning rather than, once again, having to work it through after the fact. The therapist's presence, availability and specific interventions during the course of the hospitalization partially compensated for the inability to protect Anthony more fully.

In the therapy session immediately following the hospitalization, Anthony's warm engagement with his therapist and his immediate search for the playroom magnets are evidence of the value of his therapist's hospital visit. Anthony initiates a discussion about a part of his hospital experience by telling and showing his therapist how he had used the magnets. He is more verbal than ever before and an exchange occurs in which his therapist can begin to help Anthony understand how things can be balanced and repaired, and that Anthony is in better "working order."

For the first time, Anthony can express his own confusion in a more direct fashion. There is confusion about time, confusion about his body and confusion about his mother's efforts to explain the stitches. The therapist makes an enabling comment recognizing that some of Anthony's confusion is age appropriate.

Also, for the first time, Anthony tells his therapist, directly, about some of his pain and distress, and clearly conveys another important confusion—that his distressed behavior has caused a mishap. The therapist attempts to explore this distortion a bit further. Anthony "changes the subject" but his association from the catgut to his dead cat reveals the confused connections between loss, body damage, sibling rivalry and aggression. The therapist chooses to work with two aspects of Anthony's account. He begins to lay the groundwork for a clarification about psychological processes, i.e., "Things pop into people's minds." In addition, he focuses on the theme of loss.

New material continues to appear and the themes shift to replacements, sexuality, aggression and how mothers try to protect their children. The therapist links this last issue to Anthony's hospitalization. Anthony shifts to his view of the birth process. The therapist attempts to explore this unsuccessfully and, too quickly, provides a correction of the distortion which may well close out a fuller portrayal of the aggressive component in Anthony's fantasies. Anthony is puzzled and approaches the idea of damage from another direction, this time linked again to the loss of a valued object while he was away.

The crisis event has, obviously, triggered the loosening of Anthony's constricted defenses and, accompanied by a deepened relationship with his therapist, released a floodgate of material. The tentative formulation of Anthony's difficulties which was constructed from his history and only partially glimpsed in Anthony's previous hours now seems well confirmed and well represented in this hour's therapeutic content. While less than ideal, the therapist's handling of this crisis has been sufficiently adept and competent to help this boy through a very difficult situation. At the same time, the crisis interventions have been entirely in keeping with the overall direction of therapy. The therapist's accessibility and presence during the experience were an important demonstration to Anthony that he is cared about. The post-hospitalization therapy session is a veritable table of contents of Anthony's concerns and confusions. It is almost too much material to deal with and the therapist tries to respond to some of it too quickly with reassurance and information. Anthony informs the therapist that these are ineffective interventions and shows by his persistence that he is ready to explore his concerns further and more deeply over time. It is evident that this "crisis" has become a real opportunity to move the therapy a quantum leap forward.

ALICIA COMPTON

For all of her eight years, Alicia's life has been spent in moving from one crisis to another. She has been repeatedly confronted by her mother's psychotic episodes and many psychiatric hospitalizations. Each of these has resulted in a disruption of Alicia's living arrangements, often leading to changes in her school setting or interrupting her school attendance. She has lived with her mother, Mrs. Compton, her mother's friends, occasionally with her abusive father whose whereabouts have been unknown for some time, and most often with her aunt, Miss Howell. The aunt is 15 years older than Alicia's mother and raised Mrs. Compton as well as her youngest sister. All three were orphaned when their mother died during the birth of the youngest daughter, when Mrs. Compton was five.

Miss Howell, age 50, has grown weary of "rescuing" Mrs. Compton and Alicia. She has worked all of her life and remained unmarried and the caretaker of this family throughout many of their difficulties. She cannot understand her younger sister's problems, insisting that these are largely willful acts of laziness and irresponsibility. In recent years, she has been in poor health, contributing to her decreasing willingness to step in and help her family.

Precipitated by the breakup with her most recent lover, Mrs. Compton is once again hospitalized. Although Miss Howell takes Alicia into her care again, she proceeds, on the advice of a neighbor, to call in the Child Protective Services to arrange more long-range plans for her niece. In portraying her wish for some relief from the constant caretaker role, she tells the C.P.S. worker that Mrs. Compton has "once again abandoned Alicia." Since Miss Howell has so often served as respite and rescue surrogate mother, the C.P.S. worker does not see this as an urgent crisis and fails to hear that Miss Howell is at the end of her rope. Miss Howell's guilty ambivalence has screened the urgency of her request.

Before the worker can take any action, Mrs. Compton is discharged and shortly after takes Alicia home. In the interim, the school has become alarmed by Alicia's immobilization and inability to learn. They contact Mrs. Compton and urge her to have Alicia seen for psychological assessment and treatment. Mrs. Compton follows through rapidly and on hearing that Alicia will be evaluated, the Child Protection Agency closes their case. Miss Howell accedes to this plan and agrees to participate in the psychological evaluation.

The evaluation reveals a shy, highly anxious and depressed child. She engages slowly, seems uninterested in the play equipment and whispers shyly that she hates living in so many different places. She never knows what will happen when she lives with her mother and she thinks that maybe her aunt is also getting too sick to continue taking care of her.

Alicia is entirely preoccupied and frightened by this predicament, leaving little energy for age-appropriate interests, activities or learning. In the course of the assessment, Miss Howell and Mrs. Compton are seen separately. Alicia's aunt insists that Alicia has already been through too much and should not continue to stay with her mother. She herself is too ill to care for Alicia properly. Her idea is that Alicia should be sent to live with her younger aunt who has settled in the Southwest. She acknowledges that she has not seen her youngest sister for some time, but has recently spoken with her and learned that Alicia's aunt would agree to take her. While discussing this possible plan, she mentions, casually, that Alicia would be the only child there since this aunt's two children are presently living with their father. The therapist attempts to explore why these children are not with their mother. Miss Howell becomes somewhat defensive, insisting that her youngest sister is more than able to care for Alicia.

Mrs. Compton thoroughly resists this plan. She does not want to relinquish Alicia to anyone, especially to someone who is so far away that it would be impossible for her to see her daughter. In spite of her assertions, she does have some awareness of the limits of her own ability to take care of Alicia. Each time she reviews the history of Alicia's disrupted experiences, she agonizes over what to do.

The therapist notices that whenever Mrs. Compton seems more and more determined to keep Alicia, she appears more disorganized and confused. During this period of time, she has several emergency appointments with her psychiatrist. It becomes clear to the therapist evaluating Alicia and to Mrs. Compton's psychiatrist that Alicia's mother is in no position to care for Alicia consistently, or to make the decision to relinquish her. Together, the two therapists recognize that continued exploration of Mrs. Compton's conflict will lead only to further agonizing and decompensation. Such continued exploration leaves Alicia in a state of constant terror about her future. A decision needs to be made in the interest of both patients and Alicia's therapist firmly recommends that Alicia be made a dependent ward of the court to protect her from capricious and ever-changing living arrangements and to insure that a safe, stable, predictable home will be found for her.

Mrs. Compton's relief is evident and immediate, even though she is clearly saddened. Miss Howell seems willing to yield some of her insistence on her plan to send Alicia to the younger aunt.

Alicia's therapist informs the Child Protective Services worker of the plan, making it plain that no psychotherapy can be of any utility in these unstable circumstances. He informs the C.P.S. worker that he plans to have a few meetings with Mrs. Compton to assist her in working out the questions she will want to put to the C.P.S. worker about how a new home for Alicia will be found, how her going there will be accomplished, what her visiting rights and arrangements will be, etc. Alicia's therapist tries to convey his sense of the importance of these preparatory sessions to help Mrs. Compton maintain as much of the mothering as she can while permitting her to give Alicia this opportunity for greater stability. This period of time will also permit the therapist to help Alicia prepare for the change and to introduce her to the new person at C.P.S. who will find her new home.

Unfortunately, at her first meeting with Mrs. Compton, the C.P.S. worker becomes overly concerned with the mother's ambivalence and, fearing that she will oppose court wardship, urges Mrs. Compton to bring Alicia immediately to an emergency shelter prior to finalizing placement plans. This advice is offered, in part, out of the worker's awareness that, in her city, court wardship is much easier to arrange when a child is already in "emergency" placement. Frightened and confused by this unanticipated extra step, Mrs. Compton does not appear with Alicia at the Children's Shelter, nor does she return with Alicia to Alicia's therapist. All efforts by Alicia's therapist to reestablish contact are stonewalled—at least until the next crisis. C.P.S. cannot proceed further in the absence of overt child abuse and Alicia is left with no one to act in her interest, with the possible exception of her mother's psychiatrist.

Discussion

There are countless children like Alicia who are the victims of unintended abuse and neglect. Aside from her father's overt abuse, about which little is known, Alicia's caretakers are not without concern for her. Her predicament is a consequence of her mother's chronic illness with its periodic, acute disorganized episodes and her aunt's growing weariness, age and illness.

Intended or not, Alicia's life has been severely and constantly disrupted by endless moves and unceasing instability. In such circumstances, there has been no possibility for her to develop a sense of certainty, predictability or safety. She lives in a state of continuing terror which makes it impossible for her to get on with the business of childhood—learning, building friendships, developing her talents and interests. The external chaos has, clearly, been internalized. Despite the fact that she is conscious of her terror and even somewhat aware of the realities which promote it, she is unable, in the face of continuous trauma, to construct either cognitive or affective defenses to deal with her distress. Nor is it possible—or even desirable—to begin to try to help Alicia psychotherapeutically, given the unremitting disruptions in her world. Attempts to sort out reality from fantasy or the specific distortions that Alicia may superimpose on her actual experiences would be futile until adequate protection and stability can be achieved. This principle underlies much of the thinking about the first interventions which must be made when working with abused and neglected children.

The school properly recognizes that Alicia is immobilized and in considerable psychological distress. Their referral to a psychiatric center is a logical outcome of their focus on Alicia's disturbance. Fortunately and correctly, the therapist who begins to work with Alicia recognizes the impossibility of offering psychological services alone, without simultaneously attending to this child's primary need for an ordered and safe environment. He is immediately confronted with the contesting interests of Alicia, her mother and her aunt.

Miss Howell's interests seem fairly transparent. After a lifetime of caring for her sisters and her niece, she wants out and now. The pressures upon her lead her to construct an ill-considered plan to place Alicia with her youngest sister. Only inadvertently—and perhaps under the impetus of unconscious guilt—does she reveal that her youngest sister may be an inappropriate caretaker. It is likely that this revelation, combined with the opportunity to receive some acknowledgement from the therapist for responsibilities and burdens she has shouldered for many years, permits Miss Howell to give the therapist time and room to work out an alternative plan.

Mrs. Compton's intense ambivalence poses greater difficulties. Initially, Alicia's therapist attempts to help Mrs. Compton decide whether to keep Alicia or to place her. He discovers, along with Mrs. Compton's therapist, that a therapeutically neutral stance—in the service of maximum self-determination—leads to Mrs. Compton's further disintegration. In spite of her declarations, she is clearly incapable of confronting her ambivalent dilemma. Collaboratively, the two therapists come to understand the psychodynamic necessity of making an unequivocal recommendation. Mrs. Compton's relief is evident and within these conditions she can begin to consider the ways in which she can retain as much parenting as possible, without being the primary caretaker. She can now work actively with the therapist on the many things she needs to know and plan to accomplish a satisfactory placement for Alicia.

At the initiative of Alicia's therapist, the Child Protective Services worker's help is once again enlisted. The therapist makes a considerable effort to explain the complex psychodynamics of Mrs. Compton's ambivalence, stressing the importance of remaining firm about the need for placement underwritten by court wardship. He forewarns the C.P.S. worker that Mrs. Compton will likely act out her ambivalence and urges that sufficient time be taken in arranging the placement to permit Mrs. Compton and Alicia adequate preparation for and participation in the arrangements. Regrettably, the C.P.S. worker does not grasp all of the psychological nuances and cannot resist an impulsive response to Mrs. Compton's intense and potentially disruptive ambivalence. All too aware of Alicia's need for protection and Mrs. Compton's vacillation, the worker unilaterally initiates an unnecessary step. The sudden introduction of an interim shelter placement serves to upset a very delicately balanced approach and moves the entire situation back to a crisis state. Mrs. Compton removes herself and Alicia from the people who can help.

The worker's error is in part based upon her thorough knowledge of the placement system. Her attention to the needs of the "system" rather than to the subjective realities and their imperatives has compounded the existing crisis in the Compton family.

MONICA REIFER

Four-and-a-half-year-old Monica was brought to the Emergency Room of a hospital late one Sunday evening by her father. Her anus was red, and excoriated with some bleeding, while her vaginal area was also inflamed with small breaks in the skin. The father was highly agitated and upset. Monica's 20-month-old sister had come with them to the hospital.

Mr. Reifer cried as he gave his account of being unable to control himself with Monica. She had been alternately encopretic and retentive for some time. She had gone without a bowel movement for many days. He could no longer stand it. He knew she was in pain and finally had begun to insert his fingers into her anus to get at the feces. When Monica began to shriek and bleed he became frightened and came to the hospital.

Monica and her baby sister were admitted to the pediatric ward. The father remained with them, pacing and agitated although Monica tried again and again to soothe and comfort him. She repeatedly asked him to hold her hand and stroked him lovingly whenever he would calm down.

The following morning a consultant from the child psychiatry service met with the father at the request of the pediatric staff.

Mr. Reifer wept frequently as he gave the following information. His wife had left him some three weeks ago. She insisted she could no longer tolerate his periodic drinking or his depression, since his recent "tragedy." At first he was reluctant to give details of this, but in response to some gentle inquiry he revealed that some months ago he had severely injured a pedestrian while driving, adding, "I was sober—honestly." Since then he has been beset by legal charges and other pressures including his wife's leaving. "I wish I were dead, myself," he stated.

He had become so depressed after the tragedy that he had been hospitalized briefly and was still in outpatient treatment.

The therapist acknowledged the enormous pressure Mr. Reifer had been under and noted that last night he clearly felt he could not control himself. He responded by giving a detailed account of last night's events with Monica. He loved Monica—how could he have hurt her so? He was no good—he deserved to be punished, hurt himself.

Once again the therapist acknowledged his grief, noting however that the nurses had told her that, in spite of last night's attack, Monica had tried to comfort him, suggesting that she loved her daddy very much. Mr. Reifer shook his head desolately.

The therapist asked the father's permission to contact his psychiatrist and meet with Monica. She told him that she would be calling the Child Protective Services to let them know about the problem and to enlist their help in planning for the family. She also asked if he had anything to eat that morning. He was not hungry, but accepted her offer of a cup of coffee and agreed to wait for her return shortly.

Contacting his psychiatrist, the therapist learned that the father was hospitalized because he had been potentially suicidal. She was now further convinced that the father might once again be suicidal and determined to help Mr. Reifer be seen immediately for further assessment and possible hospitalization.

She then met with Monica, a beautiful child, who was very eager to please. The therapist introduced herself to Monica as a lady who tried to help children with their troubles. Monica said she had lots of troubles. Her Daddy was so sad—she just couldn't make Daddy feel better. And Mommie wasn't home anymore. She just comes once in a while.

She wanted to go home with Daddy and her sister. The therapist told Monica that those were lots of big troubles and that last night must surely have been terrible and scarey. Monica reluctantly and shyly whispered that she was scared when Daddy got so mad—but she loved her Daddy and wanted to go home. Efforts to elicit last night's frightening events were resisted by Monica and the therapist told Monica that she would go see Daddy now and come back soon to talk again.

A second interview with Mr. Reifer followed and the therapist was successful in persuading him to see his psychiatrist with whom she had spoken and who would be able to see him. He, too, needed help. They planned together how he would tell Monica that he must leave and the therapist remained available in Monica's room while he explained that he, too, must go to the hospital for a little while.

Monica was deeply upset. The therapist promised that Monica and Daddy would talk together on the phone and that she would try to help Monica with her big troubles.

Indeed, Monica and her father, who was hospitalized, talked several times that day on the phone. Once Monica was overheard to say, "Daddy, you are in the hospital and I am in the hospital but we should be together."

Later in the afternoon, as the therapist had promised, she returned to see Monica. This time she brought with her an array of play material: paper, Scotch tape, crayons, several puppets, a doll and two telephones.

Initially Monica remained silent and morose.

The therapist commented on Monica's sadness and said that a little girl could feel all mixed up—sad and mad and hurt—when her mommie and daddy were away. Monica began to listen—but silently (in contrast to her previous quick verbal action). Maybe Monica was mad at the therapist. Did she think the therapist sent Daddy away? No response.

The therapist took two puppets and held a conversation between the two. One puppet (a little bear) asked the other if he thought maybe something bad he did made his Daddy go away. Monica was now fully attentive, as the second puppet replied that little bears could have all sorts of puzzling and mixed up ideas when bad things happened. And it's so hard when they have no one to ask and figure things out with.

Monica whispered, "The little bear is bad."

The therapist offered Monica a puppet. She chose the little bear and a puppet play ensued in which the therapist and Monica "figured" together. Drawing upon the information she had about the mother's departure, the therapist asked Monica's puppet about this. The little bear replied that she and her sister didn't always mind, Mommie got tired and then there were fights. Sometimes with Daddy; sometimes little bear got very scared too. Through the puppet play a somewhat more detailed picture was evoked about the previous night's experience. While this play went on Monica moved her puppet on and off her hand looking and poking inside. The therapist commented on this—the little bear was getting poked. What could be inside? Did he hurt inside? Monica put the puppet down. She searched in the toy kit, selecting the "sticky Scotch tape." Again and again she tore pieces and placed them on a sheet of colored paper. The therapist noted how well the Scotch tape sticks—the paper stays with it. They don't come apart. It's nice to keep things together. More and more Scotch tape was used and Monica now vigorously reported, "It's a mess." "Yup," the therapist agreed, "it's a mess, but it does stick together."

Discussion

In this instance, the pediatric ward is being used to protect and shelter Monica and her sister. Important assessments and dispositions have to be made for the entire Reifer family. It is clear that Mr. Reifer has been under enormous pressures and is breaking down under their weight. In spite of his decompensation and loss of control, he obviously loves his children and has rapidly sought help. This step is certainly motivated by his care for and wish to protect his children. Very likely it is also motivated by his overwhelming guilt which seeks retribution. His account is clear, informative and honest.

Monica demonstrates her attachment and her precocity in her efforts to comfort her father. Efforts to comfort an abusing parent are not unusual in abused children.

The therapist actively engages Mr. Reifer in the necessary steps which need to be taken. She is available to hear his story and to mobilize other important helpers—his psychiatrist and child protection services. This practical "taking care of business" also has psychological importance, conveying the message that the problems are manageable and that solutions can be sought and found. Her attention is given to Mr. Reifer and his needs, as well as to the children. A more purely psychological intervention with Mr. Reifer is her effort to relieve some of his guilt and grief by reporting the nurses' observations of Monica's obvious love and concern for him. He is not consoled by this intervention. A tangible effort is made to demonstrate concern for him, by asking if he has eaten; the effect of this intervention is unknown. However, all of these efforts in his behalf may pave the way for his acceptance of her recommendation that he see his psychiatrist immediately.

The next piece of her work is with Monica directly, taking place over two separate meetings on the same day. The first of these is aimed primarily at establishing contact with Monica, and identifying and explaining the therapist's function to Monica. Efforts to engage Monica in discussion of the previous night's events are resisted except for Monica's whispered acknowledgement that she was very scared. The therapist chooses to push no further.

In a second meeting with Mr. Reifer the therapist helps him to prepare himself and Monica for their separation. At a time when his resources are obviously depleted, remaining present and available while he talks to Monica is a vital supportive intervention for both father and child. In this second meeting Monica appears, initially, more listless, sad and less connected. The therapist finds a way to re-engage Monica through the "once-displaced" medium of the puppets. At first, Monica is a silent audience to the dialogue which the therapist assumes is present in Monica's thinking. Monica confirms the correctness of this assumption by becoming an active puppeteer and by extending the material to include issues of omnipotent, magical four-and-a-half-year-old thoughts about her responsibility for her mother's departure and her father's anger. In a more symbolic way the traumatic events of the prior evening are played out with the puppet. The therapist tries to extend this play and link it more directly with the previous night. This appears to be too much for Monica and the play is disrupted. It is replaced, however, by the Scotch tape activities which are simultaneously defensive, restitutive and communicative. Some of Monica's resiliency is evident in her vigorous report that "it's a mess," which the therapist supports by a simple agreement and extends to include the idea that whatever the mess, sticking together is possible. This is only the beginning of the crisis resolution and of the more definitive and longer-range tasks which need to be addressed. These include:

1) Provide information to C.P.S. and work with them to devise a plan of action to serve Monica's best interests.
2) Introduce C.P.S. worker to Monica and help bridge that contact.
3) Arrange for father to visit his children if he is sufficiently able to control suicidal depression.
4) Locate the mother and determine her capacity to take over the children's care.
5) Find a foster home where both children can remain together or use a shelter facility, until the parents can reestablish a home.

6) Arrange for Monica's treatment for her anxiety and depression which are starting to be manifest in her bowel symptoms and, very likely, in her costly developmental precocity.

DIVORCE

"It was the very worst day of my life," said a 15-year-old to her therapist. "The day the judge asked me to stand up and say which one of my parents I wanted to live with. He told me I could make the choice. What choice—that's no choice! I had to say I wanted to go with my mother. She looked like she needed me more; she was crying so hard. So I went with my mother, but that's not the way I wanted it to be at all."

There is a growing body of psychological and sociological literature addressing the phenomenon of divorce and its impact on children and families. Most of this literature documents the increasing prevalence of divorce as a solution to marital difficulties, with some authors likening the phenomenon to an epidemic. The psychological literature documents the profound impact which divorce has on all family members. The psychological impact on the children in divorcing families has been shown to be more extensive, more complex and more long lasting than previously believed. The literature describes in great detail the struggles with loss, separation, and realignment which characterize the crisis of divorce. Therapists who work with children and families probably encounter this crisis event more than any single other. Sometimes the therapeutic contact occurs at particularly sharp moments of the crisis such as at the point of separation or at the moment of a custody battle. At other times therapists become involved long after these intense moments are over but when some intercurrent event has revived some unresolved issues and the child's coping mechanisms are failing.

The following cases illustrate the work with two children at different points in this life crisis.

TOMMY SMITH

Tommy provides a glimpse of how a ten-year-old struggled with his anguish as a final custody hearing approached. His parents separated when Tommy was six, but they remained in regular contact and combat. As the court date neared, Tommy became so obviously depressed that his teacher referred him to a nearby psychiatric outpatient clinic.

This depression had been somewhat masked by other symptoms: a failure to learn and storms in the classroom which seemed to come out of the blue. In the initial diagnostic meetings, Tommy acknowledged that he sometimes toyed with the idea that he might escape his endless turmoil by throwing himself out of a window. He was sure the judge would ask him to select the parent with whom he wanted to live. He had no answer—if he selected one, the other would be deeply hurt and angry.

Later, he drew a picture of two angry, battling adults who hovered over the head of a small, helpless child, each pulling in his own direction. This was no fantasy; his drawing truly depicted his short-fused parents and his situation.

The therapist commented that a boy could indeed feel helpless and hopeless about such persistent struggles. Sometimes, it might feel to him that they were going on inside himself. She thought that such a boy might not always be able to concentrate on his own work. Tommy agreed, adding important detail about how hard it was to concentrate on school work; the worries simply kept coming into his mind.

After a pause, he asked if the therapist would like to know how he tried to send the thoughts away. His "imaginings" helped. Some time ago, when he could not sleep, he began these "imaginings." He had begun to think of ways of finding a big mansion. Only children would be permitted to live there—no grown-ups. They would have to find a way to become self-supporting. Somehow they would gain control of a supermarket and a particular ice cream company—his specially favorite brand. They would be able to manufacture enough ice cream to supply all the needy children in the world, even those in Africa. He had gradually shared this fantasy with a friend, who also liked to play this game they called "Controlling Companies." These two "industrialists" had extended their control over transportation systems in order to insure the distribution of their ice cream holdings. Tommy became quite immersed in detailing this complicated fantasy to his therapist.

It needs no stretch of the imagination to understand this child's efforts to escape from the realities of his daily experiences. Nor is it difficult to see why he must have a mansion from which all adults are banished. He and his friend will gain control over a vast industrial complex when, in fact, Tommy is helpless to control his painful life situation. The needy will be nourished and comforted, as he is not. In short, the realities of Tommy's life, including his own adaptational efforts, shape his fantasies while impoverishing his learning.

JULIE O'CONNOR

Julie is a nine-and-a-half-year-old girl whose parents separated when she was four. The parents have joint custody and Julie has spent alternate months at each of their homes. She has attended one school since kindergarten and has been able to maintain friends despite her monthly shifts. Julie has her own room, clothing and toys at each home but, despite this, the two households are very different. Her father remarried when Julie was six and he and his second wife live in a very ordered and scheduled way. Her mother is also remarried to a man who travels a great deal and has limited contact with Julie. The mother's household is much less organized and her schedule is erratic. Many last-minute baby-sitters and outings are a regular part of Julie's life at her mother's house. These life-style differences were a major cause of the parents' divorce and are a persistent source of disagreement about raising Julie. Julie is well aware of these disagreements and, despite her own irritation with her mother, she frequently defends her against the thinly-veiled criticisms offered by her father and stepmother. Her need to protect her mother, who is less well off, is a source of considerable conflict for Julie, who secretly longs for permanent residence in her father's more stable household while maintaining understandably strong ties to her mother.

Julie's struggle with this conflict has increased in the past year, especially since Julie learned of her stepmother's pregnancy. Her father has become concerned about her "whiney" behavior and some deterioration in the previously good relationship with her stepmother. When her teachers also expressed concern about Julie's changed behavior at school, he sought psychotherapeutic help for Julie. Surprisingly, all the adults agreed that this was a proper course of action.

The first ten hours of Julie's therapy were spent exploring several major themes:

1) Julie's unhappiness about the impending arrival of the new baby, which would, once again, change her life.
2) The corollary worry that she would no longer have as stable a place with her stepmother and, less consciously, with her father.
3) Increasing anger with her mother for not giving Julie enough—a reflection of a more general fear of not getting enough from anyone.
4) Some acute anxiety in response to her mother's invitation to "express her anger" by hitting or biting her mother. This was

particularly frightening for Julie at this time, when many complicated and disturbing feelings were very close to the surface.

The ninth and tenth hours focused on these themes in relation to Julie's upcoming month-long visit to her grandparents' ranch. In these two hours Julie described a fight with her mother about a promise which her mother had not kept. She spoke again of her mother's invitation to Julie to express her anger by retaliating with hitting or biting. Julie told the therapist that she wouldn't really hurt her mother, although she felt like it. "I only bit her finger gently. Hardly at all. Though I felt like punching her all up." Immediately thereafter, Julie made a cast for her arm out of paper. She then assured her therapist that she really could use the arm for some things and suggested that they play checkers. During this quiet game she reported that she both liked and hated to play checkers. Particularly, she hated to play checkers with her mother who "doesn't always pay attention."

The eleventh session, just before Julie's school vacation, was described by her therapist as follows:

Julie arrives with her mother. Julie is wearing a long skirt pulled up over her chest with a sweater over the skirt. She is sucking on a red candy.

Julie: It will take me 50 minutes to finish this—it takes a long time.
Th: That's how much time we have left together before you go away on vacation. That looks like good candy.
Julie: It's cherry, my favorite. I had it in my freezer for a month now. I've got 12 of them saved. Want to know what they're made of? (She reads the list of ingredients which are mostly sugar and chemicals.) Nothing real, all artificial. But, it tastes good. (She holds up the sucker and looks through it at me.) I can't see you that well now but I will be able to when it gets thinner.
Th: Yes, things do change as time passes. That makes me think that you're going away for quite a long time. When you first go away you think about all the things you will be doing and maybe it's harder to think about the people and things you've left behind. Then, as the time grows nearer to coming back home, you think about seeing everyone again and remember them more.
Julie: (laughs) Yeah.
Th: You can keep a picture of me and everyone you want to remember in your mind while you're away.
Julie: You mean *draw* a picture?

Th: Oh?

Julie: (She closes one eye and draws in the air.) I'll draw this side of you. OK? (She closes the other eye.) Now the other side . . . wait, let me get your hair right. There, now I've got you!

Th: Did you draw a picture of your family?

Julie: I did those yesterday. I've got everybody. (She puts down the sucker.) I'll finish this later. Can I go to the bathroom to wash my hands? They're all sticky.

Th: Of course.

Julie: (Returns and sits down) Do you have any horse books?

Th: No. I'll bet you're thinking about horses because there will be horses at the ranch.

Julie: And I'll wear my riding outfit I got for my birthday.

Th: I'm very interested in horses. Can you tell me about them?

Julie: My favorite horses are thoroughbreds and plough horses.

Th: How are they different?

Julie: A thoroughbred races and a plough horse works on a farm.

Th: Hmm. So one has to be very fast and the other has to work very hard.

Julie: Yes.

Th: Those sound like very different horses and yet you like both of them.

(pause)

Julie: Can we play checkers? (Goes to the drawer and opens it and sees the dart guns. She takes one and aims it at the wall and shoots it. Then she turns toward me and smiles.)

Th: That's the very first game you and I played together here.

Julie: Yes. We can use the target I made.

Th: OK. I'll get it for us.

Julie: (takes the target and tapes it on the wall and shoots at it) Now it's your turn. (therapist takes a turn)

Julie: Now, let's shoot together. We'll stand here together and I'll say one, two, three, go.

(We shoot together several times and she is delighted with this.)

Julie: Now let's stand here together and we'll shoot the birds. (referring to a rag-hanging with bird designs on it) You shoot the one on the left and I'll shoot the one on the right.

Th: It is fun to do things together. I will remember the things we have done together while you are away and I'll think of you.

(While she is shooting the long skirt she is wearing falls to her waist and drags on the floor.)

Th: You're having a difficult time with that.

Julie: Yes, it's a sundress. (She pulls up her sweater and shows me how she wears the skirt up past her chest.) It needs straps here to hold it up better. My mother gave it to me.

Th: Will she help you put the straps on?

Julie: Yes. (She puts the dart gun away and goes to take out the checkers but changes her mind.) No, let's play doctor. (Opens the doctor's bag and takes out stethoscope and listens to her heart. The earplugs hurt her and she complains.)

Th: Let's see if I can stretch them so they don't hurt. (I stretch them and hand them back to her and she listens again.)

Julie: That's better. My heart is going boom ba boom. Here, now you listen to your heart. (I do so.)

Julie: OK, now you'll be the patient and I'll be the doctor. Now, I'll take your temperature. (makes believe she puts a thermometer in my mouth) And, I'll take your blood pressure, too. (makes believe she is wrapping the blood pressure cuff around my arm) (She checks the thermometer.) Hmm, you've got a fever. Let me check your blood pressure. (She pretends to check.) Hmm, not good. I think you need an operation.

Th: What? Why?

Julie: You've got an infection in your arm. You need surgery.

Th: Surgery! Well, I need more information than that to agree to surgery.

Julie: I'll call your mother and ask for her permission. What's her name?

Th: What do you imagine it might be?

Julie: (thinks) I'll call her Mildred. (She telephones.) Hello, this is Dr. O'Connor. Your daughter needs surgery on her arm and I'll have to operate. I'd like your permission. (aside to me) She gave me it.

Th: Just a minute. I'd like to discuss this with her. A mother needs to talk with her daughter about such a big decision.

Julie: OK, here's the phone.

Th: Hello, Mom. I don't think I need surgery on my arm and I don't think you should give your permission. I think there is another way to fix my arm, without surgery, and that needs to be discussed first. (I hand the phone back to Julie.) My mother agrees.

Julie: (takes phone) Hello, Mildred this is Dr. O'Connor again and I think your daughter needs the surgery. (sinister smile) She gave me her permission again!

Th: Well, I think there must be another way to fix my arm and we haven't talked about it. Like, what caused the infection?

Julie: I don't know. (She takes the play knife from the drawer and sadistically smiles as she pretends to sharpen it.) This will really make it sharp. (Then, from a distance, she makes cutting gestures.) Chop, chop, chop, all in pieces. I have to go to the bathroom, alright?

Th: You've asked my permission about several things today—about washing your hands, playing checkers, going to the bathroom. Today you're not sure about what's OK to do. Maybe you have lots of unsure feelings.

Julie: (She leaves for the bathroom and returns quickly.) Now I'll cut the infection out right here and it will be all gone. I don't think I'll have to cut your whole arm off after all. Just this infected part.

Th: I don't think even that has to be cut out and I don't think I need any surgery. And I don't want surgery.

Julie: I won't hurt you, it won't hurt a bit, you'll only be in the hospital a few days and you'll be all better.

Th: I don't want to go to the hospital.

Julie: (sincerely) I promise it won't hurt and you won't have to go to the hospital and this is a plastic knife.

Th: Oh, I see, I'm in good hands and you wouldn't really hurt me and this is pretend.

Julie: Yes, see. (She makes believe she cuts at my arm.) Did that hurt?

Th: No. It's good to know I'm in good hands and won't be hurt.

Julie: Now I'll call your father and ask him to pay the bill. What's his name? I'll call him Jason. Hello, this is Dr. O'Connor. Your daughter had surgery and it didn't hurt and it cost $2,000. Will you pay the bill? You'd like to talk with her. (hands me the phone)

Th: Hello, Dad. Yes, I think I was in good hands with Dr. O'Connor. She was sure not to hurt me. (I hand her the phone.)

Julie: (big smile) Well, thank you, Jason, I'll send you the bill.

Th: You know Julie, there are other ways of fixing hurts than cutting them out. Last week you had a cast on your arm and this week I had surgery on my arm. I think you're worried about going away and some of those worried feelings about your mom that we talked about. I know you wish you could get rid of them so you won't have to worry about her while you're away. But I think that those feelings will be safe inside you and that when you come back we can figure them out together. Our time is almost up.

Julie: (big smile) I'll help put things away.

Th: I will miss you and I look forward to hearing all the exciting things you will have done at the ranch. Should I write to you?

Julie: Yes. (smiles)

(As I open the door Julie's mother is standing out in the hallway.)

Julie: (runs to her mother and hugs her) Mommy, Mommy, will you give her Grandma and Grandpa's address?

Mother: Both of you sure look like you've had a good time. I don't have the address with me but I'll call you and give it to you.

Th: Goodbye. Goodbye, Julie, have fun.

Discussion

Julie's experience of joint custody is, as indicated, becoming a more and more common one for today's children.* Fortunately, she is able to live in the same neighborhood so her schooling and friendships are not disrupted. As in many such instances, the difference between her parents' styles of living are sharpened by the shuffling back and forth between the two households. As a consequence, Julie's "loyalty conflict" is heightened and perpetuated.

This is evident in her secret yearning to remain in her father's more stable home and in her continuous protection of her mother. Despite this, Julie has managed reasonably well, which points to her good capabilities and adaptation. The forthcoming arrival of a new baby has threatened this adaptation and the expectable vulnerability to disruption has led to some regression and symptom formation.

Julie is an eminently treatable child. In the first ten hours, she quickly reveals the preoccupying concerns which have led to her regression. Feelings and worries are close to the surface and she is trusting enough to be able to make a good alliance with her therapist. They have gone to work rapidly and psychotherapy is well under way. The ninth and tenth hours center, in large part, on Julie's struggle with aggressive and sadistic wishes which have been seductively activated by her mother's invitation to "express her anger." Julie tries very hard to defend against these unthinkable wishes, demonstrated by immobilizing her arm. She then partly works this through by immediately avowing that her arm is still serviceable.

The work continues in the eleventh hour, which is largely structured around the impending disruption of the visit to her grandparents' ranch. Julie's cue about the sucker permits the therapist to pick up the idea of time passing, to connect it to the upcoming separation and

---

*The California State Legislature, in its 1982 session, considered a bill which would make it mandatory for the courts to award joint custody whenever possible. While the particular bill did not pass, it does seem to be a reflection of a growing sentiment.

to use it as a paradigm for the many feelings related to the constant comings and goings. Probably, in her effort to be as supportive and understanding as possible, the therapist has generalized, condensed and packaged more than she needs to for this capable child. Although this "summary" is, in all likelihood, globally correct, it does tend to obstruct and obscure the particular issues which Julie might elect to discuss about the ranch. Similarly, the therapist's introduction of keeping pictures of people in the mind takes the initiative further from Julie, who, however, recovers it by her pretend drawings. In both interchanges the therapist's intent is to support: Julie "reminds" her therapist that an exploratory approach is more productive. Her "drawings in the air" might, as readily, have been a response to a therapeutic inquiry such as, "What might you do to take with you things you wanted to remember while at your grandparents?"

Julie's request to leave the playroom may simply be, as she states, a wish to clean sticky hands. It may also be prompted by some anxiety about leaving her family. When she returns, she introduces the new theme: horses. The therapist once again ties this content to the ranch but, this time, continues in a more exploratory mode. Julie's response, and the interchange which follows, allows them to develop the idea that it is possible and acceptable to like two very different kinds of horses. The metaphor of the different horses is sufficiently close to her parents—one works very hard, the other races around—that it need not be made more explicit at this time.

The pause between this conversation and Julie's decision to start a game suggests that she has done enough work on this for the moment. Intent on finding the checkers, she goes instead to the dart guns which leads them to recall their history together, and to enjoy themselves. This "recapitulation" is a very common event in hours preceding an interruption in therapy.

A second effort to start a checker game—which is known to be a charged activity linked to ambivalence about her mother—is deflected by the discovery of the doctor kit. This heralds a long sequence concerned with Julie's struggle with aggression. Julie's play with the doctor kit appears to be more conflict-specific than the general use which children make of these play materials to portray issues of hurt, hurting and help, since it is clearly connected back to the earlier hour in which her own offending arm had to be casted. The therapist's position in this exchange sides with delay, thoughtful review and less drastic action. Under the guise of helper, Julie persists in her wish to cut off the infected arm. At first she is gleeful in her persistence but soon asks to leave—evidence of some mounting anxiety. Upon her return, she has a compromise: She won't cut the arm off, she will only excise the infection. The therapist continues to urge delay and review and Julie compromises further, first assuring that it won't hurt and then that it is only plastic and pretend. The therapist makes a very imaginative and skillful validation of their common understanding that pretend aggression is very different from real "hitting and biting," by her simple statement that she (the pretend patient) sees that she is in good hands.

In this sequence, Julie's portrayal of the differentiated roles assigned to each of her parents is of interest. The mother is called upon to give permission for the sadistic surgery. At the conclusion of the successful event, the father is called upon to foot the bill. Julie's identification with her therapist's approach is portrayed by Julie's spontaneous offer to let the patient talk to her father, an adoption of the therapist's prior "invention."

The hour ends with the therapist's effort to tie everything up in a neat bundle. This is, undoubtedly, motivated by the pressure of the upcoming long separation. It is a common effort which many therapists make in such circumstances and represents a sort of imagined innoculation against anxiety. It rarely has that effect. However, when the therapist-patient relationship is as good as this one obviously is, the patient will simply forgive and ignore whatever she cannot use.

The final moments are more productively directed at maintaining their connection and anticipating their reunion. The simple and genuine feelings in this exchange are not ignored, and are much appreciated by Julie.

REFERENCES

1. Chess, S., Thomas, A., Metheman, M., and Cohen, J., Early parental attitudes, divorce and separation and young adult outcome: Findings of a longitudinal study. *J. of Amer. Academy of Child Psychiatry*, 1983, Vol. 22(1): 47-51.
2. Connell, P. H., Suicidal attempts in childhood and adolescence. In J. H. Howells (Ed.), *Modern perspective on child psychiatry*. New York: Brunner/Mazel, 1965.
3. Egeland, B. et al., A prospective study of the antecedents of child abuse. *National Institute of Mental Health Reports*, September, 1979.
4. Egeland, B., Breitenbucher, M., and Rosenberg, D., Prospective study of the significance of life stress in the etiology of child abuse. *Journal of Consulting Clinical Psychology*, 1980, Vol. 48(2): 195-205.
5. Fraiberg, S., and Fraiberg, L., *Studies in infant mental health*. New York: Basic Books, 1981.
6. Garmezy, N., and Rutter, M. (Eds.), *Stress, coping, and development*. New York: McGraw-Hill, 1983.

7. Green, A., Psychiatric treatment of abused children. *J. of Amer. Academy of Child Psychiatry*, 1978, Vol. 17(2): 356-371.
8. Hassibi, M., Children in crisis. In I. Glick et al. (Eds.), *Psychiatric Emergencies*. New York: Grune and Stratton, 1976.
9. Hetherington, E. M., Divorce, a child's perspective. *American Psychologist*, 1979, Vol. 34: 851-858.
10. Kinard, E., Experiencing child abuse: Effects on emotional adjustment. *Amer. J. of Orthopsychiatry*, 1982, Vol. 52(1): 82-90.
11. Lau, H. G., and Cooper, S., A night crisis. *Psychiatry*, 1973, Vol. 36(1): 23-36.
12. Letourneau, C., Empathy and stress: How they affect parental aggression. *Journal of Social Work*, 1981, Vol. 26(5): 383-388.
13. Rembar, J., Novick, J., and Kalter, N., Attrition among families of divorce: Patterns in an outpatient psychiatric population. *J. of Amer. Academy of Child Psychiatry*, 1982, Vol. 21(4): 409-413.
14. Schoettle, V. C., and Cantwell, D. P., Children of divorce. *J. of Amer. Academy of Child Psychiatry*, 1980, Vol. 19: 453-475.
15. Terr, L., Psychiatric trauma in children. *Amer. J. of Psychiatry*, 1981, Vol. 138: 14-19.
16. Wallerstein, J. S., and Kelly, J. B., *Surviving the breakup: How children and parents cope with divorce*. New York: Basic Books, 1980.
17. Weiss, E. H., and Berg, R. G., Child victims of sexual assault: Impact of court procedures. *J. of Amer. Academy of Child Psychiatry*, 1982, Vol. 21(5): 513-518.

CHAPTER 8

Adolescence

Adolescence has typically been conceptualized as a time of rapid growth, often characterized by turmoil and, if all goes well, eventual integration. Physical, cognitive and emotional growth spurt ahead, creating pressure for new adaptation, as well as opportunities to reconcile and resolve older conflicts.

All adolescents struggle with a heightened awareness of body changes and body concerns. Continuous and sometimes rapid alteration in size, contours, skin texture and hair distribution make for great uncertainty about who one is, even in physical terms. Every small change, even a new blemish, takes on enormous proportions. If one's corporeal self is inconstant, how then to form a solid sense of one's personal, internal and interpersonal self? This issue, of course, transcends body concerns. From the vast array of experience, each adolescent must select and order those partial identifications out of which to fashion a coherent and cohesive identity. Inherent in this effort is the adolescent wish and fear to be like and different from one's parents—to create a unique sense of self, separate from his or her family. While this is the central task of adolescence, it is a process which continues throughout life. Not everyone succeeds, and for some the organization of a solid identity is impaired and the sense of self remains fragmented and diffuse.

Other tasks and challenges are woven into this central process.

Among these are the establishment of new peer relationships which become increasingly more important as the adolescent moves away from the nuclear family. These group relationships aid the separation-individuation process and provide opportunities for experimentation with new emotions, new allegiances, and new behaviors. This experimentation is of great value, while it is also often a source of difficulty for some adolescents and worry for most parents. For teenagers and parents alike, there is often hidden competition and jealousy.

It is commonly recognized that, while the process of separation-individuation is lifelong, it is particularly heightened during toddlerhood and adolescence. With the beginnings of cognitive maturity, the reality of wider experiences apart from the family and the development of new loyalties, the adolescent is in a position to view the family from a new vantage point. For some, the "clay feet" come into sharp focus and this new perspective can be a shameful or painful vision.

The maturing cognitive capacity also provides the adolescent with opportunities to experiment with new ideas and ideologies. Ideas about ideas lead to the formation of moral and ethical codes and systems which are tried on and discarded sometimes in bewilderingly rapid order.

While the shape of such adolescent turmoil and integration is often influenced by the ethos of the current culture, it would be naive to presume that human nature radically alters to conform with the external pressure and style of a given time. Yet, it would be equally naive to presume that general societal and more temporal cultural forces do not influence some forms of adolescent experience and behavior.

Joseph Adelson, in a charming and thoughtful paper entitled, "The Mystique of Adolescence," suggests that Americans have always been excessively preoccupied by adolescence, tending to over-generalize and thus distort this stage of life. Speaking of the Adolescent Fool, embodied in such characters as Andy Hardy, who preoccupied us in the 50s, Adelson writes: "He was represented as a figure of fun: callow, flighty, silly, given to infatuations, wild enthusiasms and transient moodiness," or as "a rather harmless Werther: sensitive, emotionally afflicted, overly sentimental." In either case: "innocent, unrelated to intrigues and corruptions, or the moral seriousness of adulthood . . . (1, p. 1).

In the early 60s, we welcomed the Adolescent as Visionary, "distinguished by the purity of his moral vision which allows him to perceive or state the moral simplicity hidden by adult complication" (1, p. 1).

Prophet and victim, this prototype is victimized by adult corruption, neglect or disinterest. Adelson notes that side by side, and as anti-type to the Visionary, the early 60s provided another prototype, the Victimizer who is "cruel, sinister, and amoral" (1, p. 1). The Visionary Innocent is contrasted to the evil and omnipotent Victimizer.

The late 60s and early 70s offered still another set of prototypes: the Rebel, the Hedonist, the Esthete.

Saintliness juxtaposed against corruption, victim against victimizer, violence against aestheticism, hedonism against renunciation, foolishness against wisdom. We are tempted by extremes, extreme portrayals and often extreme solutions. If adolescence is not a time of psychological turbulence, is it then a time of quietude? If most adolescents quietly go about their lives, is it necessary to exclude all theoretical considerations that address turmoil and turbulence?

Probably not, although Bandura's reminder of an earlier time must be heeded: He comments, "If a society labels its adolescents . . . and expects them to be rebellious, unpredictable, sloppy and wild in their behavior and if this picture is repeatedly reinforced by the mass media, such cultural expectations may very well force adolescents into the role of rebel" (3, p. 24).

It is startling to recall that a phrase so generally in use such a short time ago has seemed to slip from our language. In the 60s and early 70s, we heard a great deal about the generation gap—a gap considered profound and unbridgeable. At that time, discontinuities in human experience were sharply emphasized. Despite a mood of optimism, challenge and a sense that events could be powerfully influenced by individual action, the late 60s and early 70s represented a time when struggle with elders was avowed, expected and understood to be the norm. At the end of this decade, there was less emphasis on discontinuity, and by the late 70s, "generation gap" had all but disappeared from the vernacular. Perhaps this is always so at a time when optimism wanes, and multiple and partial solutions to problems seem more prevalent than those more sharply drawn in a more revolutionary time and with more revolutionary fervor. It is a quieter time—a less optimistic time—with no clear major themes to capture the moment.

However, continuities and discontinuities have characterized the history of human civilization and of adolescence itself. There are times of turmoil and times of quieter integration, though every decade is marked by both, no matter what we choose to emphasize. In spite of a particular temporal ethos, most adolescents participate only peripherally in the major struggles which characterize a given period. Many researchers have reported that adolescents are typically far more like their own parents than unlike them, even during those times when discontinuities and differences are sharply emphasized.

Despite the difficulty in characterizing current times, and the recognition that characterizations do oversimplify from generalizations about small minorities, it would be equally foolish to disavow trends and issues which influence all of our lives.

There *are* profound changes taking place in American family life, changes which do influence development, and adolescent development in particular, and perhaps most powerfully in affiliative experience. Urie Bronfenbrenner speaks to this: "This feeling, and fact, of disconnectedness from people and activities has a name that has become familiar: alienation . . . ," adding that this sense of alienation "is rapidly reflected in the structure and function of individual human beings, particularly those who are still in the process of development: children and young people" (5, p. 53). Bronfenbrenner recognizes that although "alienation ultimately affects the individual, it has its roots in the institutions of society" (5, p. 53) and particularly in the institution of the family. In this, Bronfenbrenner joins with Erikson, who considers the relationship between culture and the individual as the world of outer reality: "a pervasive actuality . . . not simply an environment which merely surrounds you but one which is also in you and you in it" (7, p. 24).

How powerful this actuality is, is described by Settlage:

Largely because of television, today's adolescent has been exposed to societal and cultural problems on local, national, and international levels throughout his childhood years. . . . In past eras, a person could demarcate a limited segment of the world of reality and prepare himself to deal with a limited number of problems. Living in our age of instant communication at a time when the survival of mankind would appear to depend upon our ability to effect radical social change, today's generation feels its reality includes the entire world with all of its problems. . . . Probably as a result of these same circumstances, today's adult generation is much less sure of its values than were past generations. Contradictions, duplicities, and uncertainties abound. (14, pp. 84-85)

While Settlage suggests how current culture generally impinges on adolescent internal development, Bronfenbrenner turns his attention inward toward the direction of change within the American family. He characterizes this as one of disorganization rather than constructive development. Bronfenbrenner, among others, points to the rising number of mothers in the work force, the reduction in other adults who might substitute as caretakers, the rise in divorce rates, in single parent families and the poverty line or near poverty living of so many of these families, the even higher incidence of poverty for Black and other minority families, the rise in teenage pregnancy, and the demands on working parents whose energy is drained away from child care. Bronfenbrenner adds:

> It is not only parents of whom children are deprived but also people in general. Developments of recent decades—many in themselves beneficent—conspire to isolate children from the rest of society. The fragmentation of the extended family, the separation of residential and business areas, the breakdown of neighborhoods, zoning ordinances, occupational mobility, child labor laws, the abolition of the apprentice system, consolidated schools, supermarkets, television, separate patterns of social life for different age groups, the working mother, the delegation of child care to specialists—all these manifestations of progress operate to decrease opportunity and incentive for meaningful contact between children and people older or younger than themselves. (5, p. 54)

Speaking more directly to serious manifestations of alienation among adolescents, Bronfenbrenner notes "the rising rate of youthful runaways, school dropouts, drug abuse, suicide, delinquency, vandalism and violence" (5, p. 55). He adds that if present trends continue, one in every nine youngsters will appear in juvenile court before the age of 18. While care must be taken in understanding the meaning of such information, there seems to be inescapable evidence that family life—still the most powerful crucible for socialization—is under heavy stress today.

Clearly sociocultural forces do work to shape behavior. Nowhere, however, may the impact of such forces be seen more clearly than in the development of minority young people. Here, culture within culture—often culture at odds with wider societal forces—impinges on and shapes the transitional stage of adolescence. Seventeen-and-a-half-year-old Mary illustrates this clearly.

MARY MORISHITA

Mary Morishita is a sansei (third generation) Japanese-American, the second born in a family of four children to a nisei (second generation) housewife and a kibei blue collar worker. A kibei is a Japanese-American who was born in the United States, sent to Japan for his education, and returned to the United States when this was completed.

Mary has a sister three years older, a brother two years younger and a sister four years younger than herself. Both parents came from farm families who were interned briefly during World War II. Mary's parents met as adolescents in the internment camp. Ten years later Mary's father reestablished contact with her mother and began a courtship which consisted mainly of a correspondence and infrequent meetings. After five years of courtship, they were married and settled in an urban area away from either of their rural families.

Mrs. Morishita assumed responsibility for raising the children, administering their discipline and caring for the household, while the father assumed the role of breadwinner, rarely becoming involved with household and child-rearing responsibilities. The family, living apart from their own extended families, had no intimate social contacts.

Mrs. Morishita is one of eight children. She describes her own mother as busy and hard working, a woman who spoke little English and was unavailable to her, favoring an older and a younger sister, of whom Mrs. Morishita was exceedingly jealous. The mother likened her own older daughter to one of her sisters: "fast, smart and good at things." She saw herself as being much like Mary: "slow and neat." She spent her own girlhood close to home, doing housework and school work and attending a Buddhist church with her family.

The father, a second generation kibei, was the older of two children, with a younger sister. Mrs. Morishita said of her husband's family: "He hardly ever speaks to them, but he was very spoiled by his sister. He is stubborn and has a hot temper. Now, he is more like a boarder than a husband or father. He eats and sleeps at home but rarely talks to his children." The parents have not slept together for years, and the mother shares a bedroom with Mary. Although the mother clearly resents her husband's lack of involvement with the family, she consistently assumes the blame for what goes wrong in the household.

Since Mrs. Morishita had hoped for a son, Mary's birth was a disappointment. The one early developmental milestone the mother recalled clearly was her difficulty in toilet training Mary. Mary would become uncooperative and constipated when her mother began to bowel train her. This was finally accomplished at age three-and-a-half with the aid of suppositories. With the birth of her baby sister, Mary began once again to wet until age four-and-a-half. When she began kindergarten, Mary cried a good deal, complaining that her brother and sister could remain at home. She remained home often with colds and other ailments throughout elementary school. All school changes were difficult. She was an average student, though psychological tests revealed that she was in the bright normal level of intelligence. She began to menstruate at 12½ but refused to hear her mother's or older sister's explanations.

In junior high school, she became ever more nervous. Mary had one friend at school but was advised by her mother to see the friend less often whenever they disagreed or fought. On her sixteenth birthday, Mary was asked out by a boy but because this was to be a double-date with a white couple, her mother insisted that Mary ask her father for approval. Afraid to risk this, Mary decided not to go. In the eleventh grade, Mary asked to join a school club. However, since this required bus travel after dark, Mrs. Morishita insisted that Mary's father would have to take her, but both mother and daughter were too fearful to ask the father.

Mary began having overt problems around the age of 16½. She became depressed and suicidal and was hospitalized for approximately one month before being referred to a day treatment facility.

The precipitating stresses surrounding Mary's decompensation included the following. At about 16½, Mary got a job. Her mother reported that for the first time, Mary did not ask whether she might go ahead with this independent plan; she simply avowed her determination by stating: "You can't stop me." Once at work, Mary heard a "recording" which said she had made a "big mistake" and that she was in "big trouble." After the second day at work, Mary came home feeling dizzy and headachy, and told her mother that someone at work had put poison in her drink. The parents forced her to quit the job, and this was followed by a week of crying, depression and an inability to go to school.

In relating this story, the mother reported her reaction to Mary's defiance by going to work as: "See what happened to her."

Around the same time, Mary had written for information about becoming an oceanographer and had received a reply that she would need more education. Mary saw this as a rejection and felt badly. Soon after she began to think that teachers and students were talking about and laughing at her, saying she was "lazy and dumb."

In addition, her mother reported that Mary was fighting more with her only girlfriend and becoming increasingly jealous of the mother's greater attachment to the younger sister.

One further stress seemed to be the attention paid to her younger brother's birthday, which occurred just before she decided to go to work.

Soon after these events occurred, Mary began appointments at a mental health center and was placed on Stelazine in an effort to avoid hospitalization, which the parents strongly opposed. It was not until Mary's therapist went on vacation and Mary became suicidal and grossly psychotic that the family agreed to their daughter's hospitalization. During her hospitalization, she was described as confused, grossly delusional, constantly irritating and annoying to others, acting silly, childlike and testing limits. Visual hallucinations included seeing male teachers and boys, as well as male Japanese faces coming at her.

The psychological data is replete with evidence that Mary has always been a socially isolated girl whose efforts at autonomy, affiliation and assertion were marked by fear and ambivalence. Her impulsive, rebellious effort to put these strivings into action at 16½ led to sharp regression and primitive decompensation. Hostility was projected and the annihilation anxiety surrounding her feeble and unsuccessful efforts at separation-individuation was evident in her paranoid fear that she would be killed by her co-workers.

The intense and reciprocal ambivalent ties to her mother have all the hallmarks of a hostile symbiotic attachment. Stubbornness, jealousy, retentiveness and fear of loss are suggested in her toilet training history, the needy attachment to her mother, and the decompensation following her therapist's vacation. Fearful sexual pulls are also suggested in her hallucinations. Themes of being wrong and making mistakes testify to her fear of assertion, risk-taking and learning.

In addition, Mary's experiences serve to illustrate the manner in which cultural factors influence personality organization and disorganization.

Both of Mary's parents must perceive the world as a rather friendless, harsh environment. Both have been shaken from their moorings again and again. Mary's mother grew up in a primarily Japanese-speaking family, the less preferred among her siblings. The father, although favored as a son and spoiled by his sister, bore the burden of an acculturation which required that he leave his own roots to be educated in Japan. There, he was faced with a new cultural adaptation without family supports, and later returned to his family to readjust to this reentry.

Both parents were interned during World War II, a process we, in America, have still not dared to confront as a national disgrace. To be clearly told, "You are the enemy, untrustworthy and unworthy of retaining your freedom and the goods you have earned" is a powerful event that must organize one's weltanschauung. To resist a "paranoid" view of the world under such circumstances strains human toughness, resilience and ingenuity. That the Morishitas' distrust, suspicion and fear of the wider culture would fail to be transmitted to their children seems hardly plausible. The societal pressures toward a suspicious and distrustful "world view" were compounded for the Morishita family by their unique circumstances. Their decision to settle far from rural origins exerted another powerful influence. In a new and unfamiliar place, a new family must emerge developing new traditions in an environment that provides few supports. Alone and without help, this nuclear family must inevitably have sought to meet all affiliative needs within the confines of its small, tight group. And this small, tight group was not without its own internal strains and conflicts. Before children will dare to meet and, with friendliness, greet new people, they must have some parental permission. Molded by experiences of change, hostility and little support, it seems understandable that these parents were unlikely to offer that permission or the sense of safety in assertion.

Closed away from others, the traditional roles of husband and wife in Japanese life seem to have worked to inhibit the family's progression. Mrs. Morishita, shamed by her inability to quickly produce a male child, must have experienced her "disgrace" as alienating her from her husband. Why this posture was not reversed by the birth of the third and male child is unclear, but Mr. Morishita continued to move further and further away from his family. Perhaps, by then, family patterns had been well established. Fear characterized the mother's and Mary's relationships with the father. Mary's mother seemed to cling to Mary for sexual protection from her husband and in her perception that she and Mary were alike. Mary, in turn, favored less than her older sister and less than a wanted male child, clung desperately and ambivalently to her mother. The role of shame and responsibility in Japanese families, particularly for Japanese mothers, is well documented and may well intensify the potential for hostile symbiosis in such families.

If Bronfenbrenner and others are correct that the American family is subject to stresses and strains which produce alienation, how much more true is this for families such as Mary's? They face a double jeopardy by living in a culture within a culture. It is not surprising, then, that Mary's transition into mid-adolescence was tumultuous and fragmented.

The sense of alienation is indeed a most painful one. Many factors contribute to it, keeping people at a distance from one another. Cultural styles can be a force for cohesion—giving shape, style and individuality to groups. On the other hand, when cultural difference remains suspect or is denigrated, human affiliations become more difficult. For the adolescent, who still must integrate experiences anew—whether this be done quietly or noisily—the restrictions or inhibitions of experimentation and human connection are most at risk.

Treatment

Following her discharge from the psychiatric ward, Mary was referred to a day treatment center for adolescents. The center provided activities, group and individual therapy, along with family sessions. The staff of the center included Black, Asian and Caucasian professionals. Mary continued to receive medication which had been helpful in reducing her flagrant psychotic symptoms while she was hospitalized. Her therapist saw her twice weekly in individual sessions, worked with Mary's family, participated in the group therapy program and worked closely with the activities program staff. The following is the therapist's account of the first four months of Mary's treatment and the work with Mary's family.

First month

This period was characterized by much anxiety and Mary's inability to remain in the office for an entire 50-minute session. She would shift, uncomfortably, in her chair, turn away from me and "instruct" the clock to move more rapidly. She would become quite silly and, giggling, would offer the observation that she acted silly in order to get attention. Other similar anxious observations suggested that she was "parroting" comments made by others.

When asked what might help her to be more comfortable, she proposed that we go for a walk, which I agreed to, provided we could spend some time in the office. On these walks, she would hop on one foot or shuffle along beside me with frequent inappropriate gestures to strangers on the street. I did not admonish her for this behavior or attempt to stop it, but suggested instead that when she and I knew one another better, I expected that this behavior would diminish.

In the office, I had the impression that Mary experienced my questions as both intrusive and caring. She said, "You care because you ask a lot of questions . . . because you want to understand me . . . and help me with my problems." When I would ask her what she thought some of these problems were or how we could work together on these, her typical initial responses were, "I don't know" or "Just by talking." I could not be sure whether this type of response was defensive, obstinate, or showed some deficit in social skills.

Gradually, however, several themes emerged:

1) *Fear of making friends.* Mary recounted incidents which occurred at school prior to her breakdown in which others were talking about her and reacting to her "weirdly." I acknowledged that these thoughts about others were indeed very frightening. At the same time, I made observations about Mary's behavior in the group sessions and in the center, and suggested that we could use these observations to figure out how others were really responding to her and what might be the relationship between her behavior and the reactions of others. These first efforts at reality testing would lead to obvious discomfort and I did not press them. Toward the end of the first month, Mary could acknowledge that she "felt rotten when the kids said I was behaving like a baby."

2) *Depressive feelings and lack of self-esteem.* Mary said that she felt very depressed about the troubles with her family, particularly with her mother. She thought that her family didn't want her around and that maybe they had put her in the hospital "in order to get rid of me." However, she could also say that she was hospitalized because she must have been behaving strangely and therefore it was her "own fault."

She spoke of being fat and unattractive, but expressed the longing that "When I get older, maybe I'll get skinnier." Whenever she sneezed or needed to blow her nose, she ordered me not to watch, saying with a giggle, "It's too embarrassing."

3) *Sexuality.* There were occasional references to sexual themes, such as her disgust with the "dirty pictures" in the magazines at the newsstand. She also told me about a boy who insisted that Mary kiss him, warning her that if she did not, she would go crazy. She said, "I had never kissed a boy, so I didn't." When I asked her what she thought he meant by "going crazy," she replied, "That I would like girls and not like boys."

Second month

Mary's behavior at the center became less childish and more appropriate. This was accompanied by a decrease in anxious, giggly interactions, and by the appearance of more explicit depressed and withdrawn behavior. She came promptly to each individual session and could remain for the entire 50 minutes by the middle of the second month.

Three major themes became prominent in this second month of treatment:

1) *Withdrawal and avoidance of problems and feelings.* Mary complained repeatedly of being tired and bored. Though she slept a great deal, she explained her tiredness as being due to lack of sleep. She used the tiredness as a reason for avoiding interaction with peers at the center. She said: "People are always talking about problems and feelings—it's boring."

2) *Warding off anger.* She acknowledged that she felt sad at times, but did not always know why. On two occasions, following her observation of another patient's uncontrollable anger, she spoke of becoming very sad and wanting to cry. Efforts to inquire about whether she might have also been frightened or angry were met with vigorous denial. Later in the hour, she imitated the patient's angry gestures, but insisted this was only a joke!

She gave little information about what was going on at home. However, when she did report an occasional family incident, she would often say that she wasn't sure whether these events made her sad or mad.

3) *Conflicts about growing up.* The plants in my office and elsewhere in the center became an important focus of our meetings. Mary spoke about how much safer plants are than people, commenting, "Plants are quiet. They don't fight with you. They're easy to grow." We began to discuss the conditions different plants needed for growing and how not all of them were alike.

Mary also noted that animals were also different and that one dog she knew was nice and friendly and liked to be petted, but there was another dog who was bigger and growled whenever anyone came near. These thoughts led to her remembering her collection of stuffed animals, and she said, with some shame, that she really was too old to sleep with one of these, but "it's hard to put her away."

Third and fourth month

Mary's behavior improved enough so that she could enroll in a course at a community college. This was a very important step for Mary and involved us in considerable discussion and planning about realistic goals. Despite her apprehension about returning to school, where the most flagrant psychotic behavior first appeared, she managed the enrollment and was clearly proud of this achievement. What went on in the course was reported regularly and with clear evidence that Mary was learning.

During this period, she appeared less depressed, and Mary was able to say that she felt better. Her medication was slowly reduced and finally discontinued without a regression. This served to validate for Mary that she was really getting better. She spoke of calling her former friend and beginning some social activities outside of the center.

Efforts to engage Mary in reflecting about her previous difficulties were less successful than work on present activities or future plans. She would abruptly change the subject or announce that she did not want to talk about "that." Gradually she was able to observe that it was hard to find the right words for those confusing and frightening feelings and thoughts.

However, she was able to tell me, directly, that she "didn't like it" when I changed an appointment and, though she initially denied any feelings about my vacation, she was finally able to tell me that she "was disappointed and would miss me." This discussion of my vacation permitted us to begin to address the issue of separation more generally. We were able to discuss how people could stay in touch with one another through letters, phone calls, and memories even when they were physically apart. Mary herself made the connection that she liked her class at school, even though it meant missing activities at the center. Immediately following this remark, she wondered, with some nervousness, if anyone at the center noticed her absence.

It seems to me that Mary is making good progress, although much work remains to be done to help her develop more effective coping skills and to better understand her situation and her feelings.

Work with the family

I met with the entire family for six of the eight sessions which were scheduled. The first two sessions were marked by awkward pauses and much emphasis on Mary's disruptive behavior at home. Mrs. Morishita complained about Mary's jealousy of her siblings and Mary's inability to entertain herself. She could not give Mary all the time Mary demanded. Mary's older sister also complained about Mary's excessive and unreasonable demands. Mary's brother participated very little and seemed puzzled about why he was there. Mr. Morishita was also mostly silent at first, but clearly attentive. Toward the end of the first session, he made a surprising statement. He said that he thought everyone should try to understand Mary and that, even though he was often tired from work, Mary could talk to him any time.

My efforts in these first two sessions were directed toward giving each family member an opportunity to say what this difficult time had been like for each of them and to convey the idea that we could work together so the whole family might benefit. I also tried to defuse the blaming comments directed at Mary by translating these into explanations of Mary's behavior. I tried to enlist Mary's help in doing this, but was only moderately successful. However, in the remaining sessions with the family, Mary's changed behavior was more convincing evidence to the family that Mary was improving. Her return to school, and the reduction and discontinuance of the medication served as tangible proof of her recovery. In turn, the family's anxiety diminished and some of the family members desisted in blaming Mary. In a restrained way, Mr. Morishita praised Mary for the efforts she was making. Both Mary and Mrs. Morishita were astonished by his praise, and Mary blushed with obvious pleasure.

I was able to capitalize on this noteworthy event in my next individual session with Mary. Mary acknowledged her astonishment at her father's praise, saying, "I never knew, before, what he thought." I reminded Mary of her previous belief that the family might have wanted to get rid of her, and Mary was able to wonder if some of her confused ideas were because the family didn't speak together much, except to accuse one another.

Subsequently I began to hear, in the family sessions and in the individual sessions, of increased activity with her father, such as going shopping together and also some material suggesting Mary's growing identification with him, such as taking a nap after dinner, which was a long-standing habit of his.

Mrs. Morishita seemed puzzled by Mary's growing relationship with her father. Perhaps in response to this shift, Mary's mother seemed to move toward a closer relationship with Mary's older sister.

Discussion

In the first month, the work with Mary focused on developing an alliance and helping to reduce her intense anxiety. Her therapist took note of how much anxiety Mary could tolerate and permitted Mary to regulate the amount of time they spent in the office. She permitted Mary to come to know her gradually and in a variety of settings. She did not admonish Mary or attempt to stop Mary's behavior but instead simply stated her expectation that Mary would be able to behave differently when they knew one another better. This intervention was a particular form of "limit setting." It is perhaps the least intrusive way of letting someone know what is expected and, in this instance, seems particularly deft.

Simultaneous with Mary's introduction to the center, its people, structure and activities, the therapist invited the family's participation. Implicitly this established that Mary remained a part of her family and that their help was enlisted in her behalf. The importance of this involvement was later confirmed when Mary disclosed her fear that the family wanted to get rid of her.

Concurrent with these initial steps, the therapist began the work of reality testing through her observations of Mary's behavior at the center and its impact on others. She invited Mary to join with her in making these observations but did not press them beyond Mary's capacity to take them in. The mutually shared field of observations which the full day's activities at the center provided were invaluable in this effort. The peer experiences and group pressures, along with the observations and reinforcements of other staff members, were powerful adjuncts to the individual and family therapy.

As Mary became more familiar with the center and with her therapist, her silly, anxious behavior decreased. With this, she began to express some of the preoccupying themes and fears. These included her underlying depression, her fear of her craziness and the more specific concern that sexuality and craziness were linked. In the main, the therapist listened and made little effort to interpret. Instead, she seemed to suggest that Mary's behavior could be understood in more realistic ways.

In the second month, Mary could tolerate regular meetings with the therapist for full, 50-minute sessions. Although she often expressed her resistance through being tired or bored, it became more clear that angry aggressive feelings were being warded off by depression and denial. The therapist respected these defenses, recognizing that Mary was just emerging from a psychotic state and remained quite vulnerable and fragile. Furthermore, the therapist could be confident in her decision to let these defenses be, since important new material continued to appear. In particular, Mary and her therapist began to work on Mary's conflicts about growing up. These issues were addressed through the metaphor of growing things—plants and animals—and the different conditions which different organisms need for growth. The first interpretive interventions were made within these metaphors. Mary confirmed the utility of this metaphor for her own experience and showed some insight into her wish to remain a little child, the shame this generated and her difficulty in relinquishing this posture for a more adult stance.

By the third month, the now familiar structure and order of the center and therapy helped Mary reconstitute enough to begin the progression into real world activities. The return to a "normal" environment and activity was proof for Mary that she was getting better and she acknowledged that she was feeling better. This proof was further reinforced by the discontinuance of her medication. The therapist supported these new efforts even though her attempts to explore the psychotic episode were resisted. Her therapist recognized that Mary was still too close to her frightening psychotic experience and wisely permitted time and distance to assist the recovery, rather than trying to push the exploration of the meanings of the psychotic behavior. The time was used, instead, for planning and review of present accomplishments and immediate future next steps. In spite of the resistance, Mary's ability to wonder if she was missed when she was at school and to express her sense of missing the therapist during the vacation were suggestive of a more realistic re-working of previously more psychotic themes. These can be viewed as non-psychotic substitutes for the delusion that her family wanted to get rid of her, as well as for the psychotic behavior stemming from her unsuccessful efforts to be separate and autonomous.

The family therapy sessions, occurring simultaneously with the individual therapy, the group therapy and the center's activity programs, were essential ingredients in the overall treatment. It was particularly important in light of the context in which Mary's psychotic episode evolved—Mary's precipitous efforts to separate from a confusing and symbiotic family entanglement.

It is not uncommon for many families to find the initial sessions awkward and shameful and to defend against these feelings by blaming the identified patient. The therapist's efforts were intended to demonstrate a different form of behavior by hearing out each of the family members. Rather surprisingly, Mr. Morishita was the first family member to depart from the blaming stance by indicating that he was available to talk with Mary. In another sense, this move away from the family's posture was not so surprising. He had always been the outsider.

Mary's improvement provided the family members with some hope and allowed them to perceive her as less than endlessly demanding, burdensome and bewildering. Her father's praise seemed to initiate some re-alignment in the family, allowing Mary to establish some increased closeness and identification with him, thereby loosening Mary's symbiotic attachment to her mother who then sought a new alliance with her older daughter.

The material from the family therapy sessions was useful for further work in the individual sessions. In particular, it helped Mary make some first connections to the meaning of some of her psychotic ideation.

JEFFREY MURPHY

Jeffrey's difficulties are illustrative of some of the issues which confront all adolescents. Yet his unique experiences make the move into adolescence far more complicated and conflicted.

Concerned about a serious drop in their son's academic performance and the discovery that he had been stealing, Mr. and Mrs. Murphy sought help for 13-year-old Jeffrey. Jeffrey is the third of six children in a family whose economic circumstances have always been difficult. This has been particularly stressful for the last three years since Mr. Murphy sustained an injury which made it impossible for him to continue his work as a plumber. During this time, Mrs. Murphy has tried to add to the family's income by taking part-time jobs. This has added to the burden of raising her many children and has required her to give up taking occasional courses in literature at the local community college, a pursuit she had greatly enjoyed. In the early meetings, Jeffrey's parents seemed somewhat guarded and evasive about details of family life, and particularly about Mr. Murphy's accident, in contrast to their openness about Jeffrey, their willingness to support treatment for him and their agreement to work closely with Jeffrey's therapist. Several times, when Mrs. Murphy was seen alone, she became quite sad and appeared to be on the brink of revealing something, but each time she drew back and instead proceeded to "count her blessings."

Jeffrey's developmental history was unremarkable except for some precocity up to age eight when he suffered severe injuries in a car accident. He spent months in the hospital and was forced to return for several surgical repairs. Between hospitalizations, Jeffrey attended a school for handicapped children where he and his mother felt he had learned little. Mrs. Murphy was particularly bitter about the minimal academic expectations of the school despite the students' intellectual capacities. Jeffrey wore a heavy body cast for several years, which altered his gait markedly. He became extremely skillful in maneuvering, amazing his doctors and others with his ability to overcome the cumbersomeness of the cast. Jeffrey had learned to cope by becoming a bit of a clown and a daredevil, remaining invariably cheerful and inviting playmates to compete with him in physical games.

The surgeries over and the cast removed, Jeffrey was transferred to his neighborhood school when he was 12. There, his grades began to fall. In his second semester, he began to fail subjects in which he was clearly competent. Although his language skills were considerably beyond grade level, he failed English because he would either not turn in his homework assignments or would turn in work which did not follow instructions.

The early treatment hours were spent in describing his experiences superficially and in entertaining his therapist. He steadfastly denied that he had stolen anything. When he won at games, he seemed pleased but as he came to know his therapist better, he began to wonder if the therapist was feigning incompetence in order to let him win. In describing the many surgeries and his experience with the body cast, he spoke of how admired he was for managing these bravely. Only some months later could Jeffrey talk of feeling pitied and even unjustly rewarded because of his handicap.

This acknowledgement opened a series of hours in which Jeffrey spoke in a bewildered way about somehow liking what had happened to him. He was puzzled about how someone could like an experience that contained so much pain and restriction. Yet he knew that he enjoyed the special attention and the admiration he had received. These were hard to give up. On the other hand, he had not liked being pitied nor had he always enjoyed getting things for no better reason than being injured. More hesitantly, he said that he did not like it now when he was pitied and teased for being poor. He hated that! After this revelation, he sat for a moment in silence and then announced that he had a secret which he could now tell his therapist. He said, "You know those times I told you that I didn't take things, well, I really did." He went on to say that he'd stolen things to feel less poor and to show the other kids that he was as good as they. For a while he had even enjoyed the stealing, skillfully outsmarting the storekeepers. With some increased anxiety, however, he reported that he had begun to have nightmares. Those scared him and he thought that maybe if he stopped stealing, the nightmares would go away. "In fact," he said, "I don't have many nightmares anymore."

In the hour that followed these confessions, Jeffrey immediately began a checker game. The therapist commented that Jeffrey seemed to have a very clear idea about what he wanted to do. Jeffrey began to win and, as he had done in the early sessions, he asked if the therapist was letting him win. Assuring Jeffrey again that this was not so, the therapist linked this doubt with the times that Jeffrey had felt that people pitied him and gave him things which he had not fairly earned. Jeffrey agreed that maybe that was true, but he also wondered if he could be better than a grown-up. The therapist suggested that it was not always a safe feeling to think you might be better than a grown-up; perhaps he held himself back now from doing as well as he could because of such a worry. Jeffrey puzzled over that. Could that really happen to a person? He thought he really did want to do well. In fact, he'd won a checker game just that week with the school's checker champ. He felt good! It didn't make sense that he'd want to defeat himself.

After a bit of quiet play, Jeffrey reported that he was thinking about a school assignment. The class had been asked to invite six people from various historical periods to a dinner, to learn about these characters, to plan the menu and to imagine their likely conversation. He had chosen Florence Nightingale, Rocky Marciano, Al Capone, Charlie Chaplin, Emmett Kelley and Bonnie from Bonnie and Clyde. Jeffrey hesitated before acknowledging that these were not his first choices—he changed his first choices when he realized that all of his first choices were violent people. He didn't want others to think he was violent. They teased him enough.

Jeffrey said that he sometimes got mad about having to worry about what others thought. He didn't like being poor, but why should he care what other people thought about that? He explained that his father's accident was the reason for the family's poverty, but he can't blame his father for that. He added that he does think his father managed to lose some things they owned by dumb decisions.

Hesitantly, he also told of his father's bad moods—no one knows when he will be verbally or even physically abusive. He has learned to stay out of father's way—the others and his mother have not always been so lucky. He hates it, especially when his father hits his mother.

Discussion

It is noteworthy that Jeffrey's emotional, learning and behavioral problems became manifest shortly after his chronic physical problems and restrictions abated. The onset of his difficulties were also coincident with the beginning of adolescence and his entry into a new school. Seemingly, he has the chance to be a regular, competent youngster, in a "normal" school setting for the first time in five years. However, Jeffrey's behavior demonstrated that these transitions were more than he could handle.

Despite the pain and physical limitations of the five years just past, Jeffrey had developed methods of coping with many secondary gains. These included a sense of specialness, much attention, and lots of praise and admiration. Such rewards are not easily given up. Free of his cast, Jeffrey faced the problem of yielding these gains and simultaneously adapting to marked changes in body state, part of which is relinquishing the cast as part of the body. The common adolescent concern about body changes was vastly more difficult for Jeffrey, who had already experienced his body as unreliable and painful. In spite of his heroic adaptations, he was left with profound doubts about whether his competencies were real or fraudulent. In fact, his injury resulted in reduced academic expectations, pity from others and rewards which he felt were unearned. This conflict was portrayed clearly in the therapy by his repeated questioning of whether he won fairly or was being "given the game." Related to this was another common adolescent question—again more pointed for Jeffrey—"Can I beat a grown-up?"

Jeffrey's entry into the new school required that he adapt to a whole new peer group. He encountered a good deal of teasing and pity for being poor, which he hated even more than being pitied for being injured. During the therapy hour in which Jeffrey discussed this, the therapist noted that Jeffrey was more hesitant in reporting his "hatred" of the current pity (poor) than the previous pity (injured). This "hesitancy" may seem puzzling. However, when one considers that poverty has no distinctively positive secondary gains and unconsciously contains the secret shame about and contempt for his father, the hesitancy becomes understandable. Much later, this was confirmed by Jeffrey's statements about his belief that his father bears the blame for the family's poverty.

Jeffrey's shame about his poverty seems to be one determinant in his stealing. Other factors in his behavioral symptom are his pride and pleasure in outwitting the storekeepers, which is analogous to his agility in overcoming his physical handicap and which is paralleled in the therapy by his steadfast denial of the stealing for many weeks. The stealing may also reflect, in a more active form, the conviction that he got things he didn't deserve. However, Jeffrey disclosed that the stealing became more and more dystonic. Somehow, he had figured out that his nightmares might have been his punishment for stealing and indeed, the nightmares ceased when he, experimentally, gave up his criminal career.

Some issues in Jeffrey's learning problems have already been alluded to. These include entry into a new "normal" school shortly after the loss of his body cast, competing with grown-ups and perhaps a self-inflicted punishment for competitive feelings toward a father for whom he feels pity and contempt. In adolescence, moral imperatives become pronounced and often inflexible. In addition, Jeffrey lives in a home with six other children. Is he concerned about rivalry with peers which may be rooted in some rivalry with his siblings?

In fact, Jeffrey does not suffer from true learning impairments. He can do ably what is required of him; he simply will not and does not turn in required reading assignments—behavior which seems simultaneously motivated and puzzling. Is such defiance a mix of many factors—an act of self assertion and a protection against submissive pulls? These conflicting pressures are a common adolescent preoccupation which Jeffrey struggles to integrate. Moreover, his diminished school performance probably serves to protect his inadequate father, and also to protect Jeffrey from an identification with his mother, who loves to read. Jeffrey's identifications and his efforts to confront the task of developing a cohesive identity are complicated and difficult. He and his father have both suffered body insults and both have engaged in unfair behavior. Father is abusive and irrational. Jeffrey has stolen and won unjust rewards. It is after his father's accident that the family fortunes diminished and the father became declassed, moody and violent. To be like his father may frighten Jeffrey. Will he then be violent, "dumb," impoverished and incompetent? Without an able, effective father, Jeffrey may be pushed toward a closer identification with his mother. That path is also troublesome. His mother is female, a silent, secret-keeping victim, who makes do and escapes into her love of books. The pull for submission and its costs confront Jeffrey in his daily observations of his mother's behaviors.

This boy's response to the academic assignment of inviting historical figures to dinner gives us many clues to his ego models and part-identifications which are the raw material for identity organization. On second thought, he has selected Florence Nightingale, Rocky Marciano, Al Capone, Charlie Chaplin, Emmett Kelley and Bonnie of the crime team, Bonnie and Clyde. The first set of diners have been altered and we do not have a close view of these first choices. We do know that Jeffrey worried that his first selections revealed too much interest in violence—an experience he knows about all too well, and must keep hidden and under control.

While we do not have Jeffrey's associations to his selections and thus can only speculate about the meeting of these "ego-models," it is possible that each represents a part of his experience and his inner world.

Florence Nightingale, the nurse, may derive from his illness and the many medical interventions that shaped his life for five of his 13 years. The caring, tender part of Jeffrey, seen in his wishes to protect his mother, may also reside in this choice.

Rocky Marciano, the fighter who achieves against adversity, may represent Jeffrey's struggles to overcome his own poor and damaged state through battle and physical prowess.

Al Capone and the female half of the team of Bonnie and Clyde may demonstrate the still untamed impulses to steal and gain ruthlessly while, at the same time, Bonnie may represent his emerging interest in sexuality, once again complicated by unreliable physical experiences.

Charlie Chaplin and Emmett Kelley must surely portray some of Jeffrey's efforts to smile through tears as he struggled to adapt to painful and long-lasting physical difficulties. Jeffrey is not without humor—one of human kind's most saving attributes. Both of Jeffrey's choices have earned the world's love by their clowning, which, nevertheless, has always carried a serious undertone of sadness, tenderness and being able to tolerate the stance of victim. Both are distinctive by their humor, genius, unusual posture and physical antics and by their ability to transmit messages without words.

Jeffrey clearly demonstrates the interplay between phase-specific developmental themes and the more idiosyncratic difficulties of a particular adolescent. Distinguishing between these intertwined processes is a more vexing technical problem in adolescence than in any other developmental stage because the normative adolescent processes are expressed in more vivid, dramatic and sometimes turbulent forms which tend to resemble or be perceived as psychopathology.

LARRY SCOTT

The clinical work with Larry Scott is a brief therapy illustrating many aspects of psychotherapeutic technique. The detailed account of the first eight therapy hours reveals how and why one clinician selected among many possible interventions, how the efficacy of these interventions can be assessed by the patient's subsequent responses and how each of these threads is woven into a particular therapeutic tapestry uniquely designed for this patient and this therapist.

The report permits an examination of how these interventions are tailored to fit the developmental issues of an adolescent. They also demonstrate the ways in which a white female therapist works effectively with a black young man, despite the inherent complications that may accompany such a combination.

"There Are Two Roads After All"

Larry Scott is a black 15-year-old who lives with his mother and a younger brother and sister. The Scotts are among a growing number of black families who live in a newly integrated neighborhood. The family moved into the area just prior to the current school term.

Larry's mother is a nutritionist and the sole supporter of her family. His father lives in another city and tends to see his children about once a year. The parents were divorced ten years ago.

Larry has been repeatedly getting into fist fights at his new school. When suspended, he threatened to kill school personnel. Following the next fight, which was described as an "unprovoked attack" on a smaller boy, the police were called to take Larry to Juvenile Hall. The police attempted to handcuff Larry, but he exploded and became so hysterical and threatening that he was taken instead to the psychiatric ward of the county hospital. A court hearing was held several days later, and commitment was recommended. However, when Mrs. Scott agreed to seek outpatient treatment and to take a leave of absence from work in order to care for Larry at home, the court stayed the commitment, ordered Larry to keep away from the school and placed him on probation under court wardship.

In the first outpatient interview, Larry seemed almost ostentatiously menacing as he stood over his female therapist, glowering, fists clenched, and all muscles tensed. At first he seemed to be struggling not to speak. When the therapist mentioned this, he burst out, "I'm not coming here, I don't belong here. I don't care what they do to me. I don't care, I'm not crazy. I'm going to sue the judge, he can't get away with this, let them send me to the nut house. I don't care. . . ." The therapist interrupted, "OK, so sit down and let's talk about it. I don't know whether you belong here either—all I know right now is that you are very upset." He sat down. "Now, tell me, what's been happening to you?"

His story was incoherent and interspersed with threats to kill the principal, the judge, and particularly the school counselor. He insisted that the school fights were not started by him, but that everyone was against him. In a particularly jumbled and frightened fashion, he spoke of the arrival of the police, the handcuffs and the time on the psychiatric ward. He repeated again and again, "I don't care. . . ." The therapist said, "Of course you care—you must care very much. And I agree with you, that psychiatric ward is no place for a 15-year-old boy. It's terribly frightening. You weren't prepared to go there, you didn't know what would happen next. . . ."

He said, "They were going to send me to the nut house or to Juvey or prison . . . I don't want to go anywhere, I'm not crazy, but I'm not coming here. The judge sent me here so he could laugh at me . . . the whole city's laughing at me. . . ." He stood up to leave.

The therapist responded, "Larry, I don't know what they are saying about you because I don't have their reports. But I will know in three days and during that time, I'll also want to talk with your mother. Will you come back then? That way, I'll tell you what they say and you won't have to guess."

He agreed with some reluctance, and added, "If I don't get in trouble. . . ." He was planning to accost his school counselor, to make the man sorry for the trouble he had caused. Almost pleadingly, he added, "Don't know if I can stay away from him." The therapist replied, "You are asking if you are that strong. You will have to prove to yourself you can be strong enough to stay away . . . for three days. Then we'll talk more about it."

He made some grandiose comments about his strength, then added, "I'll just stay in the house and not go nowhere."

The next day the therapist met with Larry's mother. Mrs. Scott, an attractive, intelligent woman, tended to deny that Larry had ever had problems but agreed that he needed help now because of the recent trouble. She did acknowledge that he had never been a particularly good student, but assured the therapist that none of her children had ever been in trouble before. She seemed concerned and embarrassed that Larry was on probation and also seeing a therapist. In the main, Mrs. Scott's responses, although cooperative, were rather unrevealing. She affirmed her plan to take some time off from work and readily agreed to keep Larry's therapist informed of any significant events or changes. She did not see any point in having regular interviews with the therapist or participating actively in Larry's treatment.

Larry did keep his second appointment, announcing, "I'm only going to stay five minutes." He turned the clock to face him and stared at it. He did not look at his therapist who said, "Then let's make those five minutes worthwhile. I've got the court report. You've had a lot of troubles. When you were a little kid—first and second grade, the kids picked on you and you didn't know how to make them stop. You didn't know how to make friends. You must have been very lonely—that's rough on a little kid. And you were very small and thin, in a neighborhood with a lot of bullies." He remained silent, but nodded. "And now you are obviously not weak and yet some of the same problems are there; you never got a chance to learn how to make friends. It's a sad thing." He said, "Five minutes is up," but didn't stand to leave. She repeated, "It is sad that you don't get a chance to make friends."

Larry began to talk about when he was in grade school. The bigger boys would waylay him to tease him for wearing a cap, and would knock it off his head. He told of living in a place where there was snow—this was a happy memory. He described accidentally setting fire to his mother's curtains, "when I was just a baby or a kid. I didn't mean to, but I could have burned the whole house down." He jumped from this back to early school years, and how the boys tried to trick him. Quickly he said, "But I'm not dumb, I'm smarter than anyone. I can walk along a river, jump back and forth, back and forth. . . . I'm so careful I don't fall in. . . ." The therapist said, "It sounds as if you have to be Superman. You tell yourself you have to jump farther and faster and oftener than anyone else. That's how it feels to you, I guess." "Yeah, because I used to be strong. Last year, all the time I was lifting weights. . . ." He described what the weights looked like, and how it felt lifting them. "I could lift 100, no, 150 pounds. Maybe more, if I tried. Just like that, not straining, just lifting slow, taking my time, you didn't want to get a rupture. Maybe it was only 140 pounds. I lost my strength this year. Now I don't think I can lift more than 50 pounds. Can you sweat your strength away?" The therapist commented, "Sometimes you talk yourself into believing you can do even things you know you can't do." "Yeah, that's just how it is now." "Tell me about now."

He spoke coherently of his loneliness. He had been kicked out of the recreation center, he was out of school and a month ago, he'd been told to leave the roller rink and never come back. "I got no friends, see?

Nobody wants me around, but I don't care." Then quickly, he said, "But I'm the best swimmer. You know anything about swimming? You know the freestyle, the butterfly? Well, I'm so good, no swimming pool is big enough for me. I'm so good, the lake used to be big enough, but it's not big enough anymore. I guess only the ocean is big enough for my kind of swimming." At the end of the hour, he agreed to return next week.

Prior to the next interview, the therapist heard from Larry's mother, who told her that his brother had teased Larry about coming to the clinic, which reinforced Larry's fears that everyone "knew" and considered him crazy. He refused to continue treatment.

Larry's probation officer and the therapist talked the matter over, and decided that Larry should be reminded that the court ordered him to continue until his next court hearing. His probation officer was a young black man who liked Larry and felt very strongly that the precipitating factor triggering the emotional upheaval was the move to a new school where he was treated very insensitively from the beginning. The probation officer became an increasingly important person for Larry, representing benign but firm authority. His method was to ignore pathology and instead spell out the rules of conduct, repeating them weekly and gradually allowing Larry more freedom as the boy seemed able to use it. Mrs. Scott came to trust the probation officer and supported his decisions. The therapist and the probation officer stayed in regular contact.

Larry did return and did not mention his decision to quit. When the therapist mentioned it, he grinned, acknowledging that it was all right as long as no one thought he came because he wanted to.

The next two interviews dealt with his feelings about the recent events. There was some wild threatening to get the school counselor, to sue everybody, and one or two lapses into fantasy, such as the swimming and weightlifting. As he gave a detailed account of his experiences with the police, it was obvious that he could not tolerate the feelings of helplessness associated with the handcuffs. His fears about the psychiatric ward were similar. He asked about patients who were strapped down and was particularly concerned about a patient who, from his description, was in a state of delirium tremens. Larry had been put in restraints when he first arrived. As Larry told of this, he groaned, and was visibly perspiring. The therapist answered his questions about the psychiatric ward and tried to underline the fact that, given a very difficult and frightening situation, he had handled some things very well.

He told of a second time he had been threatened with restraints. This had occurred after he had been told he could not go home prior to the court hearing and he thought that he was considered crazy and dangerous. He then began threatening to kill ward personnel and behaved in a wild manner. As they talked, he agreed that he would label someone as crazy if they behaved as he had. The therapist suggested that whenever he felt someone was criticizing him unfairly, "You seem to knock yourself out proving they are right." He was amused by the choice of words and agreed.

The therapist tried to link this with his behavior at school, but he would not accept this.

He brought the subject back to the psychiatric ward and said it wasn't just that he had to prove he was as bad as they thought . . . he was also scared. The therapist agreed. By the end of the fourth hour, Larry was speaking coherently, calmly and with surprising self-understanding.

In the next session, Larry seemed strikingly improved. He began by talking about a new friend, his age, who moved in next door, with whom he had swapped phonograph records.*

After a short silence, Larry said he was thinking about school. He wondered if they'd let him re-enroll after the court hearing. The semester was "mostly gone, and what will I do, I don't know . . . but I'll get A's, they can't stop me if I try hard enough." "Why do you have to get A's? Superman again?" He tried to deny that getting A's was impossible. The therapist replied, "It will be a triumph if you can pass any of your courses." He finally admitted this. She said, "So why do you set such goals? You know, I think when you do this, you are very mean to yourself." He said it was the school personnel who were mean to him. "You are the one who says you have to be Superman. It's you who won't give yourself credit for doing the best you can." After a long pause, he said, "You have to get A's to be a doctor. I'm going to be a doctor . . . not just any doctor, I'm going to be the head doctor. My mother says they try to keep Blacks from being doctors, so a Black has to be better than any white doctor. I'll run the whole hospital, I'll be the one who tells the white doctors what to do." He stopped, said firmly, "and don't go talking about Superman. Superman is *not* a doctor." They both smiled, and the therapist noted that, regardless of the smiles, this subject meant a great deal to him.

---

*Later, his mother telephoned to confirm this as the first time Larry had a friend for quite a while. She was extremely pleased.

He said, "Ever since I was born I guess I was going to be a doctor." He told of his mother buying him a set of encyclopedias, "when I couldn't even read much at all. And I read them, too, I read all the way to the M's." He sounded very depressed. "And then what happened?" He said, "I just stopped, that's all. I got too tired, maybe, I don't know. It's like being tired." The therapist asked when that happened and he said, "in junior high." As he talked, he told of how hard he had tried to get good grades but he never got better than a C in junior high. "Is that why you stopped reading the encyclopedia?" He said, "It wasn't any use. My brother could read all the way through them. He doesn't even have to read them, he always gets A's. I guess he will be the doctor." Long pause. "I don't know what will happen to me." He sat silent for a time, then said, "It's strange here. We talk and talk and then everything is said and there is nothing more. Only silence." "Yes, that is how it can feel when you have finally been able to tell so much about yourself."

Four days later the therapist received a frantic call from Larry's mother and one from his probation officer: Larry had been picked up by the police for attempting to shoplift. The police took Larry home and notified probation. This occurred a week-and-a-half before his next scheduled court hearing on whether or not he could return to school.

In the next hour, Larry insisted that he had been falsely accused of stealing. He had gone into the store to buy a record, had the money in his pocket, and was holding the article "in plain sight," when he decided to go out on the sidewalk to tell his brother something; he carried the record with him. He was planning to prove in court that he had stood in the doorway, rather than on the sidewalk, and therefore was not guilty, etc. He would then sue the store for false arrest. He said, "They could send me to the Youth Authority for nothing!"

The therapist said that their task was to figure out what pressures were on him that made it necessary for him to get himself in trouble. This made him quite angry and he tried to go back over old ground: everyone is against him and he is innocent. She suggested that at times it seems he has to get himself into precisely this kind of trouble: trouble in which he can feel both abused and innocent. This had happened before—he had told, in an earlier hour, of being falsely accused of vandalism. He finally admitted that maybe he had behaved in a suspicious manner in the store.

The therapist suggested that two things might have upset him this time. One was the notice of the court hearing, which came the day of the attempted theft. The other was what they had talked about last time. He said, "That's a funny thing. I can't remember anything we talked about last time." Then he said, "And I wouldn't want to do something suspicious before court—that doesn't make sense . . . I want to go back to school." She reminded him, "Last time we talked about grades." "Oh, yes, how could I forget that?" Then he said, "One other time I was out of school, and I didn't flunk. It was when I had my operation." He said he was in third grade then, and was operated on "because my navel stuck out like a pickle."

They talked about the operation and how a "little kid" would have felt about it. He said, "It's when you wake up that it's bad. I saw this scar . . . it's long enough they could have done anything inside me . . . I didn't know what they could have done. They could reach just about anywhere from so big a scar." She said, "What did you worry they had done?" With great hesitation and embarrassment, he told his fantasy. "Is there a tube, I mean a connection, from your navel to your . . . sex parts?" He felt they had shortened or somehow badly damaged his penis and that this was why he hadn't grown. "When a little kid is the smallest in the whole school, even smaller than his brother, and he sees a midget, you know what he thinks? He thinks he's a midget, too." He then asked her to tell him what had happened during the operation. She described a hernia repair, and he said with great relief, "Only muscles? Well, then, I am all right. My stomach muscles are all right . . . you use those to lift weights."

The therapist asked if he was still worried about his sexual organs. He said, "No, I think they work OK. But you can get scared of things just the same. . . ." They returned to a further discussion about the fears surrounding the operation and the therapist wondered if the operation had something to do with some of his current fears. For instance, perhaps he was afraid of being helpless, tied down and hand-cuffed in much the same way a boy is afraid of having an operation. He thought about that very seriously, and added, "I'm always afraid of being at the mercy of someone. Like someone is going to do something terrible . . . that part's like an operation." The therapist answered, "So you have to pretend to yourself that you are Superman because you are afraid of being helpless. You're really not as helpless any more. In fact, I imagine you'll be able to get through court this time without being so scared and without pretending you're Superman either."

He said, "I'm sort of worried about that." They decided they'd talk more about that next session, which would be a couple of days before the hearing.

Larry began the next session right on that topic. He said he was worried about court and what the judge might do to him. The judge would never believe he hadn't tried to steal the record. He said the probation officer was going to get a report from the therapist to give the judge. She asked if he wondered if she would say he hadn't tried to steal it. She told him she believed him when he said he hadn't, but also believed he had tried to make it look as if he were stealing, even though he wasn't aware of it at the time. They discussed how he did these things when he was upset and feeling no good and unable to defend himself. She related this again to his feelings about court and also about not being able to do as well in school as his younger brother.

After a brief silence, Larry admitted that he started that fight in school by hitting a boy who called him "brainless." He said, "But I don't want to admit this in court. The judge will think I'm no good." She said, "Again, I think you are meaner to yourself than any judge could possibly be. You look at one thing you consider a failure and you damn yourself. I think the judge will consider other things, too . . . like the fact that you have been able to go to the park and play baseball these past two weekends, and have had no fights, and that, even with the record business, you didn't lose control of yourself. I don't think he will find you a worthless person because you can't get the world's best grade, an A." He gave a short laugh, as if in relief. Then he asked what she would tell the judge. The therapist responded that she was going to tell him, "You are much less upset than when I first saw you and you seem to be doing well. In fact, I will tell him that I think you are going to be OK."

He was very touched by this, and looked as if he might weep. Instead, he stood up and said, "I have to leave early today, is that OK?" He hurried out.

Larry's probation officer and the therapist discussed the court hearing. She described the "stealing" episode as primarily a reaction to his fears of the hearing. He needed an incident that could allow him to feel injured, perhaps punished, and utterly innocent, but to allow the episode to accomplish this would only reinforce the pathology. The probation officer said he would discuss this with the judge before the hearing, and try to persuade the judge to give Larry an opportunity to tell of his successes in meeting the terms set at the first hearing: no fights, threats, etc. The probation officer and the therapist agreed that Larry should remain in his home. At the hearing, the judge was sufficiently impressed with the change in Larry that he allowed him to return to school.

Next hour, Larry described the hearing in detail and said, "This time I had a nice judge. He was the nicest white man I ever met." The therapist told him that it was the same judge at both hearings. He was dumbfounded and they were able to discuss how one's own upset can color one's view of other people—the hated judge and the liked judge were the same person.

In addition, they discussed his apprehension about returning to school and his hopes that he could stay out of trouble.

Larry was seen for six more interviews which were devoted to his real and imaginary difficulties at school, his feelings that his father had never "even cared enough about me to know how old I am," and a re-working of issues from earlier sessions, including his fears of sexual damage and inadequacy stemming from the operation. At the end of the school term, he recited Robert Frost's "A Road Not Taken." "Had to memorize it for English," he muttered. He saw the two roads as representing good and bad, or perhaps emotional sickness and health. He said, "The trouble is, they do look alike. They don't have the right markers so you can know. Or maybe you only see one road, you never know the other is there. That's when you need someone to show you there are two roads after all."

In the fall, the therapist telephoned Larry's school and learned that he was still considered a pest, a poor student and he bragged too much, but had been in no fights, had made some friends and was no longer thought to be dangerous. He was taken off probation as he had been in no further trouble.

Discussion

Larry's therapist has some information which prepares her to meet him. This creates a beginning understanding of the patient's possible concerns and the situation which precipitated his referral.

This therapist already knows some very important facts about Larry, though she cannot know a great deal about how Larry sees his situation. Larry has recently moved into a new neighborhood and a new school, often an upsetting experience for adolescents with the loss of familiar supports and friends. The current change to a new school may have revived older unresolved conflicts or brought to the fore fragments of a previous difficult transition. Larry's father left the family when Larry was about five, a time coincident with a school beginning. The connection between a most important loss for a five-year-old with a new developmental task—school entry—is very likely the background vulnerability which precipitates Larry's current difficulty when the pattern of loss and new school entry is repeated. The loss of the father may have other ramifications. While the referral material is unclear, the father's departure no doubt added to the strain in the family as Mrs. Scott assumed the role of major breadwinner and family caretaker.

Nor is the referral data informative about the racial composition of the new school—an important consideration in the identity development of an adolescent. The therapist does know that Larry's problems take the form of fights with peers and defiance of authority figures in the school. The fights with peers and, in this instance, with a smaller boy, may also have its antecedents in rivalry with his younger brother.

The therapist notes that when the authorities respond to Larry's behavior with disciplinary action, Larry's response escalates to threats to kill the school personnel. She is alerted to Larry's intense struggle for autonomy and his pattern of increasing his aggressive maneuvers each time more repression is attempted by authorities. This culminates in the final explosion and decompensation when physical restraints are used. The therapist is therefore alert to Larry's need to maintain as active a stance as possible. She can be fairly sure that Larry's recent experience on the psychiatric ward will have further threatened his sense of control and that any adolescent in such a situation will wonder about being crazy and will defend against this worry by rejecting the need for therapy and any representative of the therapeutic establishment. Consequently, the therapist knows she will face a resistant patient who probably won't permit her much time or room to work out of that difficult spot.

The mother's apparent competence to care for her family and her willingness and ability to take time from work to look after her son can be considered important assets in beginning this psychotherapy.

The opening moments of the first session confirm the very difficult task facing this therapist. Larry is menacing and rejecting. Her first comment addresses a clear conflict which releases a flow of protests, threats, and denials. Implicitly suggesting that Larry can regain some control, the therapist invites him to sit, selecting from the many protests and threats the one discussable item: whether Larry belongs there or not. She sides with neither position, offering no false reassurance, nor does she directly dispute his contentions. She begins where all treatment must begin: Can this patient and this therapist work together? The specific form of this intervention is firm, unafraid and parsimonious. Taken together, the content and the form of this intervention have the effect of calming Larry and offering the necessary support for further work. As firm as it is, it does not impose restraint; it invites control and Larry's active participation.

Larry's response confirms the effectiveness of these therapeutic comments. He can now tell his story, responding to her interest in his side of his predicament.

As the story of critical events unfolds, the therapist notes what will become a repetitive pattern: The account becomes progressively more incoherent, increasingly emotional, laced with threats, disavowals of responsibility and a dismissal of his own concern. On another level, the sequence can be described as proceeding from bluster to helplessness to omnipotence and finally to repetitive denial which appears to defend against a mounting sense of hopelessness. Among the many possible interventions, this therapist chooses to counter the denial and its underlying hopelessness. No therapy can proceed effectively without some hope. Implicitly, the therapist is conveying that Larry can care and, therefore, can have some hope. She moves a step further toward some common ground ("I agree with you") by humanizing Larry's recent traumatic experiences and by starting to make some sense of a seemingly incomprehensible situation. Once again Larry's response suggests that her remarks have landed well: He confirms and elaborates. However, in keeping with his escalating pattern, the content he offers frightens him into more and more defensive efforts which take on an increasingly paranoid and omnipotent flavor. Irrational as this is, it is Larry's effort to make sense of his plight.

Once again, the therapist does not dispute Larry's contentions. Instead, she labels this contention a guess, thus making it more available for review and reality testing. This is immediately followed by an offer to review the facts with him, providing Larry with an opportunity to return without losing face or admitting that he needs therapy and is, therefore, crazy. The offer is couched in time-limited terms and will be "paid off" in a short enough time (three days) to avert the build-up of excessive anxiety or further maladaptive defenses against this anxiety. The short time period also permits a rapid second contact with him in the hope of building a positive alliance with this very resistant, frightened and action-oriented youngster.

This intervention is validated by his agreement, by the diminution of his bravado and threats and, most significantly, by the emergence of less defended material which portrays his own doubts about his capacity to control himself. The therapist offers no false reassurance about his self-control, about which she cannot yet be certain. She tells him that, together, they will have to find out about the degree to which he can control himself. This intervention is the stuff from which therapeutic trust is built and serves as a subtle but powerful educational experience about what the business of psychotherapy is.

At that moment, Larry and his therapist seem to be more engaged than at any previous point in this first session. He concludes the hour by documenting his need to institute very repressive defenses in the face of his anxiety about self-control. He puts himself under "house arrest."

The second hour begins with Larry's confrontation. He will only stay five minutes. It is of interest that this confrontation uses time as a test, echoing the therapist's use of a time-limited arrangement for their work from the previous session. This tests whether the therapist is prepared to make good on her offer. Simultaneously, this makes it clear that he is there only for their agreed upon purpose. The therapist passes his test ("let's make the five minutes worthwhile") and proceeds to their work. She carefully selects how and what she will present from the promised reports. Notably, she begins with material from his early life. This choice serves many purposes. It avoids, for the moment, the more highly-charged present crisis; it expresses her interest in how things got to be the way they are; it humanizes Larry's difficulties as part of a life story; it states, implicitly, the therapeutic premise that the present derives from the past and that present events can be understood as part of ongoing patterns; it adds effective understanding without moral judgments.

Though Larry avows that the five minutes are up, he makes no move to leave and is clearly listening and interested. The therapist simply restates her view of the affective situation ("it is sad") and Larry picks up with new material from his earlier years. He reports a happy time, probably a screen memory of the time prior to his father's departure and possibly even before the arrival of his younger siblings. There is a poignant account of his accidental destructiveness. As his account returns to the unhappy early school years, Larry's more defensive style re-emerges with mounting grandiosity. Though the therapist can see the connection between the anxiety engendered by helpless, impotent feelings and the omnipotent defenses against these, she chooses to speak, for the moment, only to the defensive side. She labels his efforts to feel like Superman. He agrees and moves to a new area of concern. Using the now familiar mode of omnipotent defenses against anxiety, he reveals recent worries about lost strength. Larry conveys his concerns about body integrity, body damage and, very likely, sexual anxiety. In this exchange, two issues are notable: He dates this problem to one year ago, making it coincident with the recent change of school and neighborhood and, for the first time, directs a question to the therapist, soliciting advice and information.

The therapist continues to address only the defensive side, to imply a more balanced reality and ask for more information ("tell me about now").

Larry responds readily and the pattern repeats with new content. Loneliness and rejection are followed by boasting and assertion of great prowess. This appears to serve restitutive needs well enough for Larry to agree to return again.

Prior to the next session, an event occurs which, because of its confirmation of an internal worry, threatens to disrupt the treatment. This is a particularly common experience in the psychotherapy of adolescents. The therapist is obliged to mobilize important supports in Larry's environment in order to protect the treatment. Fortunately, this can be done in a way which allows Larry to continue. If Larry were adamant about discontinuing, rather than ambivalent, it is not likely that invoking the "face-saving" idea of the court's order would have succeeded.

At the start of the next therapy session, the therapist chooses to mention the recent disrupting event after observing that Larry does not bring it up. He quickly validates the assumption that there is an important part of him which would like to continue the therapy so long as he need not avow the wish.

Very important work then ensues in the remainder of this hour and in the next. In the manifest content Larry returns to the ordeal of the police and the handcuffs and the psychiatric ward. However, the form of the account this time is radically different. The focus now is on his subjective reality, with a much diminished need to resort to intense externalizations. The previous rage and threats have been replaced by fearfulness which is not only acknowledged but visibly re-experienced as he recounts the events. The themes of helplessness in the face of restraint, a persistent worry about craziness and his concern with loss of control when frustrated are evident as the underlying bases of the fearful affect.

It is possible that distance from these traumatic events has contributed to Larry's ability to describe them in a more coherent fashion. It is less likely, however, that Larry could have arrived at the more internal view of these events without the assistance of the therapist. Her capacity to help him label and accept the varied feelings permits

Larry to reveal some very frightening thematic concerns. She also assists Larry to observe and reflect upon his own behavior which he can, with appropriate distance, call "crazy." This lays the basis for calling attention to a patterned piece of Larry's behavior: He uses offense as his best defense. He agrees that this was so in the psychiatric ward, but is unwilling to accept her effort to extend the interpretation to his behavior at school. He is just not ready. However, he is ready to correct the therapist who, he believes, has underestimated how much fear plays a role in his behavior. No patient, and especially no adolescent patient, could be that revealing unless he was experiencing the therapist as truly on his side.

By the fifth session, it is clear that Larry is firmly in treatment. In addition to the work he is doing in the sessions, he has made some important strides in the real world. He now begins to address the future and to wonder about returning to school. Faced with this conflicted task, his omnipotence and perfectionistic strivings reappear. This time the therapist addresses the omnipotence directly with her remark that it would be a triumph for him to pass any of his courses. This is a firm and direct intervention, lightened by a tiny bit of humor.

Parenthetically, many therapists are typically chary of such directness, often fearing that it will humiliate or devastate the patient. There is a confusion abroad between directness and directiveness, between assertion and assault and between the seriousness of therapy and heaviness of style. This leads to a brand of tip-toe-treatment which, too often, leaves patients convinced that they ought to be fearful of their own vulnerability since they are being treated with kid gloves.

Larry demonstrates his acceptance and appreciation of her directness by agreeing with her remark. As the discussion continues the therapist is able to convey to Larry how his omnipotent expectations (Superman) are defensive and, more importantly, how they undo and demean him. This leads to Larry's revelation of the frustrated hope of being a doctor, whose roots are visible in his identification with his mother and his rivalry with his more competent brother. It is possible to connect this with his school difficulties; he cannot perform in ways that measure up to his or his mother's wishes, thwarting ethnic pride which also seems rooted in his identification with his mother's expectations. Additionally, Larry's picking on smaller students may derive from rivalry with his younger brother.

In the course of this interchange, Larry also reveals that he is on his way toward internalizing his therapist and her way of understanding experience. He tells her "and don't go talking about Superman."

While they take a moment to enjoy one another, the therapist reminds Larry that their smiles in no way diminish the serious importance of what they are discussing.

In this deepened atmosphere of understanding and acceptance, Larry can portray the depth of his frustration and hopelessness. Regrettably, the hour ends on this note—not a desirable ending for this action-oriented boy who would be better served by being allowed to take with him some modicum of hope. The subsequent events and the beginnings of the following hour tend to confirm the view of this error of omission made at the end of the fifth session. The "shoplifting" incident is, undoubtedly, also determined by the intense stress of the notification of the upcoming court hearing.

The hour begins with a defensive account of the incident. This echoes Larry's behavior in the first hour but, notably, in a more muted tone. Despite Larry's anger, the therapist persists in her stance that Larry's behavior has meaning and can be understood as another example of what they've begun to discover. Larry does engage in this discussion, reflecting on his behavior, and begins to experience it in a more dystonic way. This signals his readiness to hear a more complex interpretation of his behavior linked to stress in the outside world and stress in the therapy. Larry is intrigued by his inability to remember the previous hour. A simple reminder of the previous week's topic leads to an entirely new set of important associations and new history. Another trauma is revealed in Larry's description of the surgery he underwent for hernia repair, in which helplessness, restraint and fear are again prominent themes. They are now also related, associatively, to concerns about body damage, integrity and sexuality. Furthermore, this early traumatic event has clear links to his school career and its difficulties. This is confirmation of the earlier hints that were present in his "weight lifting" concerns. He asks again for help and information and is considerably relieved to hear a straightforward account, from someone he trusts, about what a hernia repair really is. The therapist knows that his relief cannot be complete and so she persists with further questions about this anxiety. Larry's response suggests that he can recognize that knowing something does not remove contradictory feelings.

In a further effort to demonstrate that behavior is comprehensible over time, the therapist makes a tentative link between the feelings connected to the surgery and the feelings connected to his recent predicament. Larry's thoughtfulness is mobilized and he derives a generalized insight from this comparison ("I'm always afraid of being at the mercy of someone"). She responds to this generalized expression of helplessness by again describing his maladaptive defense against it (Superman) and by suggesting that perhaps they can find better ways for him to feel safe, starting with the upcoming appearance in court. Larry is not sure but remains willing to examine the possibility further.

In the next session, Larry does indeed immediately pick up the thread of the previous hour. His fears of the court hearing center on his feeling that he will not be believed. He wants to know what his therapist will say about him. Her response is complex and addresses multiple issues and multiple psychological levels in one parsimonious reply. She responds to the manifest content by telling Larry what she will say. She also responds to the latent content ("Do *you* believe me") by telling Larry that she believes his conscious intention and then extends this by restating the interpretation of his typical defensive behavior, linking it to unconscious motives. These themes are spelled out in the ensuing discussion and are related to external stress as well as to his own feelings of worthlessness and helplessness. She connects this to his school difficulties and suggests that its origin lies, in part, in his unsuccessful competition with his more achieving younger brother. That she is correct is confirmed by Larry's admitting, for the first time, that the provocation in the original crisis occurred when a schoolmate called him "brainless." This admission is followed by a projection of his own sense of worthlessness onto the judge. The therapist interprets the projection and restates her view of his self-punitive posture. She delineates the way in which his self-punishing stance obliterates all positive achievements which she believes the judge will not overlook. This intervention serves reality testing, as well as further clarification of Larry's internal processes.

Larry's relief is obvious but not complete, and once again he wants to know more about what the therapist will tell the judge. He is clearly touched by her honest and direct response. His abrupt departure suggests that this moment of closeness is more than he can stand just yet.

This entire session represents an experience in anticipating and preparing for the upcoming stressful event. Using the transference, the therapist stands in for all those who judge Larry. Through a mixture of reality testing, support, clarification and interpretation, she helps Larry reduce his vulnerability and increases the likelihood that he will weather the court hearing in a less maladaptive fashion. It is noteworthy that at no time does she falsely reassure him. To do so would undermine her credibility and Larry's growing trust in her. Furthermore, false reassurance would rob Larry of his own tentative sense of his capacity to manage difficult situations and to judge more realistically what he can and cannot do.

The therapist and the probation officer continue their collaboration. The therapist provides her view of the relationship between the "stealing" episode and Larry's need to feel injured and innocent simultaneously. She urges that the judge's response not reinforce this maladaptive process. Together they provide important information to the judge, who, fortunately, listens and uses their advice effectively.

Naturally, the next session focuses on the experience of the court hearing. Perhaps Larry's most significant gain is made in this session when he recognizes that his emotional state altered his perception startlingly. This discovery leads to a beginning integration of the previously split representations of the hated/liked authority. The focus shifts again to the upcoming stressful task of returning to school. Larry's concern remains a much more internal one, with emphasis on controlling his behavior in the face of his apprehensions. The remaining sessions of this brief therapy are devoted largely to a reworking and consolidation of the themes and gains established in the first seven hours. In addition, two important new developments occur. A crucial piece of new material concerning his father's indifference and abandonment emerges validating the early speculation that this life event was centrally related to the current difficulties. Secondly, the material connected to the Robert Frost poem suggests that considerable repair has occurred. Larry shows a much greater ability to tolerate ambivalence in his recognition that good and bad can exist together and do not need to be split apart in absolutes. Also, this understanding is conveyed via a piece of "book-learning," suggesting that he is much more able to get on with academic tasks. Finally, he can acknowledge his need for help and his gratitude at receiving it.

This elegant brief psychotherapy provides a glimpse of almost every aspect of the psychotherapeutic armamentarium. This therapist makes effective and timely use of the real relationship, the transference, the perceptive attention to developmental issues, and environmental aids. The techniques of clarification, reality testing, confrontation, exploration, interpretation and manipulation are all skillfully used. Overall, this work can be viewed as a "supportive" therapy. The concept of support has been much maligned, misunderstood and underestimated. Maligned in that support is incorrectly presumed to require less skill and less profound understanding of psychodynamics. Misunderstood in that it is all too often confused and equated with reassurance and excessive displays of kindliness and niceness. Underestimated in that internal charge is deemed an impossible achievement of a "supportive" therapy. In fact, Larry's treatment, brief as it is and supportive as it is, belies these misconceptions.

REFERENCES

1. Adelson, J., The mystique of adolescence. *Psychiatry*, 1964, Vol. 27(1): 1-5.
2. Anthony, E. J., Normal adolescent development from a cognitive viewpoint. *J. of Amer. Academy of Child Psychiatry*, 1982, Vol. 21(4): 318-327.
3. Bandura, A., The stormy decade: Fact or fiction. In R. E. Grinder (Ed.), *Studies in adolescence*, 2nd Edition, Wisconsin: University of Wisconsin, 1969.
4. Barton, B. R., Jr., and Martin-Days, C., Adolescent depression: Significant issues in diagnosis and treatment of constricted adolescents. *Clinical Social Work Journal*, 1980, Vol. 10(4): 275-288.
5. Bronfenbrenner, U., The origins of alienation. *Scientific American*, 1974, Vol. 213: 53-61.
6. Cooper, S., A look at the effect of racism on clinical work. *Social Casework*, 1973, Vol. 54: 76-84.
7. Erikson, E., *Identity, youth and crisis*. New York: Norton, 1968.
8. Giovacchini, P., The difficult adolescent patient: Countertransference problems. In S. C. Feinstein and P. Giovacchini (Eds.), *Adolescent Psychiatry*, Vol. 3. New York: Basic Books, 1974.
9. Jackson, A. B., Berkowitz, H., and Farley, G., Race as a variable affecting the treatment involvement of children. *J. of Amer. Academy of Child Psychiatry*, 1974, Vol. 13: 20-31.
10. Kohlberg, L., and Gilligan, C., The adolescent as a philosopher: The discovery of self in a post-conventional world. *Daedalus*, 1971, Vol. 100: 1051-1086.
11. Masterson, J. F., *Treatment of the borderline adolescent: A developmental approach*. New York: Wiley Interscience, 1972.
12. Minde, K., and Minde, R., Children of immigrants. *Canadian Psychiatric Association Journal*, 1976, Vol. 23: 175-183.
13. Palumbo, J., Perceptual deficits and self-esteem in adolescence. *Clinical Social Work Journal*, 1979, Vol. 7: 34-61.
14. Settlage, C., Cultural values and the superego in late adolescence. *Psychoanalytic Study of the Child*, 1972, Vol. 27: 84-88.
15. Toolan, J. M., Depression in adolescents. In J. H. Howells (Ed.), *Modern Perspective in Adolescent Psychiatry*. New York: Brunner/Mazel, 1971, pp. 359-378.
16. Yamamoto, J., and Kubota, M., The Japanese American family. In G. Johnson Powell (Ed.), *The Psychosocial Development of Minority Group Children*. New York: Brunner/Mazel, 1983.

Index

Abandonment, 65, 153, 156
Abuse and neglect, 191-201
Achievement, 15
Adelson, Joseph, 213
Administrative regulations, 47
Adolescence, 212-251, *see also* Children
Affect, 138, 148
Aggression, 94-95, 189, 191, 209
  learning problems and, 75-76
  selectively disturbed children and, 138
  seriously disturbed children and, 94-95, 107
  sexual feelings and, 108
Alcoholism, 172-174, 197
Alienation, 215-216, 221
Alliance building techniques, 141
Ambivalence, 23-24, 78, 101-102
  attempts for autonomy and, 219
Anger
  toward the therapist, 19-20
  warding off of, 223
Anxiety, 23-24, 42, 44, 55, 100
  adolescence and, 219, 221
  loss and, 148
  separation from therapist and, 81
  stranger, 92
Assertiveness, 24, 75
Attachment, 26-27, 100, 115, 146
Authority, tolerance of, 24-25
Autonomy, 25, 37, 148

adolescence and, 219, 243
Avoidance behavior, 223

Baker, Russell, 11
Bandura, A., 214
Birth history, 33-34, 40
Body imagery and function, 22-23, 124, 189-190
  adolescence and, 212, 231, 240, 245, 248
  self-esteem and, 22-23
  seriously disturbed children and, 87, 91, 96-97
  sexual identity and, 96-97, 240
Borderline disorders, 86
Boundaries, 86, 98, 121, 126-127
  between parent and child, 102-103
Bronfenbrenner, Urie, 215-216
Bureaucracy, 47

Case plan, 36, 39
Chess, S., 129
Child development, 13-14, 130
  difference between male and female, 25
  internal stability and, 18
Children
  abused and neglected, 191-201
  difficult to engage, 81-85
  selectively disturbed, 129-163

seriously disturbed, 86-128
Clinical interchange
    patient's view of, 8-9
    therapist's view of the, 6-8
Cognitive problems, *see* Learning
        problems
Communication, 9-11, 33
Community resources, 46-47
Conflicts, 23-24, 39
    affectionate feelings and, 148
    growing up and, 223
    intra-psychic, 130
    neurotic, 140
    in seriously disturbed children, 94-97
Conscience, 105, 107
Consistency, 15, 35
    testing of, 80
Constancy, 17-20, 153
Content of communication, 10-12
Control issues, 95-96
Cooper, Shirley, 164-166
Coping mechanisms, 161
    adolescence and, 224
Countertransference, 61-64, 66, *see also*
        Transference
    treat giving and, 112
Crisis intervention, 164-210, *see also*
        Interventions
    abused and neglected children, 191-201
    consistent with overall treatment, 189
    discriminating issues and, 184
    divorce and, 201-210
    during course of therapy, 185-191
    exploring meanings of the crisis, 180
    linking family problems and, 181-183
    needs of the system and, 196
    patient relationship and, 179
Culture
    adolescence and, 213, 215-216
    distrust of the wider, 220

Death, 11-12, 139, 146
Decompensation, 195, 199, 218, 243
Defenses, 9, 55, 130
    inability to take pleasure and, 140
    motivation for therapy and, 39
    obsessive-compulsive, 96
    offense as the best, 247
    omnipotence, 245
    released by a crisis, 191
    sense of safety and, 15
Delusions, 219
Denial, 41, 55, 61, 109
    anger and, 226
Dependence, 25

Dependency needs, 138
Depression, 27-28, 55, 67
    adolescence and, 218, 222
    anger and, 226
    crisis intervention and, 197
    divorce and, 201-202
    separation anxiety and, 154
Deprivation, 20-21, 80
    attempts to overcome, 78-79
Development, *see* Child development
Developmental perspective, 13-14
Diagnosis, 43-45, 130
Dispositions, 166
Divorce and separation
    case studies, 16-17, 30, 33, 44-46, 81-
        84, 91, 117
    crisis intervention and, 201-210

Echolalic speech, 88, 91
Ego development, 102
Ego functions, 28-30, 93
    seriously disturbed and, 87
Ego models, 233
Encopresis, 22, 185
Engagement problems, 81-85, 117
Enuresis, 22, 29, 68, 88
Environment, 36, 45-46, 79
    crisis intervention and, 195
    stability and, 18-20
Erikson, E., 215
Exhibitionistic behavior, 93, 96

Family
    changes within American, 216
    chaotic environment and, 18
    differing perceptions of the problem,
        39-41
    limits on choice of interventions, 37-38
    motivation for therapy, 38-39
    values and, 41-43
    viewed as cause of child's problem, 157
    withdrawal from the, 140
Family therapy, 224-228
Fantasy, 15, 86
    seriously disturbed children and, 94-97
Fear, 8-9, 17
    divorce and, 30
    learning problems and, 27
    silent behavior and, 84
Fixation, 130
Frank, Margaret, 5
Frustration tolerance, 23-24, 62, 66
    answering questions and, 110
    learning to wait, 102

Generation gap, 214
Gratification problems, 77-81, 102, 111-112
Gratification-frustration continuum, 110
Grief, case study, 19-20
Guilt, 23, 41

Hallucinations, 219
Hassibi, M., 129
Hidden agendas, 39
Hope, 8-9
Hopelessness, 244, 248
Hypotheses testing, 7, 14
   crisis intervention and, 166

Identity, 22-23, 212
   adolescence and, 232
Illness, case study, 16-17
Impulse control, 15, 19-20, 23
   seriously disturbed children and, 98, 118
Impulse disorders, 86
Inferences, 6-7
Inhibitions, 15, 20, 55, 67
   learning problems and, 27
Intercurrent events, 11-12
Interventions, 8, *see also* Crisis intervention; Transference
   alliance building, 141
   to counter hopelessness, 244
   discordant value systems and, 43
   factors in choosing, 35-37
   use of gifts and treats, 77-81, 102, 111-112
   handling direct questions, 109-111
   internalization of, 116, 247
   to invite control, 244
   limit setting, 16, 19, 83, 109, 226
   linking content and affect, 138
   modeling, 26, 78, 111, 121, 141
   requests to take toys home, 80-81, 114-115, 119-121
   with silent children, 82-84
   trust building, 245

Jealousy, 140, *see also* Sibling rivalry

Latent content, 11, 249
Lau, Herbert G., 164-166
Learning problems, 27-28, 39, 52, 67
   adolescence and, 228, 232
   aggression and, 76
Limit setting, 16, 19, 83, 109, 226
Loneliness, 95, 236
Loss, 19-20, 65, 189

divorce and, 201
selectively disturbed children and, 138, 146, 148

Manifest content, 11, 249
Masturbation, 96
Middle level conceptualizations, 6, 9, 11-12
Modeling, 26, 78, 111, 121, 141
Morrison, Toni, 157
Motivation, 9, 38-39
Mutuality, 24-25

Narcissism, 21
Needs, appropriate expression of, 20-21
Neurosis, 130

Object constancy, 18, 154
   attainment of internal, 162
Object loss, 61
Observations, 6
Obsessive-compulsive defenses, 96
Oedipal phase, 130, 138
Omnipotent defenses, 245, 247
Overprotection, 26-27, 65

Passive resistance, 54
Peer relationships, 213, 222, 231, 236
Perfectionistic strivings, 247
Phobias, 88, 92
Play, 137, 140
   capacity for controlled, 121
Play therapy, 35
Power struggles, 65
Practice, theory and, 5-12
Primary process, 92-93, 98
Problem solving approaches, 66
Progression, 130
Projection, 94, 118, 219
Psychological testing, 55, 91
Psychosis, 86, 130
   adolescent episode of, 219
Psychotherapy, strategies and, 8
Psychotic rage, 93
Punitive conscience, 105, 107
Punitive ideas, 23

Reality, 15, 27
   understanding of time and, 102
Reality testing, 222, 226, 244
Reflection, 121
Regression, 86, 89, 105, 130
   adolescence and, 219
   divorce and, 208
Remorse, 23

Repression, 20, 61, 127
Rescue fantasy, 112
Resistance, 9, 21, 62, 147
    expressed through boredom, 226
    motivation for therapy and, 39
    passive, 54
    silent behavior and, 84
Risk-taking behavior, 15, 75, 77
Ritualistic behavior, 88-89, 91, 92

Safety, creating a sense of, 15-17
Secondary gains, 231
Secondary process, 93, 98
Secrets, 68, 74, 76
Self, psychology of the, 21
Self-condemning behavior, 23
Self-differentiation, 121, 126
Self-esteem, 22-23, 107, 124
    adolescence and, 222
    gratification problems and, 78
Self-fulfilling prophecy, 41
Self-regulatory mechanisms, 23
Sense of self, 22-23, 108, 116
Separation, *see* Divorce and separation
Separation anxiety, 153-154
Separation individuation process, 18,
        107, 159-162
    adolescence and, 213, 219, 224
Seriously disturbed, etiology of, 87-88
Settlage, C., xi, 215
Sexual identification, 92, 96-97, 98
Sexual impulses, 93
Sexuality
    adolescence and, 222, 245, 248
    aggression and, 108
    conflicts and, 148
Sibling rivalry, 153-154, 156, 190-191
    adolescence and, 247
    seriously disturbed children and, 94
Sociability, 95
Speech problems, 32-35, 88
Stability, 17-20
Stalled cases, 51-77
Stealing, 228-232, 239, 241
Stranger anxiety, 92
Stress, 4, 13, 28, 122
    family life and, 216
    precipitating a crisis, 165
    suicide attempt and, 179
Suicide, 131, 137, 197
    adolescence and, 218-219
    crisis intervention and, 167-184
Supportive therapy, 250-251
Symbiotic dyad, 26-27, 100
    hostile attachment, 219, 227

Termination of therapy, 45-46, 63-64,
        113-116
Theory, practice and, 5-12
Therapist
    alliance with the, 39
    anger toward the, 19-20
    attachment to the, 146
    choice of intervention and, 37
    clinical interchange and the, 6-8
    competition with the parents and, 112
    evoking feelings in the, 118
    feelings toward the patient, 79, 87
    identification with the, 23
    internalizing the, 247
    joins with the parents' self-blame, 157
    as a real object, 25
    risk taking and, 77
    separation from the, 81, 159-162
    style of the, 43-45
    tasks for diagnostic sessions, 44
    values and, 41-43
Therapy
    aims and goals of, 13-30
        case study, 107
        cognitive progress, 27-28
        ego functions and, 28-30
        expression of needs, 20-21
        real relationships and, 24-27
        safety and, 15-17
        self-esteem, 22-23
        with seriously disturbed, 98
        stability and constancy, 17-20
        tolerance of conflict, 23-24
    beginning stage, 131-141
    completion of, 149-163
    conditions necessary for, 32-47
    distinction between parenting and, 14
    middle phase of, 139-148
    principles for seriously disturbed, 87
    sabotage of, 112
    supportive, 250-251
    terminated precipitously, 19-20
    termination of, 45-46, 63-64, 113-116
Toilet rituals, 88-89, 92
Transference, 25, 61-63, 76, 148, 249, *see
        also* Countertransference
    crisis intervention and, 165-166
Transitional objects, 81
Treatment, *see* Therapy
Treatment resources, 46-47
Trust, 15, 71, 75-76, 245
Tutoring program, 67

Value systems, 41-43